Advanced WordPerfect Using Macro Power
A Guide for VMS and DOS Users

Advanced WordPerfect Using Macro Power
A Guide for VMS and DOS Users

Sharilyn S. Due

Digital Press

Boston   Oxford   Melbourne   Singapore   Toronto   Munich   New Delhi   Tokyo

Digital Press™ is an imprint of Butterworth–Heinemann

WordPerfect® is a registered trademark of Novell, Inc.

All trademarks found herein are property of their respective owners.

Library of Congress Cataloging-in-Publication Data

Due, Sharilyn S., 1964-
    Advanced WordPerfect using macro power / by Sharilyn S. Due
        p.   cm.
    Includes index.
    ISBN 1-55558-147-1
    1. WordPerfect (Computer file)   2. Word processing.   I. Title.
    Z52.5.W65D815   1995
    652.5'536--dc20   95-588
                                                                   CIP

The publisher offers discounts on bulk orders of this book.
For information, please write:

Manager of Special Sales, Digital Press
Butterworth–Heinemann
313 Washington Street
Newton, MA 02158–1626

Order number: EY–T817E–DP

10 9 8 7 6 5 4 3 2 1

Printed in the United States of America

This book is dedicated to

my family

and

friends.

CONTENTS

III.   ADVANCED PROGRAMMED MACROS

PREFACE

Can life include more time in the mountains or on the seashore? It can when Macro Power works for you! Almost effortlessly, you can learn to save time and improve your productivity with **Advanced WordPerfect Using Macro Power.**

Power Up WordPerfect for DOS! An appendix is included for WordPerfect 6.0 and 5.0 for DOS Users explaining how to use Macro Power in their respective environments.

Power Up WordPerfect for VMS! VMS is Digital Equipment Corporation's proprietary operating system running on a VAX or an Alpha hardware platform. WordPerfect for VMS users can use Macro Power in the VMS environment, too!

The experienced user in the DOS and/or VMS environment will find numerous step-by-step instructions incorporating the advanced features of WordPerfect into useful macros. These instructions will build the user's confidence with a basic understanding of WordPerfect macros. This acquired base knowledge will inspire the user to reach out and modify the more advanced macros in this book and to create new macros for his/her own individual use.

Using **Advanced WordPerfect Using Macro Power** will provide more time in the mountains or on the shore.

Acknowledgments

I am grateful for the assistance provided by the many individuals who have contributed to the writing of this book.

Michael Conner's recommendations and technical assistance were invaluable to this book in its early stages.

I appreciate the efforts of the reviewers, editors, and all those helping to form my manuscript into a book. A special thank you to my dad for all of his reviews and recommendations.

Also deserving of praise and appreciation are my family and friends for their loyal assistance, support and patience given toward my endeavors. A special thank you to my manager, colleagues, and friends at Digital Equipment Corporation.

INTRODUCTION

Macros CAN DO all that time consuming repetitive work for YOU!! Anyone using WordPerfect in a DOS or VMS environment can Power Up with this book and enjoy macro savings.

Computers are friendly and so is this book! Lets see how! When creating the tutorial macro examples, you should follow the step-by-step instructions under the Keystroke Action titles. When "U" the user enter a keystroke specified in the book, it will include the computer's "C" reply as it should be displayed on the user's computer screen. This type of communication between "U" the user and "C" the "computer in the book" will guide the user through easy and complex macros. It will also increase the user's confidence in the use of WordPerfect.

The **Macro Power Basics** section will introduce you to the Macro Power concept. All users should read this first chapter to acquire or review the basic methods of incorporating macros into WordPerfect.

In the **Advanced Features** section there are eleven chapters explaining how to apply Macro Power to important features of WordPerfect. Choose those macros that apply to your needs.

When you feel real confident in the use of Macro Power within WordPerfect you will want to try out the **Advanced Programmed Macros for Desk-Top Publishing and the Macro Library**.

Users of **WordPerfect 6.0 for DOS** will benefit most by first reading Appendix G entitled WordPerfect 6.0 for DOS and then progressing through the book.

Also included are a number of informational Appendices and an Index.

Have fun learning from **Advanced WordPerfect Using Macro Power** and enjoy the time and effort you save with macros!

SECTION I:

MACRO POWER BASICS

CHAPTER 1

MACRO POWER BASICS

What is a Macro?

Macros automatically execute packages of repetitive keystrokes at your command. That cumbersome heading on your weekly report can be completed in three keystrokes with WordPerfect 5.1 and Macro Power.

Benefits of Macro Power

1. *Save Time.* A macro uses your computer to save time by automatically executing repetitive keystrokes. If ten different letters need the same heading all you have to do is establish the heading, in a macro, and then invoke the macro to repeat the heading for each subsequent letter.

2. *Fewer Commands To Memorize.* A macro records all the commands you need for future reference. For example, incorporate all the routine letter writing functions of spell checking, saving, and printing in one macro and save the effort of looking up the same commands each time you need them.

3. *Fewer Keystrokes To Enter.* A macro may be invoked by using as few as two keystrokes. Complicated repetitious tasks in WordPerfect 5.1 may require many keystrokes. By using macro power the repeated keystrokes will be eliminated and exact accuracy will be maintained. For example, assume you need the same exact header including a specific graphic on all outgoing documents. All the keystrokes can be entered in one macro and then invoke the macro when you need the heading instead of typing in the same boring keystrokes each time.

4. *More Flexibility.* A powerful feature of WordPerfect 5.1 is the macro programming language. This feature provides greater flexibility for the user in the solution of a complicated task or in the creation of beneficial programs. For example, WordPerfect 5.1's programming language can be used to search your document for a certain product name and then it can insert a price for that specific item into the document. Also, you can create a helpful program that will prompt you to enter the debits and credits of your checking account into a document and then you can direct it to balance the figures for you.

5. *Easy To Remember Commands.* Macros may be named so that they are very easy to remember. For example, to print a document you can either use the normal keystrokes, Shift-F7, or you can use a mnemonically named macro, like Alternate-P, where "P" stands for Print.

Examples of Macros

Examples of Macro Power supplementing WordPerfect 5.1:

- Type a letter heading.
- Type a letter closing.
- Spell check and save a document.
- Print and save a document.
- Format the pages of a document.
- Type a form letter.
- Search and replace several items in a document.
- Sort a list of names.
- Merge an address list with a letter.
- Enter the same graphics into different documents.
- Create a database file for addresses.
- Create a database file for recipes.
- Create a customized pop-up menu.
- Create a table.

Types of Macros

There are three types of macros: temporary macros, named macros, and the PF (VMS)/ Alternate (DOS) key macros. Each type of macro can be saved on a floppy disk or hard disk and it can be copied like a file.

Type of Macros	Description
PF/Alternate	These macros are the easiest to use and remember. Saved as **ALT?.WPM**, where the question mark represents any letter of the alphabet from A to Z.
	VMS Users:
	DOS Users:
Named	Macros that are given a filename by the user and a file type/extension by WordPerfect, **.WPM**, and saved to disk.
	VMS Users:

VMS Users: *These macros are called PF Key Macros. You can use PF3 for the true Alternate macro since this key creates macros with the name of ALT?.WPM, where the question mark represents any letter of the alphabet from A to Z. Otherwise, you can use PF1 to create 26 additional macros and these macros will have the name of PF1?.WPM, where the question mark represents any letter of the alphabet from A to Z. Throughout this book the PF key is either PF1 or PF3 but assumed to be PF3.*

DOS Users: *These macros are called Alt Key Macros.*

VMS Users: *How you have set up WordPerfect 5.1 for Macro File Locations will determine whether WordPerfect 5.1 for VMS will automatically give the macros the file type of .WPM or not give them a file type. If the file specification for your Macro Files in Setup's (PF1,F7) Location of Files is, for example, DISK$DEVICE:[JENNY].WPM then all the macros you create will be saved on the device named DISK$DEVICE*

*in the directory of JENNY and have the file type of
.WPM. The examples in this book assume that you have
.WPM in the file specification for your macros. If you
have not specified .WPM in the file specification then
your macros will not have a file type.*

Temporary   Great for a one-session-only need because it is automatically erased
                             upon exit from WordPerfect 5.1. It can be saved if you choose (See
                             Temporary Macros at the end of this chapter).

Directories of Macros

When you create a named or ALT macro it will automatically be saved in your
computer's default directory unless you specify otherwise.

One way to specify a different location for your macros is to change your default drive
and directory. Remember, it is important to know where the macros are stored and to always
change the default file specification (VMS) or pathname (DOS) when you enter WordPerfect
or else to type in the file specification or pathname when you invoke those macros.

To avoid changing the default drive and directory for each new macro you can specify
a macro directory in the Setup Feature. Then WordPerfect will automatically save your macros
to a specific file specification or pathname and when you invoke these macros WordPerfect will
automatically find them.

Defining a Macro

The following series of steps are necessary to define a macro. Each step will be further
described in the Reference Keystrokes that you use when you define a macro.

If at some point while you are defining a macro you press the *Cancel key* F7 (VMS) OR
F1 (DOS) then a macro will still be saved even though you pressed Cancel.

VMS   Reference Keystrokes   DOS

PF2,F18   U: Press *Macro Define.*   Ctrl-F10
                 C: *Prints* Define macro: _.

Naming Macros

The first step in defining a macro is to name it. Each of the three types of macros are
named in a different way.

To name a temporary macro, press enter when defining the macro.

For a named macro, enter one to thirty-nine characters that are valid VMS characters
for filenames or enter one to eight characters that are valid DOS characters for filenames. It
is best to name these macros mnemonically by function for easier identification.

A PF/Alternate key macro can be named by holding down the PF1/Alt or PF3 key and
typing any letter from A to Z.

VMS Users: *PF key macros can be named by pressing either PF1 or PF3. Thus, for VMS you can have twenty-six PF1 macros and twenty-six PF3 macros for each directory. These PF1 and PF3 keys do not have to be held down while you press the corresponding alphabetical letter.*

DOS Users: *Twenty-six Alternate macros can be defined for each directory. You must hold down the Alternate key while you press the corresponding alphabetical letter. These macros are also called Alt macros.*

VMS   Reference Keystrokes   DOS

U: For a temporary macro press the *Enter key*, for a PF3/Alt or PF1 macro press PF3/Alt or PF1 and any letter from A to Z, OR for a named macro type in the name of the macro and press the *Enter key*.
C: *Prints* Description: _.

Macro Description

The next item you must enter when defining a macro is the description of the macro. You should use a functional description suitable for later reference. The description should contain a brief description of the macro's purpose because it is basically an indication of the intended use of the macro. WordPerfect 5.1 has limited this description to 39 characters.

VMS   Reference Keystrokes   DOS

U: Type in the description of the macro and press the *Enter key*.
C: *Prints* Macro Def.

Keystrokes

After you see Macro Def on your screen you can enter the keystrokes for your macro. When you define a macro this way the keystrokes will execute as you enter them into the macro.

VMS   Reference Keystrokes   DOS

U: Type in the keystrokes that you want the macro to record.
C: *Echoes keystrokes.*

Ending the Macro Definition

When you finish typing in the keystrokes for your macro you must tell WordPerfect that you are done defining your macro.

VMS	**Reference Keystrokes**	**DOS**
PF2,F18	U: Press *Macro Define* again to end the defining process. C: *Saves macro.*	Ctrl-F10

Your macro has been defined when the above series of steps have been issued.

Redefining/Replacing a Macro

If you make a mistake while defining your macro, or if you want to replace a macro with a new set of personalized keystrokes you must restart the defining process.

If *Macro Def* is still flashing in the lower left hand corner of your screen you must finish the macro definition by doing the following:

VMS	**Reference Keystrokes**	**DOS**
PF2,F18	U: Press *Macro Define* to finish defining the macro. C: *Saves macro.*	Ctrl-F10

Redefine or replace the old macro's contents with new keystrokes as follows:

VMS	**Reference Keystrokes**	**DOS**
PF2,F18	U: Press *Macro Define* to restart defining the macro. C: *Prints* Define macro: _.	Ctrl-F10
	U: Type in the macro's name and press the *Enter key.* C: *Prints Macroname* Already Exists: 1 Replace; 2 Edit; 3 Description: 0.	
	U: Press *1* to replace the old macro with the new macro. C: *Prints* Replace *File Specification (VMS) or Pathname (DOS)?* No (Yes)	
	U: Press *Y* for Yes to replace macro. C: *Prints* Description: _.	
	U: Type in the description of the macro and press the *Enter key.* C: *Prints* Macro Def.	

Redefine the whole macro from the beginning and then end the macro definition.

Enough Explanation: Let's Make a Macro!

Now is the time for a hands-on example to create your first macro. Remember to follow all the Steps in the sequential order listed below the heading of *Keystroke Action*.

This example will create a named macro for a closing paragraph that can be inserted into any letter. This is a tutorial example only, so your modifications are welcome.

Before the next step please make sure your screen is cleared and make sure the cursor is located at the top of the cleared screen.

VMS	Keystroke Action	DOS
PF2,F18	1. U: Press *Macro Define.* C: *Prints* Define macro: _.	Ctrl-F10

	2. U: Type in the name <u>CLOSE</u> and press the
	    Enter key.
	    C: *Prints* Description: _.	

	3. U: Type in <u>A letter closing</u> for the description
	    and press the *Enter key.*
	    C: *Prints* Macro Def.	

Type in the text which appears on Screen 1-1 or your own text and name.

Screen 1-1

```
     Thank you for purchasing all of your office merchandise from
Office Supplies, Inc.  Please contact us if you need further assistance.
Again, thank you for your patronage.

                              Sincerely,




                              Amanda A. Anderson
                              Manager
```

VMS	Keystroke Action	DOS

PF2,F18	4. U: Press *Macro Define* again to finish defining
	    the macro.
	    C: *Saves macro.*
		Ctrl-F10

Invoking a Macro

Invoking a macro is also referred to as executing or replaying a macro. When a macro is invoked it performs each keystroke from the beginning to the end of the macro without your help.

The correct way to invoke a macro is determined by macro type.

Invoking PF/Alt Key Macros

Do the following to invoke Alt Key macros:

VMS	Reference Keystrokes	DOS
	U: Press the *PF/Alt key* (DOS Users hold it down) and type the letter from A to Z that you used when you named the macro. NOTE: If you defined the macro with *PF3* then you must use *PF3* when you invoke that macro.	
	C: *Invokes macro.*	

PF/Alt key macros allow you to bypass the keystrokes of pressing *Macro* PF3,F18 (VMS) OR Alt-F10 (DOS) to invoke the macro.

Invoking Named Macros

Do the following to invoke named macros:

VMS	Reference Keystrokes	DOS
PF3,F18	U: Press *Macro.*	Alt-F10
	C: *Prints* Macro: _.	
	U: Type in macro's file specification (VMS) or pathname (DOS) and the name of the macro and press the *Enter key.*	
	C: *Invokes macro.*	

Invoking Temporary Macros

Do the following to invoke temporary macros:

VMS	Reference Keystrokes	DOS
PF3,F18	U: Press *Macro.*	Alt-F10
	C: *Prints* Macro: _.	
	U: Press the *Enter key.*	
	C: *Invokes macro.*	

Invoking the Close Macro

Before invoking the Close Macro please make sure your screen is cleared and make sure the cursor is located at the top of the cleared screen.

Then invoke the letter closing macro as follows:

VMS	Keystroke Action	DOS
PF3,F18	1. U: Press *Macro*. C: *Prints* Macro: _.	Alt-F10
	2. U: Type in the name of the macro which is <u>CLOSE</u> and press the *Enter key*. C: *Macro invokes*.	

Your closing paragraph will magically appear.

Congratulations! You have written and invoked your first macro.

Interrupting a Macro

To stop a macro while it is running press *Cancel* F7 (VMS) OR F1 (DOS).

Macros will stop on their own when an error is found in the macro.

Macros will also stop if a search is included in the macro and the item being searched for cannot be found unless you program the macro another way.

Macro Editor

The Macro Editor in WordPerfect 5.1 allows you to create brand new macros from scratch or to make changes to existing macros. In other words, it allows the use of the WordPerfect word processor functions within macros.

Before you can create a new macro in the Macro Editor or edit an existing macro in the macro editor you must learn how to use the macro editor.

Using the Macro Editor

Editing Keys Used in the Macro Editor

The following table, Table 1-1, shows the list of keys that you can use in the macro editor to move your cursor around and to edit your macro. These editing keys respond like they normally do in WordPerfect.

Table 1-1

Key	Description
Arrow keys	Move cursor in designated direction.
Backspace	Erases to the left of the cursor.
Ctrl	Used in combination with other editing keys for quick cursor movement.
Delete	Erases the character the cursor is currently positioned on.
End	Moves the cursor to the end of the current line.
Enter	Starts a new line in the editor.
Home	Used in combination with other editing keys for quick cursor movement.
Tab	Indents the current line in the editor.
PgDn	Moves cursor down a page.
PgUp	Moves cursor up a page.
Space Bar	Inserts a space into the editor (represented by a dot, •, in the editor).

The use of any of these editing keys will not interfere with the normal execution of the macro when you invoke it.

Inserting Text into the Macro

All you have to do to insert text into the Macro Editor is start typing! Any normal text you type in will be printed on your screen when you invoke the macro.

Inserting Function Key Commands

All you have to do to insert most of WordPerfect's function key commands is to just press the key. The key name will appear in {} and the first letter will be uppercase. See Table 1-2.

Table 1-2

Function Key	VMS Keystroke	DOS Keystroke	As Shown in Macro Editor
Block	PF3,F10	Alt-F4,F12	{Block}
Bold	F12	F6	{Bold}
Center	PF1,F12	Shift-F6	{Center}
Columns/Table	PF3,F13	Alt-F7	{Columns/Tables}
Date/Outline	PF1,F11	Shift-F5	{Date/Outline}
End Field	F17	F9	{End Field}
Flush Right	PF3,F12	Alt-F6	{Flush Right}
Font	PF2,F14	Ctrl-F8	{Font}
Footnote	PF2,F13	Ctrl-F7	{Footnote}
Format	PF1,F14	Shift-F8	{Format}
Graphics	PF3,F17	Alt-F9	{Graphics}
->Indent	F10	F4	{Indent}
->Indent<-	PF1,F10	Shift-F4	{L/R Indent}
List	F11	F5	{List}

Table 1-2 continued.

Function Key	VMS Keystroke	DOS Keystroke	As Shown in Macro Editor
Macro	-	Alt-F10	{Macro}
Mark Text	PF3,F11	Alt-F5	{Mark Text}
Merge/Sort	PF2,F17	Ctrl-F9	{Merge/Sort}
Merge Codes	PF1,F17	Shift-F9	{Merge Codes}
Move	PF2,F10	Ctrl-F4	{Move}
Print	PF1,F13	Shift-F7	{Print}
Replace	PF3,F8	Alt-F2	{Replace}
Retrieve	PF1,F18	Shift-F10	{Retrieve}
Reveal Codes	PF3,F9	Alt-F3,F11	{Reveal Codes}
Save	F18	F10	{Save}
Screen	PF2,F9	Ctrl-F3	{Screen}
<-Search	PF1,F8	Shift-F2	{Search Left}
->Search	F8	F2	{Search}
Setup	PF1,F7	Shift-F1	{Setup}
Shell	PF2,F7	Ctrl-F1	{Shell}
Spell	PF2,F8	Ctrl-F2	{Spell}
Style	PF3,F14	Alt-F8	{Style}
Switch	PF1,F9	Shift-F3	{Switch}
Tab Align	PF2,F12	Ctrl-F6	{Tab Align}
Text In/Out	PF2,F11	Ctrl-F5	{Text In/Out}
Thesaurus	PF3,F7	Alt-F1	{Thesaurus}
Underline	F14	F8	{Underline}

Some Function Key Commands cannot be inserted by just pressing the keys. These keys include the following shown in Table 1-3.

Table 1-3

Function Key	VMS Keystroke	DOS Keystroke	As Shown in Macro Editor
Cancel	F7	F1	{Cancel}
Enter	Return key	Enter key	{Enter}
Exit	F13	F7	{Exit}
Help	F9	F3	{Help}
Macro	PF3,F18	Alt-F10	{Macro}
Macro Define	PF2,F18	Ctrl-F10	{Macro Define}

To insert these Function Key Commands into the Macro Editor you must be in Command Insert mode. If you are not in Command Insert mode these keys will act like normal editing keys. There are two ways to invoke Command Insert mode.

1.   Temporarily invoke Command Insert mode. This first way allows you to invoke Command Insert mode for a one-time only keystroke. That is, it will apply to the next keystroke only. You transfer into Command Insert mode, press the Function Key Command and transfer back to resume normal editing as follows:

| **VMS** | **Reference Keystrokes** | **DOS** |

PF2

U: Press and hold down the *Ctrl key* and tap *v*, lift up, and tap the *Function Key Command key* as shown in Table 1-3.

C: *Inserts Function Command key.*

VMS Users: *The Ctrl key is also PF2. For many items these two keys work the same way. If you use the PF2 key you do not have to hold the key down while pressing another corresponding key.*

2. Permanently invoke Command Insert mode. This way allows you to permanently invoke Command Insert mode, then press the Function Key Commands and when you are done turn off Command Insert mode. This way is somewhat more limiting because some commands like the {Macro Define} command cannot be inserted into your macro this way. If you try to insert some key on a permanent basis and it does not work then insert it with the temporary way to invoke Command Insert mode. Permanently invoke Command Insert Mode as follows:

| **VMS** | **Reference Keystrokes** | **DOS** |

F2,F18

U: Press *Macro Define* and press the *Function Key Command keys.*

C: *Inserts editing keys.*

Ctrl-F10

PF2,F18

U: Press *Macro Define.*

C: *Returns to the Macro Editor.*

Ctrl-F10

Inserting Editing Keys into the Macro

The editing keys that have a certain function in the Macro Editor can also be inserted into your macro. These editing keys are shown in Table 1-4.

Table 1-4

Editing Key	*VMS Keystroke*	*DOS Keystroke*	*As Shown in Macro Editor*
Arrow keys	Arrow keys	Arrow keys	{Up},{Down},{Left},{Right}
Backspace	Delete	Backspace	{Backspace}
Ctrl	PF2	Ctrl	DOS: {Ctrl}-Corresponding Key VMS: {Macro}PF1 Corresponding Key{Enter}
Delete	Remove/KP.	Del	{Del}
End	KP1	End	{End}

Table 1-4 continued.

Editing Key	VMS Keystroke	DOS Keystroke	As Shown in Macro Editor
Enter	Return	Enter	{Enter}
Home	PF4	Home	{Home}
Next Screen	PrevScr	-	{Screen Up}
PgDn	KP3	PgDn	{Page Down}
PgUp	KP9	PgUp	{Page Up}
Prev Screen	NextScr	+	{Screen Down}
Space Bar	Space Bar	Space Bar	•
Tab	Tab	Tab	{Tab}

VMS Users: The Keystrokes labeled KP refer to the key on the Number Key Pad. Thus KP1 refers to the 1 key on the number key pad located on the far right-hand side of your keyboard.

To insert any of the above keys, besides the Space Bar, you must invoke Command Insert mode.

Editing an Existing Macro

You can use the macro editor to edit a macro you have already created. To modify any of the macros that you will create in this book use the macro editor to change them to meet your more personalized needs. To edit a macro you have created do the following:

VMS	Reference Keystrokes	DOS
PF2,F18	U: Press *Macro Define.* C: *Prints* Define macro: _.	Ctrl-F10
	U: Type in the name of the macro. C: *Prints macroname* is Already Defined. 1 Replace; 2 Edit; 3 Description: 0.	
	U: Press 2 for Edit. C: *Positions cursor in the Macro Editor.*	

By selecting *Edit,* WordPerfect 5.1 allows the macro to be edited. This is the way to make any changes that are necessary for the macro.

Creating a New Macro

To create a brand new macro using the macro editor you must first access the editor. To gain access to the editor do the following:

VMS	**Reference Keystrokes**	**DOS**

PF4   U: Press the *Home key* and then press   Home
PF2,F18   *Macro Define.*   Ctrl-F10
                   C: *Prints* Define macro: _.

                   U: Name the macro and press the *Enter key.*
                   C: *Prints* Description: _.

                   U: Type in a description and press the *Enter key.*
                   C: *Invokes the Macro Editor.*

The above commands immediately place you into the Macro Editor Screen as shown
on Screens 1-2 and 1-3.

Screen 1-2: VMS Users

```
Macro: Action

        File            MACRONAME.WPM

        Description     DESCRIPTION OF MACRO


        ┌─────────────────────────────────────────────────────┐
        │ {DISPLAY OFF}                                         │
        │                                                       │
        │                                                       │
        │                                                       │
        │                                                       │
        │                                                       │
        │                                                       │
        │                                                       │
        │                                                       │
        └─────────────────────────────────────────────────────┘

PF2,Prev Scr for macro commands;  Press Exit when done
```

Screen 1-3: DOS Users

```
Macro: Action

        File            MACRONAME.WPM

        Description     DESCRIPTION OF MACRO


        ┌─────────────────────────────────────────────────────┐
        │ {DISPLAY OFF}                                         │
        │                                                       │
        │                                                       │
        │                                                       │
        │                                                       │
        │                                                       │
        │                                                       │
        │                                                       │
        └─────────────────────────────────────────────────────┘

Ctrl-V to Insert next key as command;
Ctrl-PgUp for macro commands; Press Exit when done
```

Now whatever text, function keys, and/or editing keys you would like to insert into your new macro can be added.

Saving Macro Changes

To save any changes in your macro that you have made and return to your document do the following:

VMS	Reference Keystrokes	DOS
F13	U: Press *Exit.*	F7
VMS Users	C: *Prints* Enter Macro Name: *Macroname.*	
	C: *Returns to Document.*	*DOS Users*

VMS Users: **Perform the following Reference Keystroke Action.**

DOS Users: **Do NOT perform the following Reference Keystroke Action.**

VMS	Reference Keystrokes	DOS
	U: Type in the Macroname and/or press the *Enter key.*	
	C: *Returns to Document.*	

VMS Users: **WordPerfect will always prompt you for the macroname when you press the Exit key unless you have not made any changes.**

Canceling Macro Changes

To cancel the changes made in the macro editor and return to your document do the following:

VMS	Reference Keystrokes	DOS
F7	U: Press *Cancel.*	F1
	C: Prints Cancel changes? <u>N</u>o (Yes).	
	U: Press *Y* for Yes.	
	C: *Returns to Document.*	

Editing The Close Macro in the Macro Editor

To change the first tutorial's closing (See Chapter 1, Enough Explanation: Let's Make a Macro!) to a Block Form paragraph the macro must be edited in the macro editor.

Follow the instructions below to edit the first tutorial macro using WordPerfect 5.1's macro editor:

VMS	**Keystroke Action**	**DOS**

PF2,F18   1.   U: Press **Macro Define**.   Ctrl-F10
            C: *Prints* Define macro: _.

        2.   U: Type in the name <u>CLOSE</u> and press the **Enter key.**
            C: *Prints Macroname* Already Exists: 1 Replace; 2 Edit; 3 Description: <u>0</u>.

        3.   U: Press **2** for Edit.
            C: *Displays Macro Editor and Positions cursor in the Macro Editor Screen.*

Screen 1-4 and 1-5 shows the keystrokes that are contained in the "CLOSE.WPM" macro.

Screen 1-4: *VMS Users*

```
Macro: Action

      File          CLOSE.WPM

      Description   A letter closing

   ┌──────────────────────────────────────────────────┐
   │{DISPLAY OFF}{Tab}Thank you for purchasing all of your
   │office merchandise from Office Supplies, Inc.  Please contact
   │us if you need further assistance.  Again, thank you for your
   │patronage.{Enter}{Enter}
   │{Tab}{Tab}{Tab}{Tab}{Tab}{Tab}{Tab}Sincerely,{Enter}
   │{Enter}
   │{Enter}
   │{Enter}
   │{Enter}
   │{Tab}{Tab}{Tab}{Tab}{Tab}{Tab}{Tab}Amanda A. Anderson{Enter}
   │{Tab}{Tab}{Tab}{Tab}{Tab}{Tab}{Tab}Manager
   └──────────────────────────────────────────────────┘
PF2,Prev Scr for macro commands;  Press Exit when done
```

Screen 1-5: DOS Users

```
Macro: Action

      File          CLOSE.WPM

      Description   A letter closing

   ┌──────────────────────────────────────────────────────────┐
   │ {DISPLAY OFF}{Tab}Thank you for purchasing all of your    │
   │ office merchandise from Office Supplies, Inc.  Please contact│
   │ us if you need further assistance.  Again, thank you for your│
   │ patronage.{Enter}{Enter}                                  │
   │ {Tab}{Tab}{Tab}{Tab}{Tab}{Tab}{Tab}Sincerely,{Enter}     │
   │ {Enter}                                                    │
   │ {Enter}                                                    │
   │ {Enter}                                                    │
   │ {Enter}                                                    │
   │ {Tab}{Tab}{Tab}{Tab}{Tab}{Tab}{Tab}Amanda A. Anderson{Enter}│
   │ {Tab}{Tab}{Tab}{Tab}{Tab}{Tab}{Tab}Manager               │
   └──────────────────────────────────────────────────────────┘

Ctrl-V to Insert next key as command;
Ctrl-PgUp for macro commands; Press Exit when done
```

VMS	**Keystroke Action**	**DOS**

4. U: Press the **Right arrow key** to position the cursor on { in the first {Tab} code before Thank and press the **Delete key** to erase {Tab}.

   C: *Deletes programming code.*

5. U: Use the **Arrow keys** to position the cursor on the *m* in merchandise.

   C: *Positions cursor.*

6. U: Press the **Delete key** until merchandise is erased.

   C: *Deletes characters.*

7. U: Type in the word <u>equipment</u>.

   C: *Echoes characters.*

8. U: Use the **Arrow keys** to move the cursor to the *S* in Sincerely.

   C: *Positions cursor.*

9. U: Press the **Backspace key** until all the {Tab} codes before Sincerely are erased.

   C: *Deletes programming codes.*

10. U: Use the **Arrow keys** to move the cursor to the *A* in Amanda.

    C: *Positions cursor.*

VMS	**Keystroke Action**	**DOS**

11. U: Press the *Backspace key* until all the {Tab} codes before Amanda are erased.

    C: *Deletes programming codes.*

12. U: Use the *Arrow keys* to move the cursor to the *M* in Manager.

    C: *Positions cursor.*

13. U: Press the *Backspace* key until all the {Tab} codes before Manager are erased.

    C: *Deletes programming codes.*

F13

VMS Users

14. U: Press *Exit* to save the changes made and exit the macro editor.

    C: *Prints* Enter Macro Name: CLOSE.

    C: *Returns to Document.*

F7

DOS Users

VMS Users: Perform Keystroke Action 15.

DOS Users: Do NOT perform Keystroke Action 15.

VMS	**Keystroke Action**	**DOS**

15. U: Type in the Macroname and/or press the *Enter key.*

    C: *Returns to Document.*

Screen 1-6 and 1-7 shows the keystrokes that are contained in the new "CLOSE.WPM" macro.

Screen 1-6: VMS Users

```
Macro: Action

     File          CLOSE.WPM

     Description   A letter closing

    ┌─────────────────────────────────────────────────────────┐
    │{DISPLAY OFF}Thank you for purchasing all of your office   │
    │equipment from Office Supplies, Inc.  Please contact us if you│
    │need further assistance.  Again, thank you for your patronage.│
    │{Enter}{Enter}                                             │
    │Sincerely,{Enter}                                          │
    │{Enter}                                                    │
    │{Enter}                                                    │
    │{Enter}                                                    │
    │{Enter}                                                    │
    │Amanda A. Anderson{Enter}                                  │
    │Manager                                                    │
    └─────────────────────────────────────────────────────────┘

PF2,Prev Scr for macro commands;  Press Exit when done
```

Screen 1-7: DOS Users

```
Macro: Action

     File          CLOSE.WPM

     Description   A letter closing

    ┌─────────────────────────────────────────────────────────┐
    │{DISPLAY OFF}Thank you for purchasing all of your office   │
    │equipment from Office Supplies, Inc.  Please contact us if you│
    │need further assistance.  Again, thank you for your patronage.│
    │{Enter}{Enter}                                             │
    │Sincerely,{Enter}                                          │
    │{Enter}                                                    │
    │{Enter}                                                    │
    │{Enter}                                                    │
    │{Enter}                                                    │
    │Amanda A. Anderson{Enter}                                  │
    │Manager                                                    │
    └─────────────────────────────────────────────────────────┘

Ctrl-V to Insert next key as command;
Ctrl-PgUp for macro commands; Press Exit when done
```

Invoking the New Close Macro

Let's invoke the edited macro.

Before the next step please make sure your screen is cleared and make sure the cursor is located at the top of the cleared screen.

VMS	**Keystroke Action**	**DOS**
PF3,F18	16. U: Press *Macro.*	Alt-F10
	C: *Prints* Define macro: _	

VMS	Keystroke Action	DOS

17. U: Type in the name of the macro which is
        <u>CLOSE</u> and press the *Enter key*.
    C: *Prints* Description: _.

   The result of the edited macro will be seen on the screen. Congratulations, you have just created and edited your first macro!
   The close macro has now been saved to either your hard disk drive or to a floppy disk depending on how your WordPerfect 5.1 Software is set up. We will be using this macro again later in the book.

Macro HouseKeeping

Changing the Description of the Macro

   To change the description of your macro do the following:

VMS	Reference Keystrokes	DOS
PF2,F18	U: Press *Macro Define.* C: Prints Define macro: _.	Ctrl-F10

U: Type in the name of the macro.
C: *Prints macroname* Already Exists: 1 Replace; 2
    Edit; 3 Description: <u>0</u>.

U: Press *3* for Description.
C: *Prints* Description.

U: Type in the new description and press the *Enter key*.
C: *Returns to Macro Editor.*

   You must save your macro again in order to save your macro's description. Otherwise, if you cancel the changes in your macro the description changes also will be canceled.

Erasing a Macro

   A macro can be erased using the method for erasing a file.

Temporary Macros

   It is possible to edit and to save temporary macros.

Editing Temporary Macros

When you edit a temporary macro you must enter the name otherwise the macro will be written over automatically.

VMS	Reference Keystrokes	DOS
PF2,F18	U: Press *Macro Define*. C: *Prints* Define macro: _.	Ctrl-F10
	U: Type in the name of the macro. C: *Prints macroname* Already Exits: 1 Replace; 2 Edit; 3 Description: <u>0</u>.	

VMS Users: *Temporary   VMS   WordPerfect   macros   are   given   the   filename   of WPCORP_WP51_No.WPM where No is some sixteen-digit hexadecimal number. Depending on how your System Manager set up the system will depend on where these are stored, however, normally they will be in the directory that you log into if your manager assigned the logical name WPCORP$SCRATCH to point to that directory. See your System Manager if you cannot find the temporary macros.*

DOS Users: *Temporary DOS WordPerfect macros are given the filename of wp{wp}.wpm.*

VMS	Reference Keystrokes	DOS
	U: Press *2* for Edit. C: *Positions cursor in the Macro Editor.*	

Saving a Temporary Macro

You can save a temporary macro by changing the current filename to another filename. If you want to save this macro you must rename it before creating another temporary macro or before exiting WordPerfect.

SECTION II:

ADVANCED FEATURES OF
WORDPERFECT 5.1 USING MACROS

CHAPTER 2

SEARCH MACRO

Search Feature

The WordPerfect 5.1 search feature includes Forward Search, Reverse Search, and Search/Replace. Let's review each method along with some finer search comments before we create a macro.

Search Comments

When using WordPerfect 5.1's Search Feature you instruct WordPerfect to look through your document for a search string. The search string may include any type of character(s), WordPerfect code(s), or a combination of the two. For example, you may want to find all occurrences of a specific word in your document or you might want to find all the locations where you had defined a margin setting. In the case of margin settings you would be looking for the margin code in your document, i.e., [L/R Mar].

Codes

When entering WordPerfect codes into search strings do not literally type them in. For example, if you want to search for the Bold code, [BOLD], you should press the **Bold key.** Do not literally type in each character contained in [BOLD] like [and B, etc. When you press the **Bold key,** WordPerfect will automatically place the code into your search string for you. If you want to search for the set of the Bold codes then press the **Bold key** twice.

Case

It is important to remember that the Case of the letters typed in, either uppercase or lowercase, does make a difference when using the Search Feature. For example,

TEXT SEARCHED FOR IN FILE	TEXT FOUND IN FILE	CONCLUSION OF SEARCH
cat	cat	Found
cat	CAT	Found
CAT	CAT	Found
CAT	cat	Not Found

Note that search strings that include uppercase characters will match only with uppercase characters, not with lowercase characters. Whereas, search strings that include lowercase characters will match with both lowercase and uppercase characters. Therefore, to find all strings regardless of case you should use lowercase characters in the search string.

Search for an Unknown Character

To represent one unknown character in a search string you may use Ctrl-X. For example, you may want to search for c_t where the _ represents any character. Thus, you could enter a search string of c^Xt and WordPerfect will automatically replace ^X with any character.

To insert a ^X into a search string do the following after you define the type of search you are performing (see Forward Search, Reverse Search, and/or Search and Replace):

VMS	**Reference Keystrokes**	**DOS**
	U: Press *Ctrl-v.*	
	C: *Prints* Key = _.	
	U: Press *Ctrl-X.*	
	C: *Echoes* ^X.	

Forward Search

Forward Search will search through the user's document from the current location of the cursor to the end of the document looking for the characters and/or codes that the user has specified. Once the sequence of characters and/or codes has been located the cursor will position itself at the end of the sequence. Then the user may edit the sequence and/or continue the search process throughout the document.

To do a forward search follow the instructions below:

VMS	**Reference Keystrokes**	**DOS**
F8	U: Press *->Search.*	F2
	C: *Prints* -> Srch: _.	
	U: Type in the characters and/or codes you want to search for.	
	C: *Echoes characters and/or codes.*	
F8	U: Press *->Search.*	F2
	C: *Searches forward through document for specified characters and/or codes.*	

If an occurrence of the search string is found the cursor will position itself at the end of the string in the document. If the search string is not found, WordPerfect will quickly flash the message * Not found * in the lower left hand corner of your screen.

To search through footnotes/endnotes, headers/footers, graphics box captions, and text boxes, the user must do an extended forward search.

Extended forward search instructions follow:

VMS	Reference Keystrokes	DOS
PF4	U: Press the *Home key.* C: *Extends the search.*	Home
F8	U: Press *->Search.* C: *Prints -> Extended Srch: _.*	F2
	U: Type in the characters and/or codes you want to search for. C: *Echoes characters and/or codes.*	
F8	U: Press *->Search.* C: *Searches forward through document, footnotes/endnotes, headers/footers, graphics box captions, and text boxes for specified characters and/or codes.*	F2

Reverse Search

Reverse Search will search through the user's document from the point where the cursor is located backwards to the beginning of the document looking for the characters and/or codes that the user has specified. Once again, if the search pattern is found, the cursor will position itself at the end of the sequence of characters and/or codes. Then the user may edit the sequence of characters and/or codes and/or continue the search process. In other words, reverse search is the same as forward search except that it searches in the opposite direction.

To do a reverse search follow the instructions below:

VMS	Reference Keystrokes	DOS
PF1,F8	U: Press *<-Search.* C: *Prints <- Srch: _.*	Shift-F2
	U: Type in the characters and/or codes you want to search for. C: *Echoes characters and/or codes.*	
PF1,F8	U: Press *<-Search.* C: *Searches backward through document for specified characters and/or codes.*	Shift-F2

To reverse search through footnotes/endnotes, headers/footers, graphics box captions, and text boxes, the user must do an extended reverse search. Extended reverse search instructions follow:

VMS	Reference Keystrokes	DOS
PF4	U: Press the *Home key.* C: *Extends the search.*	Home
PF1,F8	U: Press *<-Search.* C: *Prints* <- Extended Srch: _.	Shift-F2
	U: Type in the characters and/or codes you want to search for. C: *Echoes characters and/or codes.*	
PF1,F8	U: Press *<-Search.* C: *Searches backwards through document, footnotes/endnotes, headers/footers, graphics box captions, and text boxes for specified characters and/or codes.*	Shift-F2

Search and Replace

Search and Replace will search and replace from the current location of the cursor forward to the end of the document. This is probably the most commonly used method since it allows the user to replace all occurrences of the searched for characters and/or codes with new characters and/or codes throughout the document. This process is done automatically, or with confirmation. That is, the computer replaces all the characters and/or codes in the whole document, or else the user may confirm each replacement by entering yes for the confirm option.

Follow the instructions below to do a search and automatic replacement of all occurrences of a sequence of characters and/or codes:

VMS	Reference Keystrokes	DOS
PF3,F8	U: Press *Replace.* C: *Prints* w/Confirm? No (Yes).	Alt-F2
	U: Press *n* for No. C: *Prints* -> Srch: _.	
	U: Type in the characters and/or codes you want to search for. C: *Echoes characters and/or codes.*	

VMS	**Reference Keystrokes**	**DOS**
PF3,F8	U: Press *Replace.* C: *Prints* Replace with: _.	Alt-F2
	U: Type in the characters and/or codes you want to replace the search for characters and/or codes with. C: *Echoes characters and/or codes.*	
PF3,F8	U: Press *Replace.* C: *Searches forward through document for specified characters and/or codes.*	Alt-F2

Follow the instructions below to do a search and replace if you want to confirm each replacement of a sequence of characters and/or codes:

VMS	**Reference Keystrokes**	**DOS**
PF3,F8	U: Press *Replace.* C: *Prints* w/Confirm? No (Yes).	Alt-F2
	U: Press *y* for Yes. C: *Prints* -> Srch: _.	
	U: Type in the characters and/or codes you want to search for. C: *Echoes characters and/or codes.*	
PF3,F8	U: Press *Replace.* C: *Prints* Replace with: _.	Alt-F2
	U: Type in the characters and/or codes you want to replace the search for characters and/or codes with. C: *Echoes characters and/or codes.*	
PF3,F8	U: Press *Replace.* C: *Searches forward through document for specified characters and/or codes.*	Alt-F2

Be careful with Search and Replace because the codes that you can replace the string with are limited. See the WordPerfect Reference Manual.

To search through footnotes/endnotes, headers/footers, graphics box captions, and text boxes, the user must do an extended search and replace. Extended search and replace instructions follow:

VMS	Reference Keystrokes	DOS
PF4	U: Press the *Home key.* C: *Extends the search.*	Home
PF3,F8	U: Press *Replace.* C: *Prints* w/Confirm? <u>N</u>o (Yes).	Alt-F2
	U: Press *y* for Yes or *n* for No. C: *Prints* -> Srch: _.	
	U: Type in the characters and/or codes you want to search for. C: *Echoes characters and/or codes.*	
PF3,F8	U: Press *Replace.* C: *Prints* Replace with: _.	Alt-F2
	U: Type in the characters and/or codes you want to replace the search for characters and/or codes with. C: *Echoes characters and/or codes.*	
PF3,F8	U: Press *Replace.* C: *Searches forward through document for specified* *characters and/or codes.*	*Alt-F2*

Search and Macros

If the forward or reverse search feature is included in macros and the search string is not found the macro will stop.

Creating a Search Macro

In this section, a search and replace macro will be defined. Elva, the head word processor at an investment corporation, typed in 20 different investment reports that contained an ending date of June 3. This date was stressed several times within each letter. Elva's boss, however, was told that the ending date would be extended to August 24. Therefore, Elva will have to change all the occurrences of June 3 to August 24. In order to save time, Elva can create one simple macro to invoke in each of the 20 investment reports.

Before the next step please make sure that your screen is cleared and that the cursor is located at the top of the cleared screen.

Type in the text on Screen 2-1.

Screen 2-1

```
                    Investment Report

Options Available

   Computer Consulting, Inc. has several options available through
June 3 to research for possible investment strategies.  This report
will explain the specifics of each type of available option and what
must be done by June 3 to take advantage of this great investment
opportunity.
```

VMS	Keystroke Action	DOS
PF2,F18	1. U: Press *Macro Define.* C: *Prints* Define macro: _.	Ctrl-F10
	2. U: Type in <u>SEARCH</u>. C: *Prints* Description: _.	
	3. U: Type in <u>Searches for occurrences of June 3</u> and press the *Enter key.* C: *Prints* Macro Def.	
PF4,PF4, PF4	4. U: Press the *Home, Home, Home, Up arrow* *keys.* C: *Positions cursor at top of document.*	Home, Home, Home
PF3,F8	5. U: Press *Replace.* C: *Prints* w/Confirm? <u>No</u> (Yes).	Alt-F2
	6. U: Press *n* for No. C: *Prints* -> Srch: _.	
	7. U: Type in <u>June 3</u>. C: *Prints* -> Srch: June 3_.	
PF3,F8	8. U: Press *Replace.* C: *Prints* Replace with: _.	Alt-F2
	9. U: Type in <u>August 24</u>. C: *Prints* Replace with: August 24_.	
PF3,F8	10. U: Press *Replace.* C: *Searches forward through document for all* *occurrences of June 3 and replaces it with* *August 24.*	Alt-F2
PF2,F18	11. U: Press *Macro Define.* C: *Saves macro.*	Ctrl-F10

When you define the macro in the main editing screen, the macro will execute as it is being defined.

Applications of the Search Macro

The keystrokes contained in the "SEARCH.WPM" macro are shown on Screen 2-2 or Screen 2-3.

Screen 2-2: VMS Users

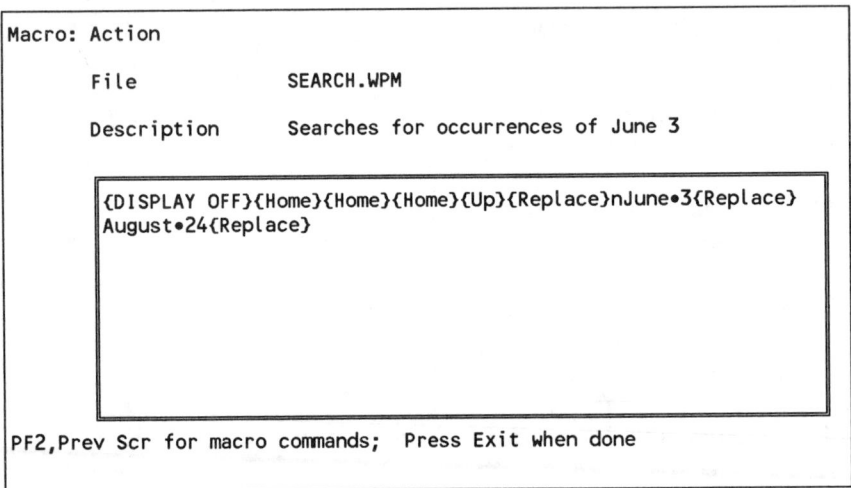

```
Macro: Action

       File            SEARCH.WPM

       Description     Searches for occurrences of June 3

       ┌─────────────────────────────────────────────────────────┐
       │ {DISPLAY OFF}{Home}{Home}{Home}{Up}{Replace}nJune•3{Replace} │
       │ August•24{Replace}                                       │
       │                                                          │
       │                                                          │
       │                                                          │
       │                                                          │
       │                                                          │
       └─────────────────────────────────────────────────────────┘

PF2,Prev Scr for macro commands;  Press Exit when done
```

Screen 2-3: DOS Users

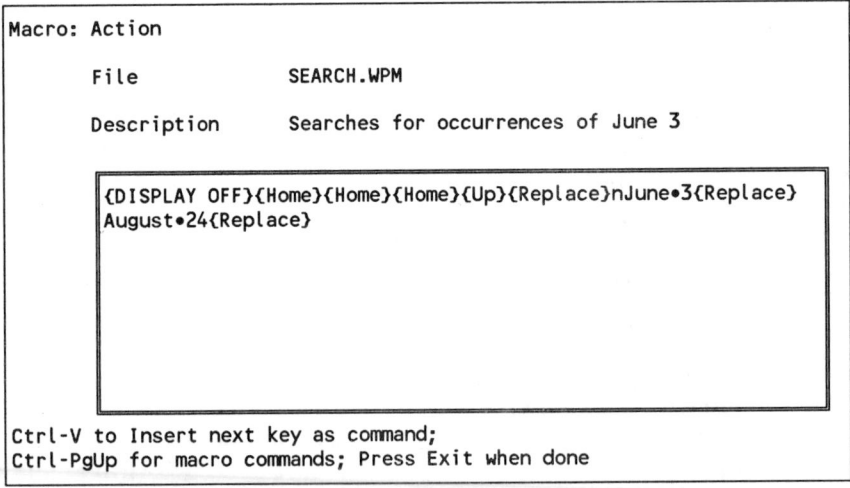

```
Macro: Action

       File            SEARCH.WPM

       Description     Searches for occurrences of June 3

       ┌─────────────────────────────────────────────────────────┐
       │ {DISPLAY OFF}{Home}{Home}{Home}{Up}{Replace}nJune•3{Replace} │
       │ August•24{Replace}                                       │
       │                                                          │
       │                                                          │
       │                                                          │
       └─────────────────────────────────────────────────────────┘

Ctrl-V to Insert next key as command;
Ctrl-PgUp for macro commands; Press Exit when done
```

This macro is ready for immediate use. It can be modified in the Macro Editor to fit your personal needs.

Using the Macro

The initial condition for this macro assumes you have a document on your screen containing the search string of June 3 that you would like to replace with August 24.

Before you invoke the macro you should see a document similar to the one shown on Screen 2-4.

Screen 2-4

```
                         European Holiday

European Travel Packages

    Several new European Travel Packages are available at a special
introductory price through June 3.  These extraordinary tour packages
are described below in explicit detail.  Please browse through the
twenty new selections.  For more information contact your travel agent
by June 3.  Don't miss out on an exciting opportunity!
```

To invoke this macro do the following:

VMS	**Keystroke Action**	**DOS**
PF3,F18	1. U: Press *Macro.* C: *Prints* Macro: _.	Alt-F10
	2. U: Type in <u>SEARCH</u> and press the *Enter key.* C: *Macro invokes.*	

When invoking this macro you will see what is shown on Screen 2-5:

Screen 2-5

```
                         European Holiday

European Travel Packages

    Several new European Travel Packages are available at a special
introductory price through August 24.  These extraordinary tour packages
are described below in explicit detail.  Please browse through the
twenty new selections.  For more information contact your travel agent
by August 24.  Don't miss out on an exciting opportunity!
```

Once the macro is invoked you can check to see that all occurrences of June 3 have automatically been changed to August 24.

Chapter 3

HEADER/FOOTER MACRO

Header/Footer Feature

Two powerful features of WordPerfect 5.1 are headers and footers. Headers and footers are often used in lengthy documents. For example, most business proposals and term papers use headers and/or footers.

A header is a heading located at the top of every page of a document. It can contain the title of the document, page numbers, author's name, graphic pictures, etc.

A footer is located at the bottom of every page of a document.

Headers and footers can contain the same items, therefore, only one is normally used in a document. However, it may be desirable to use a header for the title and a footer for the page number.

WordPerfect 5.1 includes two different headers, Header A and Header B, and two different footers, Footer A and Footer B. Headers and/or footers may be located on every page, odd pages, or even pages.

For example, the company "Investment Broker, Incorporated," that writes a daily stock market analysis, uses both a header and a footer. Every day a new report is created and the same heading is used on each page of the paper and the page number is always located at the bottom of the page. In this example, one header and one footer will be used in a four page business report. The header will contain the title of the report and the footer will contain the page numbers. A powerful macro can be created to save time for the writer of the report by adding the final touches of the header and footer to the stock market analysis report, every time it is needed. The business report will maintain consistency by using this simple macro. The layout of the four page business report is shown in Figure 3-1.

Figure 3-1

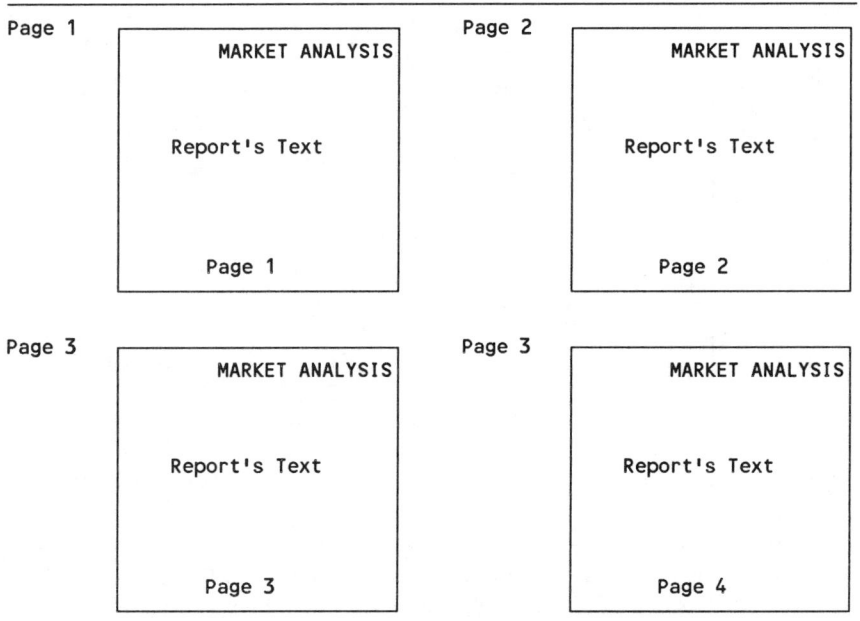

Writing a chapter for a book is an example of where two headers may be required.

The layout of the first five pages in one chapter is shown in Figure 3-2. Note that Page 2 and Page 3 are facing pages, that is, in the actual book even pages will be located on the left side and odd pages will be located on the right side.

Let Header A contain the title of the book, WORDPERFECT 5.1, and the page number and be located on every left page of the file. Let Header B contain the title of the chapter, MACRO FEATURES, and page number and be located on every right page. Header A will be inserted into the document on the first even page, page 2. Header B will be inserted into the document on the second odd page, page 3, since on the first page of the chapter the heading and page numbers are usually omitted.

Figure 3-2

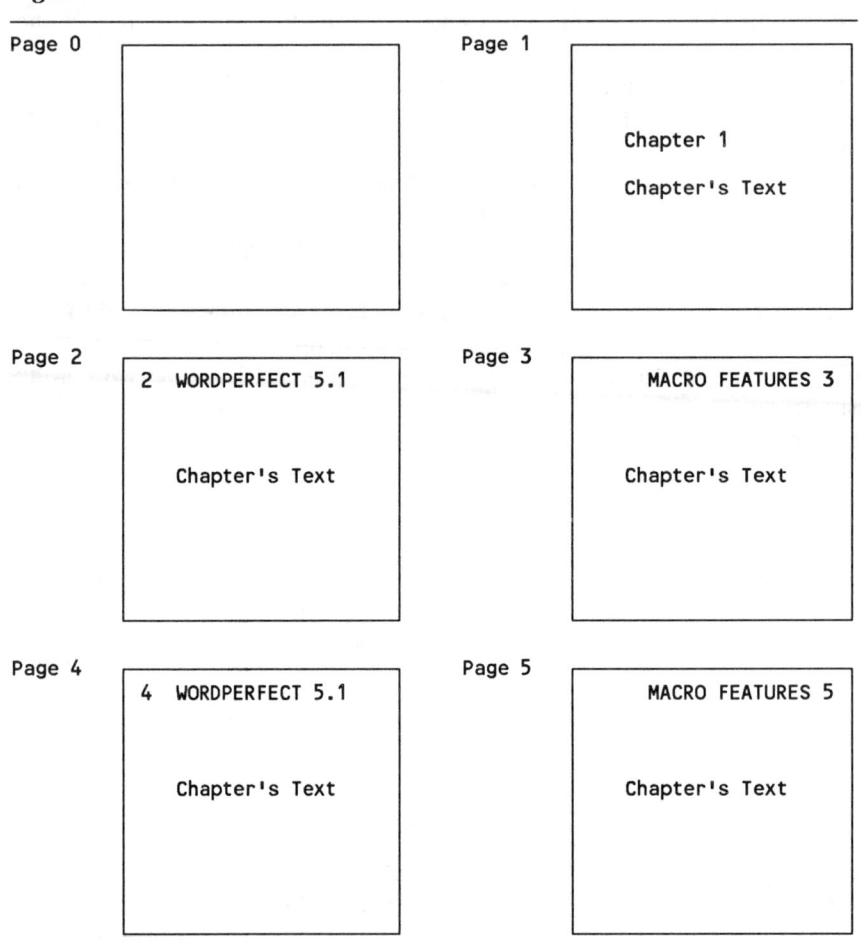

Headers and Footers are not seen on the screen. They may only be seen when the user prints or views the document.

Space is automatically allotted below the top margin or above the bottom margin for the header and/or footers on the pages of the document where they will be located. Headers and footers are located within the text and outside of your margins. Thus, the user does not need to set aside any space for these two features since they will be incorporated into the document's text.

To define a header or footer do the following:

VMS	**Reference Keystrokes**	**DOS**
PF1,F14	U: Press *Format.* C: *Displays Format Menu.*	Shift-F8
	U: Press *2* for Page. C: *Displays Format: Page Menu.*	
	U: Press *3* for Headers or *4* for Footers. C: *Prints* 1 Header A; 2 Header B; 0 *or else* 1 Footer A; 2 Footer B; 0.	
	U: Press *1* for Header A or Footer A or *2* for Header B or Footer B. C: *Prints* 1 Discontinue; 2 Every Page; 3 Odd Pages; 4 Even Pages; 5 Edit: 0.	
F13	U: Press *2* for Every Page if you want the Header/Footer displayed on every page, or press *3* if you want the Header/Footer displayed only on odd pages, or else press *4* if you want the Header/Footer displayed only on even pages. If for some reason you decide you do not want to create a Header or Footer then first press *1* for Discontinue, next press *Exit* to return back to your document. This will insert the following code into your document if you discontinue Header A for example: [Header A:Discontinue]. C: *Displays the Header or Footer Edit Screen.*	F7

Screen 3-1 shows the Footer A edit screen. This screen looks identical for both headers and footers except for the lower left-hand side status line that identifies what header or footer you are currently editing, for example, Header A, Header B, Footer A, or Footer B. In this screen we are editing Footer A.

Screen 3-1

```
┌─────────────────────────────────────────────────────────────────┐
│                                                                   │
│                                                                   │
│                                                                   │
│                                                                   │
│                                                                   │
│                                                                   │
│                                                                   │
│                                                                   │
│                                                                   │
│                                                                   │
│                                                                   │
│                                                                   │
│                                                                   │
│ Footer A:   Press Exit when done                    Ln 1" Pos 1"  │
│                                                                   │
└─────────────────────────────────────────────────────────────────┘
```

VMS	Reference Keystrokes	DOS
PF2	U: Type in the information you want in your Header or Footer. To include the consecutive page numbering in the Header or Footer press *^B* (Control-B) in the location where you want the page number to be displayed. C: *Echoes characters.*	Ctrl
F13	U: Press *Exit* when you are done. This will save the Header or Footer. C: *Displays Format: Page Menu.*	F7
F13	U: Press *Exit.* C: *Returns to Document.*	F7

When typing in the information for your header and/or footer you can make use of WordPerfect's features including fonts, underline, bold, and center.

After you have defined one or two Headers and/or Footers a HA, HB, FA, and/or FB will appear along with Every page, Odd pages, and/or Even pages on the Format: Page Menu. Thus, you will know which Headers and/or Footers you have defined.

If you want the header to be shown on the very first page of your document you must define the header at the very top of your document before any visible text.

To edit a Header or Footer after you have already defined it do the following:

VMS	Reference Keystrokes	DOS
PF1,F14	U: Press *Format.* C: *Displays Format Menu.*	Shift-F8

VMS   Reference Keystrokes   DOS

U: Press *2* for Page.
C: *Displays Format: Page Menu.*

U: Press *3* for Headers or else *4* for Footers.
C: *Prints* 1 Header A; 2 Header B: <u>0</u> *or else*
1 Footer A; 2 Footer B: <u>0</u>.

U: Press *1* for Header A or Footer A or *2* for
Header B or Footer B.
C: *Prints* 1 Discontinue; 2 Every Page; 3 Odd
Pages; 4 Even Pages; 5 Edit: <u>0</u>.

U: Press *5* for Edit.
C: *Displays Header or Footer Edit Screen.*

U: Edit the Header or Footer.
C: *Echoes characters.*

F13   U: Press *Exit* when you are done. This will save   F7
the new Header or Footer.
C: *Displays Format: Page Menu.*

F13   U: Press *Exit.*   F7
C: *Returns to Document.*

WordPerfect automatically searches backwards through your document and the first occurrence of a header or footer will be the one selected for you to edit. If WordPerfect does not find a header or footer then it will search forward through your document until it reaches the end of the document. If a header or footer is not found WordPerfect will display a *Not found* message.

Creating a Header/Footer Macro

In this section, a macro will be created which automatically inserts the same header and/or footer into any document.

Before the next step please make sure that your screen is cleared and that the cursor is located at the top of the cleared screen.

A document must first be created before you can establish a header and footer.

First, in order to type as little as possible, the left and right margins will be increased. Change your left and right margins to 2" each.

Second, the top and bottom margins need to be increased, so that you do not have to type in a very long document in order to see how this macro works. Change your top and bottom margins to 2" each.

Third, WordPerfect 5.1's default single line spacing needs to be changed to double spacing. Change line spacing to 2.

Now, since the margins and spacing settings have been changed, each page will contain only a small amount of text. Type in enough text to fill a few pages in order to see how your headers and footers work. This text may be about anything. If you do not want to type anything in you can also press the *Enter key* until you reach Page 3 of your document.

After your document is created you should save the document before continuing. Save your document by typing in the correct file specification (VMS) or pathname (DOS) and give it the filename of wpdoc.

Now we can create the header and footer macro. We will begin with a Footer on the first page in order to have a footer on every page including the first. The Footer will contain the page number and will be located at the bottom of every page.

VMS	**Keystroke Action**	**DOS**
PF2,F18	1. U: Press *Macro Define.* C: *Prints* Define macro: _.	Ctrl-F10
	2. U: Type in <u>HEADFOOT</u> and press the *Enter key*. C: *Prints* Description: _.	
	3. U: Type in <u>Document header and footer</u> and press the *Enter key*. C: *Prints* Macro Def.	
PF4,PF4, PF4	4. U: Press the *Home, Home, Home, Up arrow keys*. C: *Moves the cursor to top of document.*	Home, Home, Home
PF1,F14	5. U: Press *Format.* C: *Displays Format Menu.*	Shift-F8
	6. U: Press *2* for Page. C: *Displays Format: Page Menu.*	
	7. U: Press *4* for Footers. C: *Prints* 1 Footer A; 2 Footer B: <u>0</u>.	
	8. U: Press *1* for Footer A. C: *Prints* 1 Discontinue; 2 Every Page; 3 Odd Pages; 4 Even Pages; 5 Edit; <u>0</u>.	
	9. U: Press *2* for Every Page. C: *Displays Footer Edit Menu.*	
	10. U: Press the *Tab key* four times. C: *Inserts programming codes.*	
	11. U: Type in <u>Page</u>. C: *Echoes characters.*	

VMS	**Keystroke Action**	**DOS**
	12. U: Press the *space bar* once. C: *Inserts code.*	

PF2	13. U: Hold down the *Ctrl key* and tap *b,* then lift
	       hand up.
	       C: *Inserts ^B code into the Footer.*
		Ctrl

F13	14. U: Press *Exit.* C: *Displays Format: Page Menu.*	F7
F13	15. U: Press *Exit.* C: *Returns to Document.*	F7
KP3	16. U: Press the *PgDn key.* C: *Positions cursor on the next page.*	PgDn

The Header will be defined on Page 2 in order to have the first header on the second page. The header will contain your last name since you typed in the document.

VMS	**Keystroke Action**	**DOS**
PF1,F14	17. U: Press *Format.* C: *Displays Format Menu.*	Shift-F8
	18. U: Press *2* for Page. C: *Displays Format: Page Menu.*	
	19. U: Press *3* for Headers. C: *Prints* 1 Header A; 2 Header B: <u>0</u>.	

	20. U: Press *1* for Header A.
	       C: *Prints* 1 Discontinue; 2 Every Page; 3 Odd
	       Pages; 4 Even Pages; 5 Edit: <u>0</u>.	

	21. U: Press *2* for Every Page. C: *Displays Header Edit Screen.*	
	22. U: Press the *Tab key* 7 times. C: *Inserts programming codes.*	
	23. U: Type in your last name. C: *Echoes characters.*	
F13	24. U: Press *Exit.* C: *Displays Format: Page Menu.*	F7

VMS	Keystroke Action	DOS
F13	25. U: Press *Exit*. C: *Returns to Document*.	F7

PF2,F18	26. U: Press *Macro Define* to finish defining the
	       macro.
	       C: *Saves macro*.
		Ctrl-F10

Applications of the Header/Footer Macro

The keystrokes contained in the "HEADFOOT.WPM" macro are shown on Screen 3-2 or Screen 3-3.

Screen 3-2: VMS Users

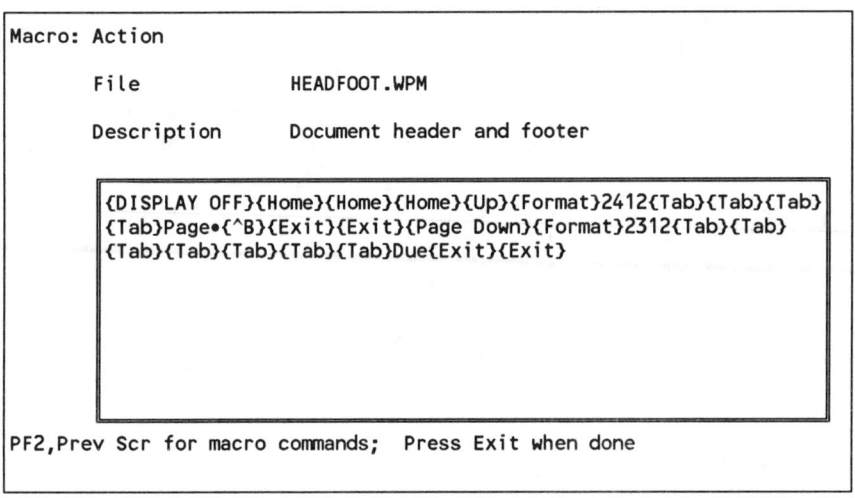

```
Macro: Action

        File            HEADFOOT.WPM

        Description     Document header and footer

    ┌─────────────────────────────────────────────────────────┐
    │ {DISPLAY OFF}{Home}{Home}{Home}{Up}{Format}2412{Tab}{Tab}{Tab}│
    │ {Tab}Page•{^B}{Exit}{Exit}{Page Down}{Format}2312{Tab}{Tab} │
    │ {Tab}{Tab}{Tab}{Tab}{Tab}Due{Exit}{Exit}                  │
    │                                                           │
    └─────────────────────────────────────────────────────────┘

PF2,Prev Scr for macro commands;   Press Exit when done
```

Screen 3-3: DOS Users

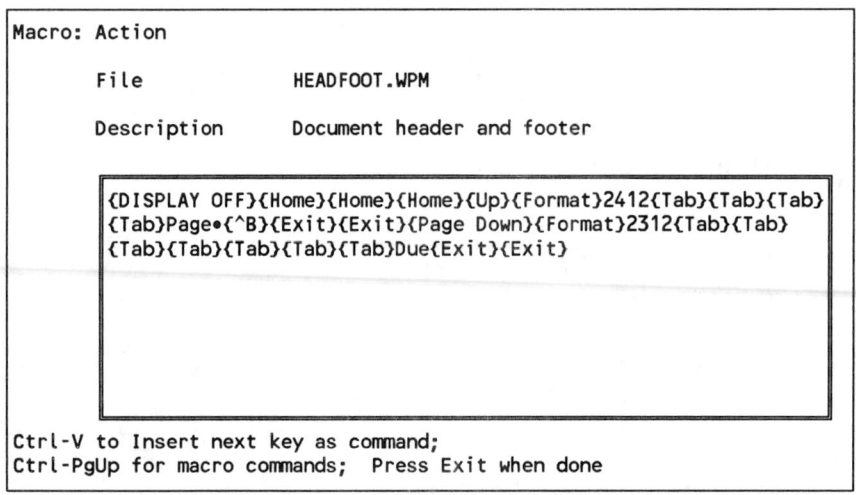

```
Macro: Action

        File            HEADFOOT.WPM

        Description     Document header and footer

    ┌─────────────────────────────────────────────────────────┐
    │ {DISPLAY OFF}{Home}{Home}{Home}{Up}{Format}2412{Tab}{Tab}{Tab}│
    │ {Tab}Page•{^B}{Exit}{Exit}{Page Down}{Format}2312{Tab}{Tab} │
    │ {Tab}{Tab}{Tab}{Tab}{Tab}Due{Exit}{Exit}                  │
    │                                                           │
    └─────────────────────────────────────────────────────────┘

Ctrl-V to Insert next key as command;
Ctrl-PgUp for macro commands;   Press Exit when done
```

This macro is ready for immediate use if you have inserted your last name into the document. It can be modified in the Macro Editor to fit your personal needs.

Using the Macro

The initial conditions for this macro assume you are starting a new document or that you are currently editing a document to include a header that contains your last name and this particular footer that contains the Page number.

To invoke this macro do the following:

VMS	Keystroke Action	DOS
PF3,F18	1. U: Press *Macro.* C: *Prints* Macro: _.	Alt-F10
	2. U: Type in <u>HEADFOOT</u> and press the *Enter key.* C: *Macro invokes.*	

When this macro invokes you will not see the actual header and footer on your screen. To see the actual header and footer you must print or view the document.

CHAPTER 4

FONT MACROS

Font Feature

WordPerfect 5.1 allows the user to choose from a variety of different fonts within any document. These include resident, soft, and hard fonts. Also, WordPerfect 5.1 lets the user change the current font's size and/or appearance. These features help the user create distinctive and professional looking documents.

Postscript and laser printers use these font capabilities to their maximum potential. Other printers may not have a wide font variety from which to choose.

Fonts

A **font** refers to a set of letters, numbers, and special symbols sharing the same typeface, style, and point size.

Typeface refers to the same type of image for all the characters in the font set. There are many different typefaces available such as Courier, Helvetica, Times Roman, etc. The two major typefaces are the serif and sans serif families. The serif typeface family contains beginning and/or ending tails on the characters, like the characters you are currently reading in this book. This typeface is traditional and people prefer it since the characters are easy to read. The sans serif typeface family does not contain tails and the characters are more rounded and, therefore, blend into each other. This typeface is often used for headings since it is very modern looking and attracts people's attention. However, this typeface is harder to read over an extended length of time.

Style refers to a modification of the typeface. For example, styles include italic, bold, bold italic, and normal.

Point size refers to the height measurement of the characters as opposed to the pitch, or the number of characters per inch. Point size is used by most computer users, while pitch is used more by stenographers. Many different point sizes are available, usually in the range from 8 to 96. The most common point size used is somewhere between 10 and 12 point. The 72 point size refers to characters with the height measurement of one inch. The 10 point size, 10/72, is approximately equal to 10 pitch.

A **resident font** is a printer's internal font. It is the default typeface for the printer.

A **soft font,** also known as a **downloadable font,** is a typeface which is stored on a floppy or hard disk and must be downloaded into the printer's memory before it can be used by the printer. Some printers do not accept soft fonts.

A **hard font,** also known as a **font cartridge,** is a small piece of hardware that contains a circuit board with different typefaces stored on it. This cartridge must be inserted into a laser printer for use.

Selecting Fonts to Use in WordPerfect 5.1

In order to select a soft font you must have the file(s) containing that specific font on your hard disk or your floppy disk drive. To select a hard font you must have the font cartridge containing that specific font. To select soft or hard fonts do the following:

VMS   Reference Keystrokes   DOS

PF1,F13   U: Press *Print*.   Shift-F7
                   C: *Displays Print Menu.*

The Print Menu is shown on Screen 4-1, Screen 4-2, or Screen 4-3.

Screen 4-1: VMS Users - Digital LN03 Plus

```
Print

     1 - Full Document
     2 - Page
     3 - Document on Disk
     4 - Control Printer
     5 - Multiple Pages
     6 - View Document
     7 - Initialize Printer

Options

     S - Select Printer              Digital LN03 Plus
     B - Binding Offset              0"
     N - Number of Copies            1
     G - Graphics Quality            Medium
     T - Text Quality                High

     J - Job Priority                100
     O - Notify Job Started/Completed   Yes
     L - Flag Pages                  None
     H - Hold                        No
         Automatic Release Time
     A - Alternating Pages           No

Selection: 0
```

Screen 4-2: VMS Users - Digital LN03R (ScriptPrinter)

```
Print

    1 - Full Document
    2 - Page
    3 - Document on Disk
    4 - Control Printer
    5 - Multiple Pages
    6 - View Document
    7 - Initialize Printer

Options

    S - Select Printer              Digital LN03R (ScriptPrinter)
    B - Binding Offset              0"
    N - Number of Copies            1
    G - Graphics Quality            Medium
    T - Text Quality                High

    J - Job Priority                100
    O - Notify Job Started/Completed Yes
    L - Flag Pages                  None
    H - Hold                        No
        Automatic Release Time
    A - Alternating Pages           No

Selection: 0
```

Screen 4-3: DOS Users - HP LaserJet IIP

```
Print

    1 - Full Document
    2 - Page
    3 - Document on Disk
    4 - Control Printer
    5 - Multiple Pages
    6 - View Document
    7 - Initialize Printer

Options

    S - Select Printer              HP LaserJet IIP
    B - Binding Offset              0"
    N - Number of Copies            1
    U - Multiple Copies Generated by WordPerfect
    G - Graphics Quality            Medium
    T - Text Quality                High



Selection: 0
```

VMS   **Reference Keystrokes**   **DOS**

U: Press *S* for Select Printer.
C: *Displays Print: Select Printer Menu.*

The Print: Select Printer Menu looks similar to Screen 4-4 or Screen 4-5, depending on what types of printers you have installed. The * printer is the printer that is currently being used by WordPerfect for your document.

If you do not have a printer connected to your computer select one anyway so you can see how the fonts would appear on that selected printer. Preferably select a laser or postscript printer in order to take full advantage of Wordperfect 5.1's font feature.

Screen 4-4: VMS Users

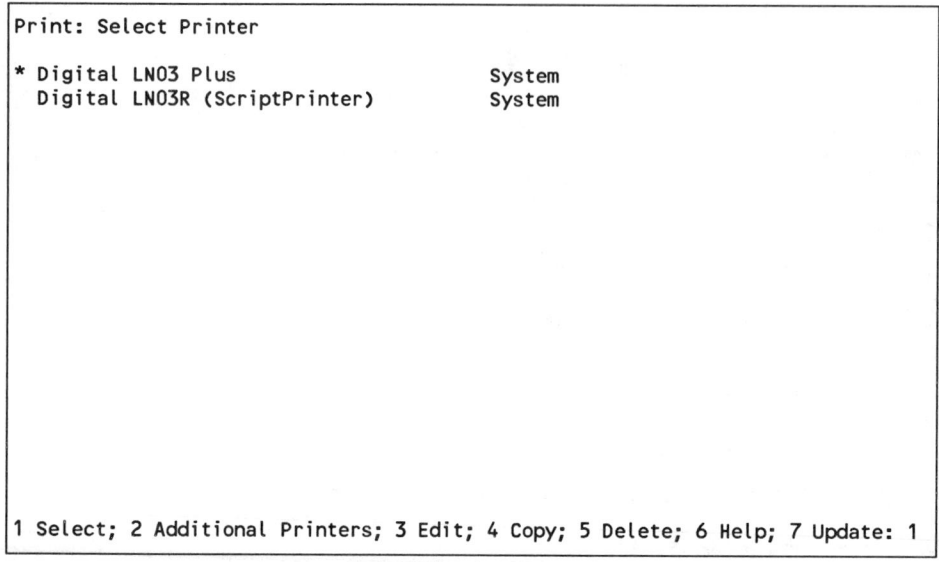

```
Print: Select Printer

* Digital LNO3 Plus                        System
  Digital LNO3R (ScriptPrinter)            System
```

```
1 Select; 2 Additional Printers; 3 Edit; 4 Copy; 5 Delete; 6 Help; 7 Update: 1
```

VMS Users: System means that a queue has been associated with the printer, however if a queue has not been associated with the printer you will see: No Output Type.

Screen 4-5: DOS Users

```
Print: Select Printer

* HP LaserJet IIP
  HP LaserJet Series II
  Panasonic KX-P1124
```

```
1 Select; 2 Additional Printers; 3 Edit; 4 Copy; 5 Delete; 6 Help; 7 Update: 1
```

VMS Users: Editing is shown in the following step. Please note that it might not be possible for you to Edit your printer. This is because you might not have enough VMS privileges. Ask your system manager about this function. If you try to edit your printer and you see the following: ***ERROR:*** *No privileges to edit PRS file (PTR51-NOEDIT) then at that point WordPerfect has verified that you do not have the correct privilege.*

VMS   Reference Keystrokes   DOS

U: Press *3* for Edit.
C: *Displays Select Printer: Edit Menu.*

The Select Printer: Edit Menu is shown on Screen 4-6, Screen 4-7, or Screen 4-8.

Screen 4-6: VMS Users - Digital LN03 Plus

```
Select Printer: Edit

        Filename                DILNOPLU.PRS

    1 - Name                    Digital LN03 Plus

    2 - Output Type             System Queue

    3 - Sheet Feeder            None

    4 - Cartridges and Fonts

    5 - Initial Base Font       Courier 10cpi

    6 - Path for Downloadable   N/A
        Fonts and Printer
        Command Files

Selection: 0
```

Screen 4-7: VMS Users - Digital LN03R (ScriptPrinter)

```
Select Printer: Edit

        Filename                DILNOSCR.PRS

    1 - Name                    Digital LN03R (ScriptPrinter)

    2 - Output Type             System Queue

    3 - Sheet Feeder            None

    4 - Cartridges and Fonts

    5 - Initial Base Font       Courier 12 pt

    6 - Path for Downloadable   N/A
        Fonts and Printer
        Command Files

Selection: 0
```

Screen 4-8: DOS Users - HP LaserJet IIP

```
Select Printer: Edit

        Filename                      HPLASIIP.PRS

    1 - Name                          HP LaserJet IIP

    2 - Port                          LPT1:

    3 - Sheet Feeder                  None

    4 - Cartridges/Fonts/Print Wheels

    5 - Initial Base Font             Courier 10cpi

    6 - Path for Downloadable
          Fonts and Printer
          Command Files

    7 - Print to Hardware Port        No

Selection: 0
```

Downloadable Fonts Location

If you have downloadable fonts available on your computer to download to your printer then you must specify where they are located. Do the following:

VMS	**Reference Keystrokes**	**DOS**
	U: Press *6* for Path for Downloadable Fonts and Printer Command Files if you are going to select downloadable fonts instead of a font cartridge.	
VMS Users	C: *Prints* Location of Printer Files: _.	
	C: *Positions cursor to right of* Path for Downloadable Fonts and Printer Command Files.	*DOS Users*
	U: Enter file specification/pathname for location of downloadable fonts and press the *Enter key.*	
	C: *Echoes characters and Returns you to Select Printer: Edit Menu.*	

VMS Users: *On your Select Printer: Edit Menu Next to Path for Downloadable Fonts and Printer Command Files you might see N/A this means that this option does not apply. The reason why this option does not apply pertains to the way the print queues were created. Your system manager created integrated print queues which finds any downloadable fonts by always using the logical WPCORP$PTR51DOWNLOAD that points to the file specification, thus this option will not allow you to enter in a different file specification.*

Cartridges and Fonts

The fourth option of the Select Printer: Edit Menu (Screens 4-6 to 4-8) allows you to specify what cartridges and fonts you would like to use with your particular printer.

VMS	**Reference Keystrokes**	**DOS**

VMS Users   U: Press *4* for Cartridges and Fonts.
               U: Press *4* for Cartridges/Fonts/Print Wheels.   *DOS Users*
VMS Users   C: *Displays Select Printer Menu.*
               C: *Displays Select Printer: Cartridges/Fonts/Print*   *DOS Users*
               Wheels Menu.

The Menu displayed looks like Screen 4-9, Screen 4-10, or Screen 4-11.

Screen 4-9: VMS Users - Digital LN03 Plus

```
Select Printer:

Font Category                    Quantity    Available

Built-In
Cartridges                          2           2




NOTE: Most fonts listed under the Font Category (with the exception of Built-In)
are optional and must be purchased separately from your dealer or manufacturer.

Font Selection and Printer Initialization methods vary with selected output
types.  Refer to the Reference Manual or System Manager's Guide for
information regarding Font Selection and Printer Initialization.

If soft fonts are not located in the same directory as your printer files, you
must specify a Path for Downloadable Fonts in the Select Printer: Edit menu.



1 Select 2 Change Quantity; N Name search: 1
```

Screen 4-10: VMS Users - Digital LN03R (ScriptPrinter)

```
Select Printer:

Font Category                         Quantity      Available

Built-In
Soft Fonts                            470 K         470 K




NOTE: Most fonts listed under the Font Category (with the exception of Built-In)
are optional and must be purchased separately from your dealer or manufacturer.

Font Selection and Printer Initialization methods vary with selected output
types.  Refer to the Reference Manual or System Manager's Guide for
information regarding Font Selection and Printer Initialization.

If soft fonts are not located in the same directory as your printer files, you
must specify a Path for Downloadable Fonts in the Select Printer: Edit menu.




1 Select 2 Change Quantity; N Name search: 1
```

Screen 4-11: DOS Users - HP LaserJet IIP

```
Select Printer: Cartridges/Fonts/Print Wheels

Font Category                         Quantity      Available

Built-In
Cartridges                               1             1
Soft Fonts                            350 K         350 K




NOTE: Most fonts listed under the Font Category (with the exception of Built-In)
are optional and must be purchased separately from your dealer or manufacturer.
If you have fonts not listed, they may be supported on an additional printer
diskette.  For more information call WP at (801) 225-5000

If soft fonts are marked '*', you must run the Initialize Printer option in WP
each time you turn on your printer.  Doing so deletes all soft fonts in printer
memory and downloads those marked with '*'.

If soft fonts are not located in the same directory as your printer files, you
must specify a Path for Downloadable Fonts in the Select Printer: Edit menu.

1 Select; 2 Change Quantity; N Name search: 1
```

In Screen 4-9 through Screen 4-11 the following options are available:

Select: Allows you to modify the types of Fonts available through Built-In, Cartridges, or Soft Fonts. Different printers will have different Font types available.

| Change Quantity: | Lets the user change the quantity of Cartridges, number of slots available for font cartridges, or change the amount of memory available for downloadable fonts. |
| **Name search:** | Provides the means to search for a preferred item. |

Depending on what type of printer you are using will determine what type of Font Categories you will see. All printers have the Built-In Font Category. Whether you have Cartridges, Soft Fonts, and/or any other type of Font Category depends on your printer.

Described below are three possible options.

1. Built-In

The Built-In fonts are the fonts that come with your printer.

To modify the Built-In fonts available for your printer do the following:

VMS   Reference Keystrokes   DOS

U: Highlight the *Built-In* option.
C: *Highlights Built-In option.*

U: Press *1* for Select.
C: *Displays Select Printer: Built-In Menu.*

The Select Printer: Built-In Menu for the Built-In option looks like Screen 4-12, Screen 4-13, or Screen 4-14.

Screen 4-12: VMS Users - Digital LN03 Plus

```
Select Print: Built-In

*  Courier 10.3cpi
*  Courier 10.3cpi (Land)
*  Courier 10cpi
*  Courier 10cpi (Land)
*  Courier 13.6cpi
*  Courier 13.6cpi (Land)
*  Elite 12cpi
*  Elite 12cpi (Land)
*  Line Draw 10cpi
*  Modern Gothic 08cpi
*  Modern Gothic 08cpi (Land)




Mark:  * Present when print job begins        Press Exit to save
                                             Press Cancel to cancel
```

Screen 4-13: VMS Users - Digital LN03R (ScriptPrinter)

```
Select Print: Built-In

*  Courier
*  Courier Bold
*  Courier Bold Oblique
*  Courier Oblique
*  Helvetica
*  Helvetica Bold
*  Helvetica Bold Oblique
*  Helvetica Narrow
*  Helvetica Narrow Bold
*  Helvetica Narrow Oblique
*  Helvetica Oblique
*  ITC Avant Garde Gothic Book
*  ITC Avant Garde Gothic Book Oblique
*  ITC Avant Garde Gothic Demi
*  ITC Avant Garde Gothic Demi Oblique
*  ITC Lubalin Graph Book
*  ITC Lubalin Graph Book Oblique
*  ITC Lubalin Graph Demi

Mark:  * Present when print job begins          Press Exit to save
                                             Press Cancel to cancel
```

Screen 4-14: DOS Users - HP LaserJet IIP

```
Select Printer: Built-In

*  Courier 10cpi
*  Courier 10cpi Bold
*  Courier 10cpi Italic
*  Courier 12cpi
*  Courier 12cpi Bold
*  Courier 12cpi Italic
*  Line Printer 16.67cpi


















Mark:  * Present when print job begins          Press Exit to save
                                             Press Cancel to cancel
```

Initially, all of the base fonts are available in your printer (as marked by the *) whenever you print a document unless you modify the Built-In fonts. To modify the Built-In fonts by specifying that they be available always (indicated by the *) do the following:

VMS	Reference Keystrokes	DOS

U: Use the *Arrow keys* to highlight preferred built-in font.
C: *Highlights font.*

U: Place * next to the built-in font you wish to select.
C: *Echoes *'s.*

To erase an * highlight the cartridge and press the *Delete key.*

When a font is selected with an asterisk (*) it means that the font is available when a print job begins.

Do the following after you have selected the fonts you want to use.

VMS	Reference Keystrokes	DOS

F13   U: Press *Exit* five times.   F7
C: *Returns to Document.*

2. Cartridges

To modify the cartridges available for your printer do the following (when you are located on Screen 4-9 to 4-11):

VMS Users: Note that the Cartridges option is not available for the Digital LN03R (ScriptPrinter).

VMS	Reference Keystrokes	DOS

U: Highlight the *Cartridges* option.
C: *Highlights Cartridges option.*

U: Press *1* for Select.
C: *Displays Select Printer: Cartridges Menu.*

The Select Printer: Cartridges Menu for the **Cartridges** option looks like Screen 4-15 or Screen 4-16.

Screen 4-15: VMS Users - Digital LN03 Plus

```
Select Printer: Cartridges          Quantity
                        Total:          2
                    Available:          2

Cartridge Fonts                              Quantity Used

    CG Times (14-18pt) Cartridge                   1
    CG Times 24pt Cartridge                        1
    CG Times Cartridge                             1
    CG Triumvirate (14-18pt) Cartridge             1
    CG Triumvirate 24pt Cartridge                  1
    English 116 Embassy Cartridge                  1
    ITC Souvenir Cartridge                         1
    Letter Gothic Cartridge                        1
    Monospace Swiss Large Cartridge                1
    Monospaced Swiss (14-18pt) Cartridge           1
    OCR A/OCR B Cartridge                          1
    US Legal Cartridge                             1

Mark:  * Present when print job begins      Press Exit to save
                                            Press Cancel to cancel
```

Screen 4-16: DOS Users - HP LaserJet IIP

```
Select Printer: Cartridges          Quantity
                        Total:          1
                    Available:          1

Cartridge Fonts                              Quantity Used

    HP A Courier 1                                 1
    HP B Tms Proportional 1                        1
    HP Bar Codes & More                            1
    HP C International 1                           1
    HP D Prestige Elite                            1
    HP E Letter Gothic                            1
    HP F Tms Proportional 2                        1
    HP Forms Etc.                                  1
    HP G Legal Elite                              1
    HP Global Text                                1
    HP Great Start                                1
    HP H Legal Courier                            1
    HP J Math Elite                                1
    HP K Math Tms                                  1
    HP L Courier P&L                               1
    HP M Prestige Elite P&L

Mark:  * Present when print job begins      Press Exit to save
                                            Press Cancel to cancel
```

VMS   Reference Keystrokes   DOS

U: Use the *Arrow keys* to highlight preferred cartridge.

C: *Highlights cartridge.*

VMS	**Reference Keystrokes**	**DOS**

U: Place ***** next to the cartridges you wish to select.
C: *Echoes *'s.*

To erase an ***** highlight the cartridge and press the ***Delete key.***

The **Total Quantity** in the upper right hand corner of Screen 4-12 or Screen 4-13 equals the total number of font cartridge slots available. The **Available Quantity** equals the number of font cartridge slots not in use.

When a font is selected with an asterisk (*) it means that the font cartridge is in the slot when a print job begins.

Do the following after you have selected the cartridge you want to use.

VMS	**Reference Keystrokes**	**DOS**
F13	U: Press *Exit* five times. C: *Returns to Document.*	F7

3. Soft Fonts

Allows you to select specific fonts, if you have soft fonts available, that you can download from your computer system into your printer's memory. These are called soft fonts.

VMS Users: Note that the Soft Fonts option is not available for the Digital LN03 Plus.

VMS	**Reference Keystrokes**	**DOS**

U: Highlight the *Soft Fonts* option.
C: *Highlights font option.*

U: Press *1* for Select.
C: *Displays Select Printer: Cartridges or Select Printer: Soft Fonts Menu.*

VMS Users: ***When you select soft fonts for the Digital LN03R (ScriptPrinter) you will see Screen 4-18 immediately (bypassing Screen 4-17).***

DOS Users: ***The Select Printer: Soft Fonts Menu for the Soft Fonts option looks like Screen 4-17.***

Screen 4-17: DOS Users - HP LaserJet IIP

```
Select Printer: Soft Fonts

Font Groups:

  HP AC TmsRmn/Helv US (P/L)
  HP AD TmsRmn/Helv R8 (P/L)
  HP AE TmsRmn/Helv US (P/L)
  HP AF TmsRmn/Helv R8 (P/L)
  HP AG Helv Headlines PC-8 (P/L)












1 Select; N Name search: 1
```

If you select the soft font group of HP AC TmsRmn/Helv US (P/L) then you would see the following Soft Fonts available (See Screen 4-19).

Screen 4-18: VMS Users - Digital LN03R (ScriptPrinter)

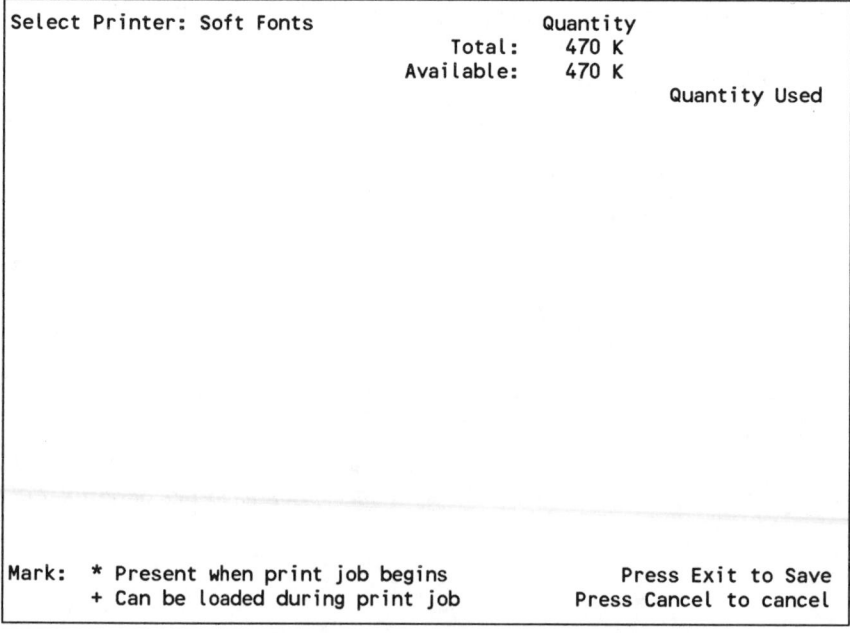

```
Select Printer: Soft Fonts              Quantity
                             Total:     470 K
                         Available:     470 K
                                                 Quantity Used












Mark:  * Present when print job begins        Press Exit to Save
       + Can be loaded during print job     Press Cancel to cancel
```

Screen 4-19: DOS Users - HP LaserJet IIP

```
Select Printer: Soft Fonts                  Quantity
                                 Total:      350 K
                             Available:      350 K

HP AC TmsRmn/Helv US (P/L)                    Quantity Used
    (AC) Helv  6pt                                 8 K
    (AC) Helv  6pt Bold                            8 K
    (AC) Helv  6pt Italic                          8 K
    (AC) Helv  8pt                                 9 K
    (AC) Helv  8pt Bold                           11 K
    (AC) Helv  8pt Italic                         10 K
    (AC) Helv 10pt                                13 K
    (AC) Helv 10pt Bold                           13 K
    (AC) Helv 10pt Italic                         14 K
    (AC) Helv 12pt                                15 K
    (AC) Helv 12pt Bold                           16 K
    (AC) Helv 12pt Italic                         16 K
    (AC) Helv 14pt                                18 K
    (AC) Helv 14pt Bold                           19 K
    (AC) Helv 14pt Italic                         20 K
    (AC) Helv 18pt Bold                           29 K


Mark:  * Present when print job begins        Press Exit to Save
       + Can be loaded/unloaded during job   Press Cancel to cancel
```

VMS   Reference Keystrokes   DOS

U: Use the *Arrow keys* to highlight preferred font.
C: *Highlights cartridge or font.*

U: Place * or + next to the fonts you wish to select.
C: *Echoes *'s or +'s.*

To erase an * or +, highlight the cartridge or font and press the *Delete key*.

The **Total Quantity** in the upper right-hand corner of Screen 4-18 or Screen 4-19 equals the total amount of memory available for downloadable fonts. The **Available Quantity** equals the remaining amount of memory currently available for downloadable fonts after subtracting the size of the fonts that you tagged for initialization.

When a font is selected with an asterisk (*) it means that the soft font is in the printer's memory when a print job begins. To place these fonts in the printer's memory they must be downloaded before printing. Fonts are downloaded when you initialize the printer (see below).

When a downloadable font is selected with a plus (+) it means that WordPerfect 5.1 will automatically load/unload a soft font during the print job. After the print job is finished the original soft font should be reinstated.

Do the following after you have selected the fonts you want to download:

VMS	Reference Keystrokes	DOS
F13	U: Press *Exit* four times. C: *Displays the Print Menu.*	F7

Do only one of the following depending on if you used *'s or +'s in Screen 4-14 or Screen 4-15.

1.   If *'s were used in the Select Printer: Cartridges and Fonts Menu in Screen 4-14 or 4-15 then you must initialize the printer by doing the following step:

VMS	Reference Keystrokes	DOS
	U: Press *7* for Initialize Printer. C: *Prints* Proceed with Printer Initialization? <u>N</u>o (Yes).	
	U: Press *Y* for Yes. C: *Begins Initialization process and Returns to Document.*	

2.   If +'s were used in the Select Printer: Cartridges and Fonts Menu in Screen 4-14 or 4-15 then you do not have to initialize the printer so you can do the following to return back to your document:

VMS	Reference Keystrokes	DOS
F13	U: Press *Exit.* C: *Returns to Document.*	F7

Changing Initial Font

The initial font, also known as the default typeface, is used throughout a document when a specific font has not been selected within the document. To change the initial font do the following:

VMS	Reference Keystrokes	DOS
PF1,F13	U: Press *Print.* C: *Displays Print Menu.*	Shift-F7
	U: Press *S* for Select Printer. C: *Displays Print: Select Printer Menu.*	
	U: Highlight printer you want to edit. C: *Highlights printer.*	

VMS   Reference Keystrokes   DOS

U: Press *3* for Edit.
C: *Displays Select Printer: Edit Menu.*

U: Press *5* for Initial Base Font.
C: *Displays the Select Printer: Initial Font Menu.*

The Select Printer: Initial Font Menu will look similar to Screen 4-20, Screen 4-21 or Screen 4-22 depending on what type of printer you have installed.

Screen 4-20: VMS Users - Digital LN03 Plus

```
Select Print: Initial Font

*  Courier 10.3cpi
   Courier 10cpi
   Courier 13.6cpi
   Elite 12cpi
   Line Draw 10cpi
   Modern Gothic 08cpi












1 Select; N Name search: 1
```

Screen 4-21: VMS Users - Digital LN03R (ScriptPrinter)

```
Select Print: Initial Font

*  Courier
   Courier Bold
   Courier Bold Oblique
   Courier Oblique
   Helvetica
   Helvetica Bold
   Helvetica Bold Oblique
   Helvetica Narrow
   Helvetica Narrow Bold
   Helvetica Narrow Oblique
   Helvetica Oblique
   ITC Avant Garde Gothic Book
   ITC Avant Garde Gothic Book Oblique
   ITC Avant Garde Gothic Demi
   ITC Avant Garde Gothic Demi Oblique
   ITC Lubalin Graph Book
   ITC Lubalin Graph Book Oblique
   ITC Lubalin Graph Demi


1 Select; N Name search: 1
```

Screen 4-22: DOS Users - HP LaserJet IIP

```
Select Printer: Initial Font

* Courier 10cpi
  Courier 10cpi Bold
  Courier 10cpi Italic
  Courier 12cpi
  Courier 12cpi Bold
  Courier 12cpi Italic
  Line Printer 16.67cpi




1 Select; N Name search: 1
```

VMS	Reference Keystrokes	DOS

U: Highlight the preferred font and press *1* to Select.
C: *Displays Select Printer: Edit Menu.*

VMS Users: **Prints Point size: 12. This is for the Digital LN03R (ScriptPrinter) only. Not for the Digital LN03 Plus or the HP LaserJet IIP. You can enter in a different value for the point size.**

VMS	Reference Keystrokes	DOS
F13	U: Press *Exit* three times.	F7
	C: *Returns to Document.*	

Note that the Initial Base Font selection in the Select Printer: Edit Menu (See Screen 4-6, Screen 4-7, or Screen 4-8) now displays the new initial font you just selected in the steps above.

Changing Base Fonts

Your document will initially be using the Initial Base Font. Other base fonts can be inserted into a document in different desired locations so that you can have a variety of fonts in your document. Keep a document simple to read yet professional looking by using only a few different fonts in a document. To change the base font in a document do the following:

VMS   Reference Keystrokes   DOS

PF2,F14   U: Press *Font*.   Ctrl-F8
                 C: *Prints* 1 Size; 2 Appearance; 3 Normal; 4 Base
                    Font; 5 Print Color: <u>0</u>.

                 U: Press *4* for Base Font.
                 C: *Displays Base Font Menu.*

     The Base Font Menu will look similar to Screen 4-23, Screen 4-24, or Screen 4-25. The exact base fonts displayed will vary depending on the printer used.

Screen 4-23: VMS Users - Digital LN03 Plus

```
Base Font

*   Courier 10.3cpi
    Courier 10cpi
    Courier 13.6cpi
    Elite 12cpi
    Line Draw 10cpi
    Modern Gothic 08cpi












1 Select; N Name search: 1
```

Screen 4-24: VMS Users - Digital LN03R (ScriptPrinter)

```
Base Font

*   Courier
    Courier Bold
    Courier Bold Oblique
    Courier Oblique
    Helvetica
    Helvetica Bold
    Helvetica Bold Oblique
    Helvetica Narrow
    Helvetica Narrow Bold
    Helvetica Narrow Oblique
    Helvetica Oblique
    ITC Avant Garde Gothic Book
    ITC Avant Garde Gothic Book Oblique
    ITC Avant Garde Gothic Demi
    ITC Avant Garde Gothic Demi Oblique
    ITC Lubalin Graph Book
    ITC Lubalin Graph Book Oblique
    ITC Lubalin Graph Demi
    ITC Lubalin Graph Demi Oblique
1 Select; N Name search: 1
```

Screen 4-25: DOS Users - HP LaserJet IIP

```
Base Font

* Courier 10cpi
  Courier 10cpi Bold
  Courier 10cpi Italic
  Courier 12cpi
  Courier 12cpi Bold
  Courier 12cpi Italic
  Line Printer 16.67cpi




1 Select; N Name search: 1
```

VMS   **Reference Keystrokes**   **DOS**

U: Highlight the preferred font and press *1* to
Select.
C: *Returns to Document.*

VMS Users: *Prints Point size: 12. This is for the Digital LN03R (ScriptPrinter) only. Not for the Digital LN03 Plus or the HP LaserJet IIP. At this point you should enter in a point size if you want a point size different than the one offered and press the Enter key.*

Changing Base Font's Size and Appearance

The Base Font's size and appearance may be modified without actually changing the base font. In some cases WordPerfect 5.1 will automatically change the font for the user.

For example, a user may create an official business newsletter for his/her supervisor using Helvetica as the base font. In some locations the user may want to select the appearance attribute bold to emphasize certain words. When the user selects the appearance attribute bold, WordPerfect 5.1 will look for a corresponding font, like Helvetica 8 point Bold, in the Base Font Menu. If WordPerfect 5.1 finds the font in its memory it will automatically change the font to Helvetica 8 point Bold.

Also, if the user makes a change in the original base font then WordPerfect 5.1 will automatically change all the fonts wherever the size and appearance attributes were previously chosen for font changes. If the user had not used the attributes and had manually changed each base font then the user would have to go through the whole document manually and change each font.

Fonts may be modified by using the following size attributes:

1. Superscript: x^2
2. Subscript: H_2O
3. Fine: Fine
4. Small: Small
5. Large: Large
6. Very Large: Very Large
7. Extra Large: Extra Large

Fonts may also be modified by using the following appearance attributes:

1. Bold: **Bold**
2. Underline: Underline
3. Double Underline: Double Underline
4. Italic: *Italic*
5. Outline: Outline
6. Shadow: **Shadow**
7. Small Caps: SMALLCAPS
8. Redline: Redline
9. Strikeout: ~~Strikeout~~

The Bold and Underline appearance attributes are used so often that WordPerfect has assigned Bold to F12 in VMS or F6 in DOS and Underline to F14 in VMS or F8 in DOS.

To change the attributes of the text that you are currently typing into WordPerfect 5.1 do the following:

VMS   Reference Keystrokes   DOS

PF2,F14		Ctrl-F8

U: Press *Font.*
C: *Prints* 1 Size; 2 Appearance; 3 Normal; 4 Base Font; 5 Print Color: 0.

U: Press either *1* for Size attributes or *2* for Appearance attributes.
C: *For option 1 prints* 1 Suprscpt; 2 Subscpt; 3 Fine; 4 Small; 5 Large; 6 Vry Large; 7 Ext Large: 0 *or for option 2 prints* 1 Bold 2 Undln 3 Dbl Und 4 Italc 5 Outln 6 Shadw 7 Sm Cap 8 Redln 9 Stkout: 0.

U: Press the preferred option.
C: *Turns preferred option on.*

The text can then be typed in and the text will reflect the size or appearance that you have specified.

VMS	Reference Keystrokes	DOS
	U: Type in characters.	
	C: *Echoes characters.*	

Do one of the following to turn the preferred option off:

VMS	Reference Keystrokes	DOS
	U: Press **Right arrow key** once to move to the right of the attribute code in **Reveal Codes.**	
	C: *Turns option off.*	

OR

VMS	Reference Keystrokes	DOS
PF2,F14	U: Press **Font.**	Ctrl-F8
	C: *Prints* 1 Size; 2 Appearance; 3 Normal; 4 Base Font; 5 Print Color: 0.	
	U: Press *3* for Normal.	
	C: *Turns option off.*	

To change the attributes of text that is **ALREADY TYPED** you must block the text by doing the following:

VMS	Reference Keystrokes	DOS
PF3,F10 OR F20	U: Press **Block.**	Alt-F4 OR F12
	C: *Prints Block on.*	
	U: Highlight the block by using the **Arrow keys.**	
	C: *Highlights specified text.*	
PF2,F14	U: Press **Font.**	Ctrl-F8
	C: *Prints* Attribute: 1 Size; 2 Appearance 0.	
	U: Press either *1* for Size attributes or *2* for Appearance attributes.	
	C: *For option 1 prints* 1 Suprscpt; 2 Subscpt; 3 Fine; 4 Small; 5 Large; 6 Vry Large; 7 Ext Large: 0 *or for option 2 prints* 1 Bold 2 Undln 3 Dbl Und 4 Italc 5 Outln 6 Shadw 7 Sm Cap 8 Redln 9 Stkout: 0.	

VMS   **Reference Keystrokes**   **DOS**

U: Press the preferred option.
C: *Turns preferred option on.*

The type of monitor being used will determine whether or not all of the above size and appearance attributes will appear on your main editing screen without viewing the document.
Also, the attributes your printer supports will determine what the text looks like on paper.

Creating a Font Macro

A useful macro will be created in this section. This macro will italicize a word for you. When you define this macro place your cursor on some word on your screen.

VMS   **Keystroke Action**   **DOS**

PF2,F18	1. U: Press *Macro Define.* C: *Prints* Define macro: _.	Ctrl-F10
	2. U: Type in <u>IT</u> and press the *Enter key.* C: *Prints* Description: _.	

	3. U: Type in <u>Italicize a word</u> and press the
	      Enter key.
	   C: *Prints* Macro Def.	

PF2,Right arrow	4. U: Press *Word Right.* C: *Positions cursor on the word to the right of the word the cursor is currently positioned on.*	Ctrl-Right arrow
PF3,F10 OR F20	5. U: Press *Block.* C: *Prints* Block on.	Alt-F4 OR F12
PF2,Left arrow	6. U: Press *Word Left.* C: *Positions cursor on the word to the left of the word the cursor is currently positioned on.*	Ctrl-Left arrow
PF2,F14	7. U: Press *Font.* C: *Prints* Attribute: 1 Size; 2 Appearance: <u>0</u>.	Ctrl-F8

	8. U: Press *2* for Appearance.
	   C: *Prints* 1 Bold 2 Undln 3 Dbl Und 4 Italc
	      5 Outln 6 Shadw 7 Sm Cap 8 Redln
	      9 Stkout: <u>0</u>.	

VMS	**Keystroke Action**	**DOS**
	9. U: Press *4* for Italc. C: *Italicizes blocked word.*	
PF2,F18	10. U: Press **Macro Define** to finish defining the macro. C: *Saves macro.*	Ctrl-F10

Applications of the Font Macro

The keystrokes that are contained in the "IT.WPM" macro are shown on Screen 4-26 or Screen 4-27.

Screen 4-26: VMS Users

```
Macro: Action

       File          IT.WPM

       Description   Italicize a word


      ┌──────────────────────────────────────────────────────┐
      │{DISPLAY OFF}{Word Right}{Block}{Word Left}{Font}24     │
      │                                                      │
      │                                                      │
      │                                                      │
      │                                                      │
      │                                                      │
      └──────────────────────────────────────────────────────┘

PF2,Prev Scr for macro commands;   Press Exit when done
```

Screen 4-27: DOS Users

```
Macro: Action

        File            IT.WPM

        Description     Italicize a word


        ┌──────────────────────────────────────────────────────┐
        │ {DISPLAY OFF}{Word Right}{Block}{Word Left}{Font}24   │
        │                                                      │
        │                                                      │
        │                                                      │
        │                                                      │
        └──────────────────────────────────────────────────────┘

PF2,Prev Scr for macro commands;   Press Exit when done
```

These macros are ready for immediate use. They can be modified in the Macro Editor to fit your personal needs.

Using the Macro

The initial condition for this macro assume that your cursor is positioned in your document on a word you want to italicize. On Screen 4-28, the cursor is positioned on the "s" in "emphasize" since emphasize is the word that we want to italicize.

Screen 4-28

```
    Computer Training, Incorporated would like to emphasize that in
order to produce a competent computer operator you must send them to
the proper training class.
```

To invoke this macro do the following:

VMS	**Keystroke Action**	**DOS**
PF3,F18	1. U: Press ***Macro***. C: *Prints* Macro: _.	Alt-F10
	2. U: Type in <u>IT</u> and press the ***Enter key***. C: *Macro invokes*.	

When invoking this macro you will see what is shown on Screen 4-29:

Screen 4-29

```
      Computer Training, Incorporated would like to emphasize that in
order to produce a competent computer operator you must send them to
the proper training class.
```

Note that the word "emphasize" is now italicized.

CHAPTER 5

COLUMN MACRO

Column Feature

The WordPerfect 5.1 column feature allows the user to set up any document in a column format. Some examples are newsletters, magazine articles, inventory lists, and address lists.

Defining Columns

The columns must be defined by WordPerfect or by your requirements before you can use them. WordPerfect will automatically calculate the size of each column and the distances between the columns depending upon your current margin settings; or, you can create a new and different column definition to meet your needs.

The initial WordPerfect default column definitions are:

1. Newspaper Type Columns
2. 2 - 3" Columns
3. .5 inches between columns
4. If your left and right margins are currently set at the default of 1" each then Column 1 will have a left margin of 1" and right margin of 4" and Column 2 will have a left margin of 4.5" and right margin of 7.5". These are all measured from the left edge of your paper.

To create a new column definition do the following:

VMS	**Reference Keystrokes**	**DOS**
	U: Move the cursor to the location where you want the column to begin.	
	C: *Positions cursor.*	
PF3,F13	U: Press *Columns/Table.*	Alt-F7
	C: *Prints* 1 Columns; 2 Tables; 3 Math: <u>0</u>.	
	U: Press *1* for Columns	
	C: *Prints* Columns: 1 On; 2 Off; 3 Define: <u>0</u>.	
	U: Press *3* for Define.	
	C: *Displays the Text Column Definition Menu.*	

The Text Column Definition Menu is shown on Screen 5-1.

Screen 5-1

```
Text Column Definition

   1 - Type

   2 - Number of Columns                        Newspaper

   3 - Distance Between Columns                  2

   4 - Margins

   Column      Left      Right      Column     Left      Right
     1:        1"        4"          13:
     2:        4.5"      7.5"        14:
     3:                              15:
     4:                              16:
     5:                              17:
     6:                              18:
     7:                              19:
     8:                              20:
     9:                              21:
    10:                              22:
    11:                              23:
    12:                              24:

Selection: 0
```

In Screen 5-1, above, there are several options to define. These options include Type, Number of Columns, Distance Between Columns, and Margins.

Type

Refers to the three types of columns offered by WordPerfect 5.1: Newspaper, Parallel, or Parallel with Block Protect.

Newspaper

Columns that flow like a newspaper or magazine article. The text flows down the first column, then down the second, and then down any remaining columns.

```
┌─────────────────────────────────┐
│        WEEKLY NEWSLETTER         │
├─────────────────┬───────────────┤
│ Budget Report   │This increase  │
│                 │is needed      │
│    The new      │since many     │
│ budget, that    │new hardware   │
│ will take       │and software   │
│ effect in       │products will  │
│ July of 1989,   │have to be     │
│ will be         │purchased to   │
│ increased by    │keep up with   │
│ $5,000 per      │the new        │
│ Department.     │technology.    │
└─────────────────┴───────────────┘
```

Parallel

Inventory, names and addresses and similar items are normally arranged in WordPerfect's parallel type columns. The text flows across the columns in order to keep the separate items that are related together. This arrangement is similar to the WordPerfect 5.1 Tables Feature (See Chapter 6).

```
┌─────────────────────────────┐
│     INVOICE ORDER FORM       │
├─────────────────────────────┤
│ Product   Quantity   Amount  │
├─────────────────────────────┤
│ Disks:    100       $ 60.00  │
│   3 1/2"                     │
│                             │
│ Ribbons   6         $ 55.10  │
│                             │
│ Deluxe    5         $790.99  │
│   Chairs                    │
│                             │
│ Total               $905.99  │
└─────────────────────────────┘
```

Parallel with Block Protect   Columns with Block Protect are Parallel columns that keep blocks of text together. For example, if you were typing in a paragraph of text Block Protect would keep the paragraph together in one column regardless of column.

Number of Columns
The maximum number is 24.

Distances Between Columns
The distance between each of the columns you define.

Margins
Allows you to change the left and right margins to the adjacent column or to the paper's edge.

VMS	Reference Keystrokes	DOS
	U: Define the columns to meet your needs.	
	C: *Defines Columns.*	
F13	U: Press *Exit* twice.	F7
	C: *Returns to Document.*	

Turning Columns On

Columns is a WordPerfect 5.1 option that must be turned on when it is needed. After you define the columns you can turn them on as follows:

VMS	Reference Keystrokes	DOS
PF3,F13	U: Press *Columns/Table.*	Alt-F7
	C: *Prints* 1 Columns; 2 Tables; 3 Math: 0.	
	U: Press *1* for Columns.	
	C: *Prints* Columns: 1 On; 2 Off; 3 Define: 0.	

VMS 　 **Reference Keystrokes** 　 **DOS**

U: Press *1* for On.
C: *Turns Columns On.*

Columns will reveal a [Col On] code on your screen if you invoke Reveal Codes.

Entering Information into Newspaper Columns

If Newspaper Columns is selected as the column type you can immediately start typing the information into the columns. The WordPerfect 5.1 Column feature will automatically wrap the data into the second line of the column for you.

Entering Information into Parallel Columns

If Parallel Columns is selected as the column type a *Hard page* (PF2,Enter for VMS and Ctrl-Enter for DOS) must be placed at the end of each separate item. Consider the example of an address list which includes the name, address, and telephone numbers of fifty people. After typing in each name the user must press *Hard page,* after typing in each address the user must press *Hard page,* and after typing in each telephone number the user must press *Hard page.*

Using Other WordPerfect Features Within Columns

Within your columns you can use headers and footers (See Chapter 3). You can also include graphic text boxes (See Chapter 7). If you want to include a table (See Chapter 6) within a column you must first place the table in a graphic text box and then place the graphic text box in the column.

Editing Within Columns

The following comments should help to explain movement in and between columns when editing in Newspaper, Parallel, and Parallel with Block Protect.

Moving Within a Column

The *up* and *down arrow keys* move up and down within the column your cursor is located in.

The *left* and *right arrow keys* move the cursor to the right or left only in that particular column.

To move to the top or bottom of a column you must press the *Goto key* (PF2,PF4 (Home) for VMS and Ctrl-Home for DOS) and then the *up* or *down arrow keys* to move the cursor to the top or bottom of the column.

Moving Through Columns

The *up* and *down arrow keys* move up and down through all the columns in consecutive order.

Moving Between Adjacent Columns

To move to the left or right between the columns you must press the *Goto key* (PF2,PF4 (Home) for VMS and Ctrl-Home for DOS) and then the *left* or *right arrow keys* respectively.

Moving to the First or Last Column

To move the cursor to the first or last column of the group of columns you must press the *Goto key* (PF2,PF4 (Home) for VMS and Ctrl-Home for DOS), the *Home key,* and then the *left* or *right arrow key.*

Turning Columns Off

Columns must be turned off in order to return WordPerfect back to normal. To turn columns off do the following:

VMS	Reference Keystrokes	DOS
PF3,F13	U: Press *Columns/Table.* C: *Prints* 1 Columns; 2 Tables; 3 Math: <u>0</u>.	Alt-F7
	U: Press *1* for Columns. C: *Prints* Columns: 1 On; 2 Off; 3 Define: <u>0</u>.	
	U: Press *2* for Off. C: *Turns Columns Off.*	

Turning columns off will reveal a [Col Off] code on your screen if you invoke *Reveal Codes.*

Displaying One Column Per Page

An alternative way to use columns is to have each column on a separate page of your WordPerfect 5.1 document. The columns can then be reviewed sequentially like a regular document. Between each column you will see a single dotted line and between pages you will see a double dotted line. Change through *Setup* (See Addition B: Template Reference under Setup).

Columns will always be printed side-by-side even if the side-by-side column display is set to No, for not having a side-by-side column display.

Creating a Column Macro

In this section a macro will be created defining a set of parallel columns. An inventory list will be created that will include a person's name, the number of computers ordered, and the number of disks ordered.

Before the next step please be sure to clear your screen and move the cursor to the top of your cleared screen.

VMS	Keystroke Action	DOS
PF2,F18	1. U: Press *Macro Define.* C: *Prints* Define macro: _.	Ctrl-F10
	2. U: Type in <u>COLUMNS</u> and press the *Enter key.* C: *Prints* Description: _.	
	3. U: Type in <u>Set up a parallel column file</u> and press the *Enter key.* C: *Returns to Document.*	
PF3,F13	4. U: Press *Columns/Table.* C: *Prints* 1 Columns; 2 Tables; 3 Math: <u>0</u>.	Alt-F7
	5. U: Press *1* for Columns. C: *Prints* Columns: 1 On; 2 Off; 3 Define: <u>0</u>.	
	6. U: Press *3* for Define. C: *Displays Text Column Definition Menu.*	

	7. U: Press *1* for Type.
	   C: *Prints* Column Type: 1 Newspaper;
	   2 Parallel; 3 Parallel with Block Protect: <u>0</u>.	

	8. U: Press *2* for Parallel. C: *Returns to Command Line.*	
	9. U: Press *2* for Number of Columns. C: *Positions cursor to right of* Number of Columns.	
	10. U: Press *3* for three columns and press the *Enter key.* C: *Returns to Command Line.*	

The Left and Right Margins and the Distance Between Columns will be automatically calculated by WordPerfect.

VMS	**Keystroke Action**	**DOS**

F13

11. U: Press *Exit.*
    C: *Prints* Columns: 1 On; 2 Off; 3 Define: <u>0</u>.

F7

12. U: Press *1* On.
    C: *Returns to Document.*

In this next section of keystroke actions the heading for the inventory list will be created.

VMS	**Keystroke Action**	**DOS**

13. U: Press the *Tab key.*
    C: *Inserts programming code.*

PF2,Enter

14. U: Type in <u>NAMES</u> and press *Hard Page.*
    C: *Echoes characters and moves cursor to second column.*

Ctrl-Enter

PF2,Enter

15. U: Type in <u>COMPUTERS ORDERED</u> and press *Hard Page.*
    C: *Echoes characters and moves cursor to third column.*

Ctrl-Enter

PF2,Enter

16. U: Type in <u>DISKS ORDERED</u> and press *Hard Page.*
    C: *Echoes characters.*

Ctrl-Enter

PF2,F18

17. U: Press *Macro Define.*
    C: *Saves macro.*

Ctrl-F10

Now you are all set for the entry of people's names, number of computers ordered, and number of disks ordered.

Enter the data listed in Screen 5-2 to see how this macro works. Remember to press *Hard page* (PF2,PF4 (Home) for VMS and Ctrl-Enter for DOS) after each entry in order to move to the next column. Also, press the *Tab key* each time before you start typing in a name.

Screen 5-2

NAMES	COMPUTERS ORDERED	DISKS ORDERED
Jimmy Jones	30	300
Sandi Sanders	15	350
Barb Lavery	50	50
Jim Rogers	20	20
Todd Peters	30	100
Greg Scorpio	15	50

Application of the Column Macro

The keystrokes contained in the "COLUMNS.WPM" macro are shown on Screen 5-3 or Screen 5-4.

Screen 5-3: VMS Users

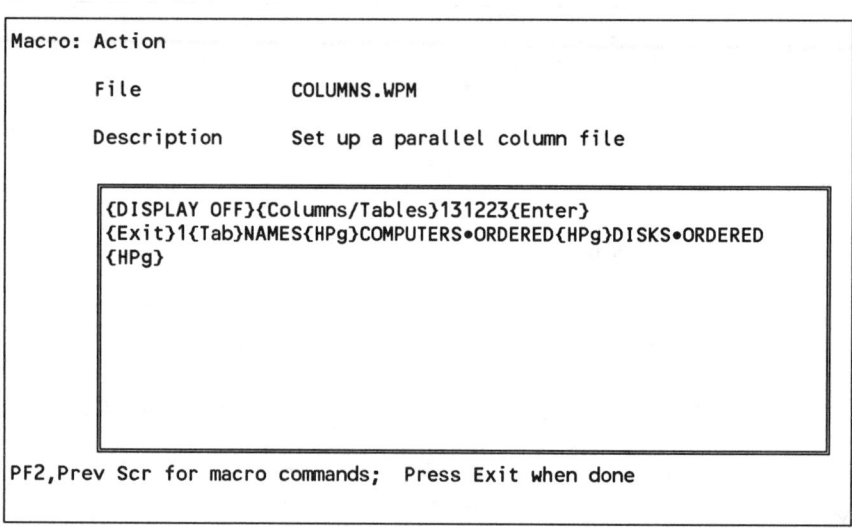

```
Macro: Action

      File            COLUMNS.WPM

      Description     Set up a parallel column file

    {DISPLAY OFF}{Columns/Tables}131223{Enter}
    {Exit}1{Tab}NAMES{HPg}COMPUTERS•ORDERED{HPg}DISKS•ORDERED
    {HPg}




PF2,Prev Scr for macro commands;   Press Exit when done
```

Screen 5-4: DOS Users

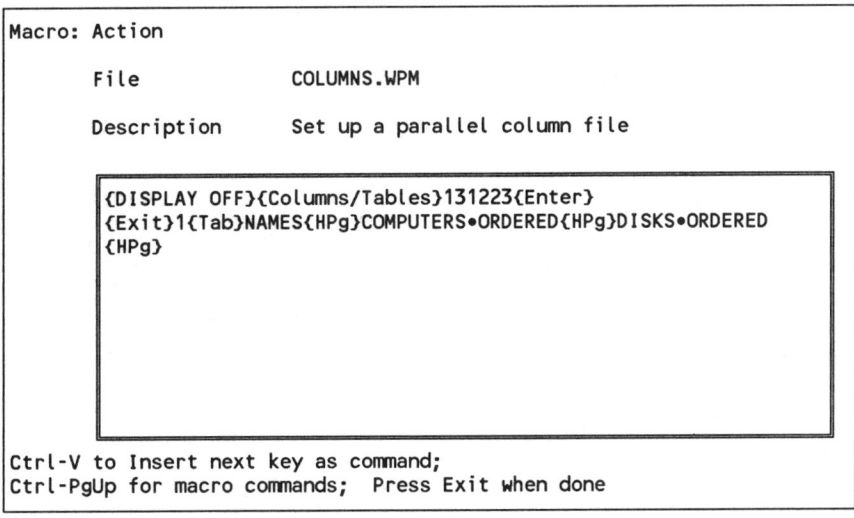

```
Macro: Action

        File              COLUMNS.WPM

        Description       Set up a parallel column file

    ┌─────────────────────────────────────────────────────────┐
    │ {DISPLAY OFF}{Columns/Tables}131223{Enter}               │
    │ {Exit}1{Tab}NAMES{HPg}COMPUTERS•ORDERED{HPg}DISKS•ORDERED │
    │ {HPg}                                                     │
    │                                                          │
    │                                                          │
    │                                                          │
    │                                                          │
    └─────────────────────────────────────────────────────────┘

Ctrl-V to Insert next key as command;
Ctrl-PgUp for macro commands;  Press Exit when done
```

This macro was used for tutorial purposes only. It can be modified in the Macro Editor to fit your personal needs.

Using the Macro

The initial conditions for this macro assume you are starting a new document or that you are currently editing a document to include a particular column heading.

To invoke this macro do the following:

VMS	Keystroke Action	DOS
PF3,F18	1. U: Press *Macro*. C: *Prints* Macro: _.	Alt-F10
	2. U: Type in <u>COLUMNS</u> and press the *Enter key*. C: *Macro invokes*.	

When invoking this macro you will see what is shown on Screen 5-5:

Screen 5-5

```
        NAMES                COMPUTERS ORDERED      DISKS ORDERED
```

Now you can add Customer Names, Computers Ordered, and Disks Ordered into the columns.

Then your screen will look similar to Screen 5-6:

Screen 5-6

NAMES	COMPUTERS ORDERED	DISKS ORDERED
Mary Peters	50	300
Mark Matthews	55	300
Stella Anderson	30	400
Marshall Johnson	25	100
Jim Paul	35	100
Laura Luke	40	300
Holly Thompson	50	200
Maureen Robin	40	200

CHAPTER 6

TABLES MACRO

Tables Feature

The new WordPerfect 5.1 table feature provides a powerful way to organize, store, and even calculate data. Tables allows you to organize and store your data in a rows and columns structure. This arrangement allows you to create separate columns of information easier than setting your own tabbed column locations or using the parallel column feature of WordPerfect as discussed in Chapter 5. Table 6-1 is an example of what a table may look like in WordPerfect 5.1.

Table 6-1

Departure	Destination	Departure Time	Arrival Time
Milwaukee, WI	London, England	1:37 p.m.	7:00 a.m.
Chicago, IL	Washington, D.C.	8:30 a.m.	9:30 p.m.
Los Angeles, CA	Milwaukee, WI	7:00 a.m.	2:35 p.m.

Table 6-1 contains four separate vertical columns of information consisting of:

1)   Departure
2)   Destination
3)   Departure Time
4)   Arrival Time

The first horizontal row in the table provides a title for each of the different columns. Each of the other three rows contains information about one complete flight from its origin to its destination.

The table keeps all of our data in a nice, neat, and organized manner. It is easy to read and it simplifies interpretation of the flight data.

Every intersection of a row and column (every box) in the table is called a cell. Every cell is given a name or address as shown in Table 6-2.

Table 6-2

A1	B1	C1	D1
A2	B2	C2	D2
A3	B3	C3	D3
A4	B4	C4	D4

The address of each cell consists of an alphabetical letter and a number. The alphabetical letter represents the column and the number represents the row. The first column is normally designated Column A and the first row is designated Row 1. The first cell in the upper left hand corner (Column A and Row 1) thus receives the cell name or address of A1.

The maximum number of columns you may have in a table is 32 labeled A to Z and then AA, BA, CA, DA, EA, and FA and the maximum number of rows is 32,765.

Creating a Table

A table can be created in any document as follows:

VMS	Reference Keystrokes	DOS
PF3,F13	U: Press *Columns/Table.* C: *Prints* 1 Columns; 2 Tables; 3 Math: <u>0</u>.	Alt-F7
	U: Select *2* for Tables. C: *Prints* Table: 1 Create; 2 Edit: <u>0</u>.	
	U: Select *1* for Create. C: *Prints* Number of Columns: <u>3</u>.	
	U: Enter the number of columns you would like in your table and press the *Enter key.* C: *Prints* Number of Rows: <u>1</u>.	
	U: Enter the number of rows you would like in your table and press the *Enter key.* C: *Displays your table in your document along with the Table Edit menu.*	

For example, on Screen 6-1 or Screen 6-2 you can see a 4 column and 4 row table. The Table Edit Menu is shown on the lower portion of the screen. The Table Edit Menu allows you to alter the actual structure of your table.

Screen 6-1: VMS Users

```
        On your screen you will see the document you were editing along
with your brand new table.  On the lower portion of your screen you will
see the Table Edit Menu.


  ┌─────────────────────┬─────────────────────┬─────────────────────┐
  │░░░░░░░░░░░░░░░░░░░░░░│                     │                     │
  │                     │                     │                     │
  ├─────────────────────┼─────────────────────┼─────────────────────┤
  │                     │                     │                     │
  │                     │                     │                     │
  ├─────────────────────┼─────────────────────┼─────────────────────┤
  │                     │                     │                     │
  │                     │                     │                     │
  └─────────────────────┴─────────────────────┴─────────────────────┘



Table Edit:  Press Exit when done  Cell A1 Doc 1 Pg 1 Ln 1.86" Pos 1.12"

PF2-Arrows Column Widths; Ins Insert; Del Delete; Move Move/Copy;
1 Size; 2 Format; 3 Lines; 4 Header; 5 Math; 6 Options; 7 Join;8 Split:0
```

Screen 6-2: DOS Users

```
        On your screen you will see the document you were editing along
with your brand new table.  On the lower portion of your screen you will
see the Table Edit Menu.


  ┌─────────────────────┬─────────────────────┬─────────────────────┐
  │░░░░░░░░░░░░░░░░░░░░░░│                     │                     │
  │                     │                     │                     │
  ├─────────────────────┼─────────────────────┼─────────────────────┤
  │                     │                     │                     │
  │                     │                     │                     │
  ├─────────────────────┼─────────────────────┼─────────────────────┤
  │                     │                     │                     │
  │                     │                     │                     │
  └─────────────────────┴─────────────────────┴─────────────────────┘



Table Edit:  Press Exit when done  Cell A1 Doc 1 Pg 1 Ln 1.86" Pos 1.12"

Ctrl-Arrows Column Widths; Ins Insert; Del Delete; Move Move/Copy;
1 Size; 2 Format; 3 Lines; 4 Header; 5 Math; 6 Options; 7 Join;8 Split:0
```

Table Edit: Cursor Movement

When the Table Edit Menu is displayed on your screen the cursor will be located within one cell. Actual data or information can be entered into your table only when the Table Edit Menu has been removed from your screen.

To move your cursor around in the table all you have to do is use your arrow keys (Up, Down, Left, and Right). This will move your cursor to the next cell in the corresponding arrow direction.

To move your cursor to the beginning of a row or end of a row press the Home Key and the corresponding left or right arrow key. To move your cursor to the top of a column or bottom of a column press the Home Key and the corresponding up or down arrow key.

To move your cursor to Cell A1 (upper left hand corner of table) press Home, Home, Up Arrow Key.

To move your cursor to the last cell in your table (lower right hand corner of table) press Home, Home, Down Arrow Key.

To move to a specific Cell Address (any of the available Cell Address, for example see Table 6-2) do the following:

VMS   Reference Keystrokes   DOS

VMS	Reference Keystrokes	DOS
PF2,PF4	U: Press *Goto.* C: *Prints* Go to _.	Ctrl-Home
	U: Type in the Cell Address (i.e., C5) and press the *Enter key.* If that cell is not in the table WordPerfect will go to the last cell. C: *Positions cursor.*	

The Table Edit Screen helps you modify the physical structure of your table. The options shown in the menu may be described as follows:

Table Edit: Ctrl/PF2-Arrows Column Widths

This option allows you to change the width of any column. Place your cursor in any cell in that column and press PF2,Right arrow key for VMS OR Ctrl-Right arrow key for DOS to widen the column or PF2,Left arrow key for VMS OR Ctrl-Left arrow key for DOS to make the column narrow.

Table Edit: Ins (Insert)

If you need more columns or rows all you have to do is use the Insert key as follows.

VMS   Reference Keystrokes   DOS

VMS	Reference Keystrokes	DOS
	U: Press the *Insert key.* C: *Prints* Insert: 1 Rows; 2 Columns: 0.	
	U: Press either *1* for Rows or *2* for Columns. C: *Prints* Number of Rows: 1 *if you selected Rows else Prints* Columns: 1 *if you selected Columns.*	
	U: Enter the total number of Rows or Columns you want to insert and press the *Enter key.* C: *Prints* Updating Table *and inserts rows or columns.*	

The table will be updated to contain the new row(s) or column(s). Any new rows that are added will be placed above the row that the cursor is positioned in and any columns added will be placed to the left of the column where the cursor is located.

Table Edit: Del (Delete)

If you need fewer columns or rows all you have to use is the Delete key as follows:

VMS   Reference Keystrokes   DOS

U: Press the *Delete key.*
C: *Prints* Delete: 1 Rows; 2 Columns: <u>0</u>.

U: Press either *1* for Rows or *2* for Columns.
C: *Prints* Number of Rows: <u>1</u> *if you selected Rows else Prints* Columns: <u>1</u> *if you selected Columns.*

U: Enter the number of Rows or Columns you want to delete and press the *Enter key.*
C: *Prints* Updating Table *and deletes rows or columns.*

The table will be updated eliminating the old row(s) or column(s). Any old rows that were deleted will be removed below the row that the cursor is positioned in and any columns removed will be removed to the right of the column where the cursor is located. Caution, remember that rows or columns changes may affect cell address and contents.

Table Edit: Move (Move/Copy)

Similar to the Move feature in WordPerfect. The Move feature allows you to move, copy, or delete the block, row, or column along with all the text contained within that section.
To move either a row or column do the following:

VMS   Reference Keystrokes   DOS

U: Position your cursor in the row or column you want to move.
C: *Positions cursor.*

PF2,F10   U: Press *Move.*   Ctrl-F4
C: *Prints* Move: 1 Block; 2 Row; 3 Column; 4 Retrieve: <u>0</u>.

U: Press either *2* for Row or *3* for Column.
C: *Prints* 1 Move; 2 Copy; 3 Delete: <u>0</u>.

VMS	**Reference Keystrokes**	**DOS**

VMS Users

U: Press *1* for Move.

C: *Prints* Updating table, *Deletes the Row or Column, and Prints* Move cursor; press Return to retrieve.

C: *Prints* Updating table, *Deletes the Row or Column, and Prints* Move cursor; press Enter to retrieve.   *DOS Users*

U: Position cursor in new location and press the **Enter key**.

C: *Retrieves Row or Column.*

To copy either a row or column do the following:

VMS	**Reference Keystrokes**	**DOS**

U: Position your cursor in the row or column you want to copy.

C: *Positions cursor.*

PF2,F10

U: Press **Move**.

C: *Prints* Move: 1 Block; 2 Row; 3 Column; 4 Retrieve: 0.   Ctrl-F4

U: Press either *2* for Row or *3* for Column.

C: *Prints* 1 Move; 2 Copy; 3 Delete: 0.

VMS Users

U: Press *2* for Copy.

C: *Prints* Updating table, *Copies the Row or Column and Prints* Move cursor; press Return to retrieve.

C: *Prints* Updating table, *Copies the Row or Column and Prints* Move cursor; press Enter to retrieve.   *DOS Users*

U: Position cursor in new locations and press the **Enter key**.

C: *Retrieves Row or Column.*

To delete either a row or column do the following:

VMS	**Reference Keystrokes**	**DOS**

U: Position your cursor in the row or column you want to move.

C: *Positions cursor.*

VMS	Reference Keystrokes	DOS
PF2,F10	U: Press *Move.* C: *Prints* Move: 1 Block; 2 Row; 3 Column; 4 Retrieve: 0.	Ctrl-F4
	U: Press either *2* for Row or *3* for Column. C: *Prints* 1 Move; 2 Copy; 3 Delete: 0.	
	U: Press *3* for Delete. C: *Prints* Updating table *and Deletes the Row or* *Column.*	

To move, copy, or delete a block of the table you must first block the section you want to move.

To block a portion of the table do the following:

VMS	Reference Keystrokes	DOS
PF3,F10 OR F20	U: Press *Block.* C: *Prints* Block on.	Alt-F4 OR F12
	U: Use *Arrow keys* to highlight portion of table you want to block. C: *Highlights text.*	

To move a section of text that has been **BLOCKED** do the following:

VMS	Reference Keystrokes	DOS
PF2,F10	U: Press *Move.* C: *Prints* Move: 1 Block; 2 Row; 3 Column; 4 Retrieve: 0.	Ctrl-F4
	U: Press *1* for Block. C: *Prints* 1 Move; 2 Copy; 3 Delete: 0.	
VMS Users	U: Press *1* for Move. C: *Deletes the Block and Prints* Move cursor; press Return to retrieve. C: *Deletes the Block and Prints* Move cursor; press Enter to retrieve.	*DOS Users*
	U: Position cursor and press the *Enter key* to retrieve Block. C: *Retrieves Block.*	

To copy a block, **FIRST BLOCK** the portion of the table you want to copy, then do the following:

VMS   Reference Keystrokes   DOS

PF2,F10

U: Press *Move.*   Ctrl-F4
C: *Prints* Move: 1 Block; 2 Row; 3 Column;
    4 Retrieve: 0.

U: Press *1* for Block.
C: *Prints* 1 Move; 2 Copy; 3 Delete: 0.

VMS Users

U: Press *2* for Copy.
C: *Copies the Block and Prints* Move cursor; press
    Return to retrieve.
C: *Copies the Block and Prints* Move cursor; press   *DOS Users*
    Enter to retrieve.

U: Position cursor and press the *Enter key* to
    retrieve Block.
C: *Retrieves Block.*

To delete a block, **FIRST BLOCK** the portion of the table you want to delete, then do the following:

VMS   Reference Keystrokes   DOS

PF2,F10

U: Press *Move.*   Ctrl-F4
C: *Prints* Move: 1 Block; 2 Row; 3 Column;
    4 Retrieve: 0.

U: Press *1* for Block.
C: *Prints* 1 Move; 2 Copy; 3 Delete: 0.

U: Press *3* for Delete.
C: *Deletes the Block.*

To retrieve the block, row, or column you already retrieved again into another location do the following:

VMS   Reference Keystrokes   DOS

U: Position cursor.
C: *Positions cursor.*

PF2,F10

U: Press *Move.*   Ctrl-F4
C: *Prints* Move: 1 Block; 2 Row; 3 Column;
    4 Retrieve: 0.

VMS   **Reference Keystrokes**   **DOS**

U: Press *4* for Retrieve.
C: *Prints* Retrieve: 1 Block; 2 Row; 3 Column: 0.

U: Press *1* for Block or *2* for Row or *3* for Column.
C: *Retrieves the last block, row, or column.*

Table Edit: Size

Size allows you to alter the number of rows or columns in your table structure. To change the number of rows or columns in your table do the following:

VMS   **Reference Keystrokes**   **DOS**

U: Press *1* for Size.
C: *Prints* Table Size: 1 Rows; 2 Columns: 0.

U: Press *1* for Rows or *2* for Columns.
C: *Prints either* Number of Rows: 3 *(Defaults to current number or rows) or Prints* Number of Columns: 3 *(Defaults to current number of columns).*

U: Enter the new number for Rows or Columns and press the *Enter key.*
C: *Inserts new Rows or Columns.*

Any new rows or columns that are added to or deleted from the table will be placed or taken from the end of the table. Thus, please note that size is different from Insert or Delete. The table size of the columns or rows will be adjusted to contain the new total number of row(s) or column(s).

If you enter a Row or Column number that is less than the current Row or Column number then WordPerfect will display the following: Prints Cells will be deleted. Continue? No (Yes). At this point you must make a decision with whether you want to continue or not and then enter *N* for No or *Y* for Yes.

Table Edit: Format

This option allows you to format either your cells, columns, or row heights. It is possible to set the format for your text in several locations. The order of precedence in which WordPerfect decides how to format the text is by:

1. How you formatted the text when you entered it into your cell.
2. The cell format options default.
3. The cell column options default.

Thus if you Bold some data as you enter it into your table, WordPerfect will print out the table's text the same way you entered the text. The way you format the text as you enter it supersedes the Column format options.

Table Edit: Format: Cells

To format your cell according to Type, Attributes, Justification, Vertical Alignment, or Lock do the following:

VMS	Reference Keystrokes	DOS

U: Press *2* for Format.
C: *Prints* Format: 1 Cell; 2 Column; 3 Row Height: <u>0</u>.

U: Press *1* for Cell.
C: *Displays Cell Format Menu including* Cell: 1 Type; 2 Attributes; 3 Justify; 4 Vertical Alignment; 5 Lock: <u>0</u>.

The Cell Format Menu is shown on Screen 6-3.

Screen 6-3

```
┌─────────────────────────────────────────────────────────────────┐
│        On your screen you will see the document you were editing along │
│  with your brand new table.  On the lower portion of your screen you will │
│  see the Table Edit Menu.                                          │
│                                                                   │
│   ┌───────────────────┬───────────────────┬───────────────────┐  │
│   │▒▒▒▒▒▒▒▒▒▒▒▒▒▒▒▒▒▒▒│                   │                   │  │
│   ├───────────────────┼───────────────────┼───────────────────┤  │
│   │                   │                   │                   │  │
│   ├───────────────────┼───────────────────┼───────────────────┤  │
│   │                   │                   │                   │  │
│   └───────────────────┴───────────────────┴───────────────────┘  │
│                                                                   │
│                                                                   │
│  Table Edit:  Press Exit when done  Cell A1 Doc 1 Pg 1 Ln 1.86" Pos 1.12" │
├───────────────────────────────────────────────────────────────────┤
│  Cell:   Top;Left;Normal                    Col: 2.17";Left;Normal │
│  Cell:   1 Type; 2 Attributes; 3 Justify; 4 Vertical Alignment; 5 Lock: 0 │
└───────────────────────────────────────────────────────────────────┘
```

Cell: Top;Left;Normal, located on the lower left of the above screen, identifies the format for the text that is entered into this cell.

Top: Vertical Alignment of your text within a cell.
Left: Justification of your text within a cell.
Normal: Attributes of your text within a cell.

The Cell Format Menu in WordPerfect 5.1 includes the following options: Type, Attributes, Justify, Vertical Alignment, and Lock.

Table Edit: Format: Cells
1 Type

WordPerfect 5.1 automatically considers all cells containing numbers as numeric and those numbers are usable in all calculations.

If you want to change a standard numeric cell to a text cell, that is, a non-numeric cell or you want to change a text cell back to a numeric cell you may do the following:

VMS	**Reference Keystrokes**	**DOS**

U: Press *2* for Format.
C: *Prints* Format: 1 Cell; 2 Column; 3 Row
   Height: <u>0</u>.

U: Press *1* for Cell.
C: *Displays Cell Format Menu including* Cell: 1
   Type; 2 Attributes; 3 Justify; 4 Vertical
   Alignment; 5 Lock: <u>0</u>.

U: Press *1* for Type (See Screen 6-3).
C: *Prints* Cell Type: 1 Numeric; 2 Text: <u>1</u>.

U: Press *1* for Numeric or *2* for Text.
C: *Returns to Table.*

Any time your cursor is located in a text cell you will see on the status line in front of the Cell's address a quotation mark (") as shown below on Screen 6-4 or Screen 6-5.

Screen 6-4: VMS Users

```
      On your screen you will see the document you were editing along
with your brand new table.  On the lower portion of your screen you will
see the Table Edit Menu.
```

```
Table Edit:  Press Exit when done Cell "A1 Doc 1 Pg 1 Ln 1.86" Pos 1.12"
```
```
PF2-Arrows Column Widths; Ins Insert; Del Delete; Move Move/Copy;
1 Size; 2 Format; 3 Lines; 4 Header; 5 Math; 6 Options; 7 Join;8 Split:0
```

Screen 6-5: DOS Users

```
        On your screen you will see the document you were editing along
with your brand new table.  On the lower portion of your screen you will
see the Table Edit Menu.
```

┌─────────────────────┬────────────────┬────────────────┐
│ ░░░░░░░░░░░░░░░░░░░░░ │   │   │
├─────────────────────┼────────────────┼────────────────┤
│   │   │   │
├─────────────────────┼────────────────┼────────────────┤
│   │   │   │
└─────────────────────┴────────────────┴────────────────┘

```
Table Edit:  Press Exit when done Cell "A1 Doc 1 Pg 1 Ln 1.86" Pos 1.12"
```

```
Ctrl-Arrows Column Widths; Ins Insert; Del Delete; Move Move/Copy;
1 Size; 2 Format; 3 Lines; 4 Header; 5 Math; 6 Options; 7 Join;8 Split:0
```

Table Edit: Format: Cells
2 Attributes - Size

In this option you may choose the attributes for the text in the cells such as Size, Appearance, Normal, or Reset.

If you want to change the size attribute for the text contained within the cell do the following:

VMS	**Reference Keystrokes**	**DOS**

U: Press *2* for Format.
C: *Prints* Format: 1 Cell; 2 Column; 3 Row Height: <u>0</u>.

U: Press *1* for Cell.
C: *Displays* Cell Format Menu including Cell: 1 Type; 2 Attributes; 3 Justify; 4 Vertical Alignment; 5 Lock: <u>0</u>.

U: Press *2* for Attributes.
C: *Prints* 1 Size; 2 Appearance; 3 Normal; 4 Reset: <u>0</u>.

U: Press *1* for Size.
C: *Prints* 1 Suprscpt; 2 Subscpt; 3 Fine; 4 Small; 5 Large; 6 Vry Large; 7 Ext Large: <u>0</u>.

U: Press the appropriate number for the attribute size.
C: *Reformats the cell.*

Table Edit: Format: Cells
2 Attributes - Appearance

If you want to change the appearance attribute for the text contained within the cell do the following:

VMS	**Reference Keystrokes**	**DOS**

U: Press *2* for Format.
C: *Prints* Format: 1 Cell; 2 Column; 3 Row Height: <u>0</u>.

U: Press *1* for Cell.
C: *Displays Cell Format Menu including* Cell: 1 Type; 2 Attributes; 3 Justify; 4 Vertical Alignment; 5 Lock: <u>0</u>.

U: Press *2* for Attributes.
C: *Prints* 1 Size; 2 Appearance; 3 Normal; 4 Reset: <u>0</u>.

U: Press *2* for Appearance.
C: *Prints* 1 Bold 2 Undln 3 Dbl Und 4 Italc 5 Outln 6 Shadw 7 Sm Cap 8 Redln 9 Stkout: <u>0</u>.

U: Press the appropriate number for the appearance.
C: *Reformats the cell.*

Table Edit: Format: Cells
2 Attributes - Normal

If you want to return all the attributes for the text contained within the cell to normal do the following:

VMS	**Reference Keystrokes**	**DOS**

U: Press *2* for Format.
C: *Prints* Format: 1 Cell; 2 Column; 3 Row Height: <u>0</u>.

U: Press *1* for Cell.
C: *Displays Cell Format Menu including* Cell: 1 Type; 2 Attributes; 3 Justify; 4 Vertical Alignment; 5 Lock: <u>0</u>.

VMS　　　　　**Reference Keystrokes**　　　　　**DOS**

　　U:　Press *2* for Attributes.
　　C:　*Prints* 1 Size; 2 Appearance; 3 Normal;
　　　　4 Reset: <u>0</u>.

　　U:　Press *3* for Normal.
　　C:　*Reformats the cell.*

Table Edit: Format: Cells
2 Attributes - Reset

　　　　If you want to reset all the attributes for the text contained within the cell to the same as the column attributes do the following:

VMS　　　　　**Reference Keystrokes**　　　　　**DOS**

　　U:　Press *2* for Format.
　　C:　*Prints* Format: 1 Cell; 2 Column; 3 Row
　　　　Height: <u>0</u>.

　　U:　Press *1* for Cell.
　　C:　*Displays Cell Format Menu including* Cell:
　　　　1 Type; 2 Attributes; 3 Justify; 4 Vertical
　　　　Alignment; 5 Lock: <u>0</u>.

　　U:　Press *2* for Attributes.
　　C:　*Prints* 1 Size; 2 Appearance; 3 Normal; 4
　　　　Reset: <u>0</u>.

　　U:　Press *4* for Reset to change the attributes to
　　　　the column's attributes.
　　C:　*Reformats the cell.*

Table Edit: Format: Cells
3 Justify

　　　　This option allows you to choose the type of justification (left or right alignment) for the text in the cells.
　　　　To change the justification for the text contained within the cell do the following:

VMS　　　　　**Reference Keystrokes**　　　　　**DOS**

　　U:　Press *2* for Format.
　　C:　*Prints* Format: 1 Cell; 2 Column; 3 Row
　　　　Height: <u>0</u>.

VMS   **Reference Keystrokes**   **DOS**

U: Press *1* for Cell.
C: *Displays Cell Format Menu including* Cell:
    1 Type; 2 Attributes; 3 Justify; 4 Vertical
    Alignment; 5 Lock: <u>0</u>.

U: Press *3* for Justify.
C: *Prints* Justification: 1 Left; 2 Center; 3 Right;
    4 Full; 5 Decimal Align; 6 Reset: <u>1</u>.

U: Press the appropriate number for the
    justification.
C: *Reformats the cell.*

Choice 6 for Reset will reset the cell justification to the same setting as the column justification.

Table Edit: Format: Cells
4 Vertical Alignment

In this option you can choose how your text material will be aligned vertically in the cell.

To change the vertical alignment of the text contained within the cell do the following:

VMS   **Reference Keystrokes**   **DOS**

U: Press *2* for Format.
C: *Prints* Format: 1 Cell; 2 Column; 3 Row
    Height: <u>0</u>.

U: Press *1* for Cell.
C: *Displays Cell Format Menu including* Cell:
    1 Type; 2 Attributes; 3 Justify; 4 Vertical
    Alignment; 5 Lock: <u>0</u>.

U: Press *4* for Vertical Alignment.
C: *Prints* Vertical Alignment: 1 Top; 2 Bottom;
    3 Center: <u>1</u>.

U: Press the appropriate number for the vertical
    alignment.
C: *Reformats the cell.*

Table Edit: Format: Cells
5 Lock

This feature prevents the accidental erasure of a cell's contents. You can choose whether or not you would like the information currently stored in the cell to be locked so that no one can change the information, on purpose or by accident, or unlocked so that you can alter the cell's contents.

To lock a cell do the following:

VMS   Reference Keystrokes   DOS

U: Press *2* for Format.
C: *Prints* Format: 1 Cell; 2 Column; 3 Row Height: 0̲.

U: Press *1* for Cell.
C: *Displays Cell Format Menu including* Cell: 1 Type; 2 Attributes; 3 Justify; 4 Vertical Alignment; 5 Lock: 0̲.

U: Press *5* for Lock.
C: *Prints* Lock: 1 On; 2 Off: 0̲.

U: Press *1* for On.
C: *Locks the cell.*

Any time your cursor is located in a cell that is locked you will see [ ] surrounding the Cell's address on the status line as shown below on Screen 6-6 or Screen 6-7.

Screen 6-6: VMS Users

```
      On your screen you will see the document you were editing along
with your brand new table.  On the lower portion of your screen you will
see the Table Edit Menu.




┌─────────────────────┬───────────────────┬───────────────────┐
│░░░░░░░░░░░░░░░░░░░░░░│                   │                   │
├─────────────────────┼───────────────────┼───────────────────┤
│                     │                   │                   │
├─────────────────────┼───────────────────┼───────────────────┤
│                     │                   │                   │
└─────────────────────┴───────────────────┴───────────────────┘




Table Edit: Press Exit when done Cell [A] [1] Doc 1 Pg 1 Ln 1.86" Pos 1.12"

PF2-Arrows Column Widths; Ins Insert; Del Delete; Move Move/Copy;
1 Size; 2 Format; 3 Lines; 4 Header; 5 Math; 6 Options; 7 Join; 8 Split:0
```

Screen 6-7: DOS Users

```
         On your screen you will see the document you were editing along
with your brand new table.  On the lower portion of your screen you will
see the Table Edit Menu.

  ┌────────────────────────┬───────────────┬───────────────┐
  │▒▒▒▒▒▒▒▒▒▒▒▒▒▒▒▒▒▒▒▒▒▒▒▒│               │               │
  ├────────────────────────┼───────────────┼───────────────┤
  │                        │               │               │
  ├────────────────────────┼───────────────┼───────────────┤
  │                        │               │               │
  └────────────────────────┴───────────────┴───────────────┘




Table Edit: Press Exit when done Cell [A][1] Doc 1 Pg 1 Ln 1.86" Pos 1.12"
─────────────────────────────────────────────────────────────────────────
Ctrl-Arrows Column Widths; Ins Insert; Del Delete; Move Move/Copy;
1 Size; 2 Format; 3 Lines; 4 Header; 5 Math; 6 Options; 7 Join; 8 Split:0
```

To unlock a cell do the following:

VMS   Reference Keystrokes   DOS

U: Press *2* for Format.
C: *Prints* Format: 1 Cell; 2 Column; 3 Row Height: <u>0</u>.

U: Press *1* for Cell.
C: *Displays Cell Format Menu including* Cell: 1 Type; 2 Attributes; 3 Justify; 4 Vertical Alignment; 5 Lock: <u>0</u>.

U: Press *5* for Lock.
C: *Prints* Lock: 1 On; 2 Off: <u>0</u>.

U: Press *2* for Off.
C: *Unlocks the cell.*

You can now change the text in the cell.

Table Edit: Format: Columns

To format your columns according to Width, Attributes, Justification, or Number of Digits do the following:

VMS   **Reference Keystrokes**   **DOS**

U: Press **2** for Format.
C: *Prints* Format: 1 Cell; 2 Column; 3 Row Height: <u>0</u>.

U: Press **2** for Column.
C: *Displays Column Format Menu including* Column: 1 Width; 2 Attributes; 3 Justify; 4 # of Digits: <u>0</u>.

The Column Format Menu is shown on Screen 6-8.

Screen 6-8

```
      On your screen you will see the document you were editing along
with your brand new table.  On the lower portion of your screen you will
see the Table Edit Menu.





Table Edit:  Press Exit when done  Cell A1 Doc 1 Pg 1 Ln 1.86" Pos 1.12"

Cell:  Top;Left;Normal                    Col: 2.17";Left;Normal
Column:  1 Width; 2 Attributes; 3 Justify; 4 # of Digits: 0.
```

Col: 2.17";Left;Normal, located on the lower right of the above screen, represents the width of your column and the format for the text you enter into this column.

2.17":   Width of the column.
Left: Justification of the column.
Normal: Attributes of the column.

The Column Format Menu in WordPerfect 5.1 contains the following options: Width, Attributes, Justify, and # of Digits.

Table Edit: Format: Columns
1 Width

In this option you can change the width of the column your cursor is located in as follows:

VMS   **Reference Keystrokes**   **DOS**

U: Press *2* for Format.
C: *Prints* Format: 1 Cell; 2 Column; 3 Row
   Height: 0.

U: Press *2* for Column.
C: *Displays Column Format Menu including*
   Column: 1 Width; 2 Attributes; 3 Justify; 4 *#*
   of Digits: 0.

U: Press *1* for Width.
C: *Prints* Column width: 2.17" *(Current column
   width)*.

U: Press the appropriate number for the width.
C: *Reformats the column.*

The other columns' widths will not be altered.

Table Edit: Format: Columns
2 Attributes

In this option you can choose the attributes for the text in the columns such as Size, Appearance, or Normal.

If you want to change the size attribute for the text contained within all the column's cells do the following:

VMS   **Reference Keystrokes**   **DOS**

U: Press *2* for Format.
C: *Prints* Format: 1 Cell; 2 Column; 3 Row
   Height: 0.

U: Press *2* for Column.
C: *Displays Column Format Menu including*
   Column: 1 Width; 2 Attributes; 3 Justify; 4 *#*
   of Digits: 0.

U: Press *2* for Attributes.
C: *Prints* 1 Size; 2 Appearance; 3 Normal: 0.

U: Press *1* for Size.
C: *Prints* 1 Suprscpt; 2 Subscpt; 3 Fine; 4 Small;
   5 Large; 6 Vry Large; 7 Ext Large: 0.

U: Press the appropriate number for the size.
C: *Reformats the column.*

Table Edit: Format: Columns
2 Attributes - Appearance

If you want to change the appearance attribute for the text contained within the column do the following:

VMS   Reference Keystrokes   DOS

U: Press *2* for Format.
C: *Prints* Format: 1 Cell; 2 Column; 3 Row Height: <u>0</u>.

U: Press *2* for Column.
C: *Displays Column Format Menu including* Column: 1 Width; 2 Attributes; 3 Justify; 4 *#* of Digits: <u>0</u>.

U: Press *2* for Attributes.
C: *Prints* 1 Size; 2 Appearance; 3 Normal: <u>0</u>.

U: Press *2* for Appearance.
C: *Prints* 1 Bold 2 Undln 3 Dbl Und 4 Italc 5 Outln 6 Shadw 7 Sm Cap 8 Redln 9 Stkout: <u>0</u>.

U: Press the appropriate number for the appearance.
C: *Reformats the column.*

Table Edit: Format: Columns
2 Attributes - Normal

If you want to return all the attributes to normal for the text contained within the column do the following:

VMS   Reference Keystrokes   DOS

U: Press *2* for Format.
C: *Prints* Format: 1 Cell; 2 Column; 3 Row Height: <u>0</u>.

U: Press *2* for Column.
C: *Displays Column Format Menu including* Column: 1 Width; 2 Attributes; 3 Justify; 4 *#* of Digits: <u>0</u>.

U: Press *2* for Attributes.
C: *Prints* 1 Size; 2 Appearance; 3 Normal: <u>0</u>.

VMS   **Reference Keystrokes**   **DOS**

U: Press *3* for Normal.
C: *Reformats the column.*

Table Edit: Format: Columns
3 Justify

In this option you can choose the type of justification for the text in the column.

If you want to change the justification for the text contained within the column do the following:

VMS   **Reference Keystrokes**   **DOS**

U: Press *2* for Format.
C: *Prints* Format: 1 Cell; 2 Column; 3 Row Height: <u>0</u>.

U: Press *2* for Column.
C: *Displays Column Format Menu including* Column: 1 Width; 2 Attributes; 3 Justify; 4 # of Digits: <u>0</u>.

U: Press *3* for Justify.
C: *Prints* Justification: 1 Left; 2 Center; 3 Right; 4 Full; 5 Decimal Align: <u>1</u>.

U: Press the appropriate number for the appearance.
C: *Reformats the column.*

Table Edit: Format: Columns
4 # of Digits

In this option you can choose the number of digits to the right of the decimal point for all calculated numbers in the column.

If you want to change the number of digits for the number contained within the column do the following:

VMS   **Reference Keystrokes**   **DOS**

U: Press *2* for Format.
C: *Prints* Format: 1 Cell; 2 Column; 3 Row Height: <u>0</u>.

VMS	**Reference Keystrokes**	**DOS**

U: Press *2* for Column.
C: *Displays Column Format Menu including* Column: 1 Width; 2 Attributes; 3 Justify; 4 # of Digits: 0.

U: Press *4* for # of Digits.
C: *Prints* Number of decimal places (0-15): 2 *(Current number of decimal places).*

U: Press the appropriate number for the number of digits and press the *Enter key.*
C: *Reformats the column.*

Table Edit: Format: Row Height

You can also format the height of any row.
Some cautions include the following:

1.   A single line of text in a row means that if your text extends beyond the edge of the cell it will not wrap around to the second line in the cell. That portion of thc text will be lost.

2.   Setting a row's height to a fixed measurement will disregard text size. It is then possible to set the font of the text contained in that fixed row to a point size that is larger than the row. Thus, the text may be too large to fit into a fixed row. If this happens you will see a blank cell on the document when you print it out on your printer.

To change the height of a row that may only contain one line of text to a fixed height disregarding text size do the following:

VMS	**Reference Keystrokes**	**DOS**

U: Press *2* for Format.
C: *Prints* Format: 1 Cell; 2 Column; 3 Row Height: 0.

U: Press *3* for Row Height.
C: *Prints* Row Height -- Single line: 1 Fixed; 2 Auto; add Multi-line: 3 Fixed; 4 Auto: 4.

U: Press *1* for Fixed.
C: *Prints* Enter fixed height for row: 0.293 *(Defaults to current row height).*

VMS   Reference KeystrokesDOS

U: Press the appropriate number for the row's height and press the *Enter key.*
C: *Adjusts the row's height.*

To let WordPerfect automatically adjust the height of a row that may contain **ONLY ONE LINE** of text do the following:

VMS   Reference Keystrokes   DOS

U: Press *2* for Format.
C: *Prints* Format: 1 Cell; 2 Column; 3 Row Height: <u>0</u>.

U: Press *3* for Row Height.
C: *Prints* Row Height -- Single line: 1 Fixed; 2 Auto; Multi-line: 3 Fixed; 4 Auto: <u>4</u>.

U: Press *2* for Auto.
C: *Adjusts the row's height.*

To change the height of a row that may contain **MULTIPLE LINES** of text within a cell to a fixed height disregarding text size do the following:

VMS   Reference Keystrokes   DOS

U: Press *2* for Format.
C: *Prints* Format: 1 Cell; 2 Column; 3 Row Height: <u>0</u>.

U: Press *3* for Row Height.
C: *Prints* Row Height -- Single line: 1 Fixed; 2 Auto; Multi-line: 3 Fixed; 4 Auto: <u>4</u>.

U: Press *3* for Fixed.
C: *Prints* Enter fixed height for row: <u>0</u>.293 *(Defaults to current row height).*

U: Press the appropriate number for the row's height and press the *Enter key.*
C: *Adjusts the row's height.*

To let WordPerfect automatically adjust the height of a row that may contain multiple lines of text do the following:

VMS	Reference Keystrokes	DOS

U: Press *2* for Format.
C: *Prints* Format: 1 Cell; 2 Column; 3 Row
Height: <u>0</u>.

U: Press *3* for Row Height.
C: *Prints* Row Height -- Single line: 1 Fixed;
2 Auto; Multi-line: 3 Fixed; 4 Auto: <u>4</u>.

U: Press *4* for Auto.
C: *Adjusts the row's height.*

Table Edit: Lines

This option allows you to choose the type of lines that you would like to have in and around your table's cells, rows, and columns.

You can block, or highlight, a section of the table whose lines you would like to change or you can move to the cell whose lines you would like to change.

Remember, to block a section of the table do the following:

VMS	Reference Keystrokes	DOS
PF3,F10		Alt-F4
OR		OR
F20		F12

U: Press **Block.**
C: *Prints* Block on.

U: Use *Arrow keys* to highlight cells.
C: *Highlights cells.*

Table Edit: Lines
Changing Line Display

To change the lines surrounding a block or a cell do the following:

VMS	Reference Keystrokes	DOS

U: Press *3* for Lines.
C: *Prints* Lines: 1 Left; 2 Right; 3 Top; 4 Bottom;
5 Inside; 6 Outside; 7 All; 8 Shade: <u>0</u>.

The Lines Menu is shown on Screen 6-9.

Screen 6-9

```
        On your screen you will see the document you were editing along
with your brand new table.  On the lower portion of your screen you will
see the Table Edit Menu.
```

Table Edit: Press Exit when done   Cell A1 Doc 1 Pg 1 Ln 1.86" Pos 1.12"

```
Top=Double; Bottom=None; Left=Double; Right=None
Lines: 1 Left;2 Right;3 Top;4 Bottom;5 Inside;6 Outside;7 All;8 Shade: 0
```

Top=Double; Bottom=None; Left=Double; Right=None represents WordPerfect's built in defaults for the cell or block of cells.

Inside represents all the lines inside the blocked area of cells, whereas, outside represents all the lines that surround the blocked cells.

VMS   Reference Keystrokes   DOS

U: Press the appropriate number between 1 and 7.
C: *Prints* 1 None; 2 Single; 3 Double; 4 Dashed;
      5 Dotted; 6 Thick; 7 Extra Thick: <u>0</u>.

U: Press the appropriate number.
C: *Reformats the lines.*

Table Edit: Lines
Changing Cell Shading

Shade will color in the cell or cells interior section.

VMS   Reference Keystrokes   DOS

U: Press *3* for Lines.
C: *Prints* Lines: 1 Left; 2 Right; 3 Top; 4 Bottom;
      5 Inside; 6 Outside; 7 All; 8 Shade: <u>0</u>.

U: Press *8* for Shade.
C: *Prints* Shading: 1 On; 2 Off: <u>0</u>.

VMS	Reference Keystrokes	DOS

U: Press *1* for On or *2* for Off.
C: *Turns shading in the cell on or off.*

Table Edit: Header

This WordPerfect option provides for the repetition of column headings on subsequent pages. Usually the top few lines of your table will contain the labels, or titles, for all your columns in the table. If you would like those labels to be repeated on any succeeding pages you must specify what rows should be contained in your header.

To tell WordPerfect the number of header rows in your table (starting from Row 1 at the top of your table) do the following:

VMS	Reference Keystrokes	DOS

U: Press *4* for Headers.
C: *Prints* Number of header rows: <u>0</u>.

U: Enter the number of header rows you would
     like in your table and press the *Enter key*.
C: *Returns to table.*

Table Edit: Math

WordPerfect's Math feature (see Chapter 8) includes math calculations. Table Math, new with WordPerfect 5.1, provides calculations within tables.

Table Math may be preferred if you had created the following table, Table 6-3, and want to include the Total Amount of your expenses in Cell B5.

Table 6-3

Major Expenses for July	Amount
Rent	700.00
Food	150.00
Miscellaneous	350.00
Total	Cell B5

Insertion of a math formula in Cell B5 can instruct WordPerfect 5.1 to calculate and print the total of all your expenses in that cell.

Table Edit: Formulas

A formula consists of the address(es) of the cell(s) whose contents you want to include in the calculation and the appropriate math operator(s). Math operators include the following:

Math Operators	Description
*	Used for multiplication
/	Used for division
+	Used for addition
-	Used for subtraction

In the above example you would want the following type of formula contained in Cell B5: B2+B3+B4. This formula would add the numbers contained in Cells B2, B3, and B4 together to get the sum of the expenses. Since the formula will be located in Cell B5 the result of the calculation will be shown in Cell B5.

To enter a formula into a Cell do the following:

VMS   Reference Keystrokes   DOS

U: Press *5* for Math.
C: *Prints* Math: 1 Calculate; 2 Formula; 3 Copy
Formula; 4 +; 5 =; 6 *: 0.

U: Press *2* for Formula.
C: *Prints* Enter formula: _.

U: Enter formula and press the *Enter key.*
C: *Echoes formula and displays calculation result in table.*

If you change one or more of the numbers in the table that is used in a formula you must recalculate the formula to make the corresponding calculation change in the correct Cell. To recalculate formulas do the following:

VMS   Reference Keystrokes   DOS

U: Press *5* for Math.
C: *Prints* Math: 1 Calculate; 2 Formula; 3 Copy
Formula; 4 +; 5 =; 6 *: 0.

U: Press *1* for Calculate.
C: *Recalculates formulas and displays new calculation results in tables.*

An example of a different type of formula is shown in Table 6-4.

Table 6-4

Months	Low Temperature	High Temperature	Average Temperature
June	54	85	70
July	71	100	87
August	75	102	95
Averages			

Cells A1, B1, C1, and D1 all contain the titles for their columns. Cells A2, A3, and A4 contain the names of the months for the summer season.

In Row 5 in Cells B5, C5, and D5 a formula should be placed to calculate out the averages of each column. The formulas you should place in the above Cells is listed below.

Cell Address	Formula
B5	(B2+B3+B4)/3
C5	(C2+C3+C4)/3
D5	(D2+D3+D4)/3

The order of precedence in formula calculations, as to what is computed first, etc. in a numerical calculation is as follows:

1. Left to right.
2. Parentheses
3. Multiplication and/or Division
4. Addition and/or Subtraction

If you enter a portion of a Cell Address, for example only the Column Letters without the corresponding Row Numbers, then WordPerfect will presume that you are referring to the current Row Number in which your formula is placed.

A generic formula may also be used in any Cell in your table. The generic formula does not make references to any Cells it just performs its own calculations. For example, in Cell S5 you could have the formula: (77*11) - 26.

Table Edit: Copying Formulas

It is possible to copy a formula and place it in another location. There are two ways to copy formulas either copy from one cell to another cell or copy from one cell to a group of cells beneath or to the right of the cell being copied.

To copy a formula from one cell to another do the following:

VMS   **Reference Keystrokes**   **DOS**

U: Press *5* for Math.
C: *Prints* Math: 1 Calculate; 2 Formula; 3 Copy
   Formula; 4 +; 5 =; 6 *: 0.

U: Press *3* for Copy Formula.
C: *Prints* Copy formula To: 1 Cell; 2 Down;
   3 Right: 0.

U: Press *1* for Cell.

VMS Users   C: *Prints* Move cursor; press Return to retrieve.
C: *Prints* Move cursor; press Enter to retrieve.   *DOS Users*

U: Move cursor to the cell you want to copy the
   formula into and press the *Enter key.*
C: *Retrieves formula.*

If you want to copy a formula from one cell to a group of cells beneath or to the right of the cell being copied it is easier to do the following:

VMS   **Reference Keystrokes**   **DOS**

U: Press *5* for Math.
C: *Prints* Math: 1 Calculate; 2 Formula; 3 Copy
   Formula; 4 +; 5 =; 6 *: 0.

U: Press *3* for Copy Formula.
C: *Prints* Copy formula To: 1 Cell; 2 Down; 3
   Right: 0.

U: Press *2* for Down or *3* for Right.
C: *Prints* Number of times to copy formula: 1.

U: Enter number of times to copy formula and
   press the *Enter key.*
C: *Retrieves formula specified number of times
   down or to the right of cell being copied.*

Table Edit: Functions

There are three functions you can use in Table Math just like they are used in the Math feature. These functions are the Subtotal function, Total function, and the Grand Total function.

The Subtotal function is represented by the +. When this function is placed in a Cell it will add all the numbers contained in the cells directly above the Cell with the Subtotal function in it. To enter a Subtotal function in a Cell do the following:

VMS	**Reference Keystrokes**	**DOS**

U: Press *5* for Math.
C: *Prints* Math: 1 Calculate; 2 Formula; 3 Copy
Formula; 4 +; 5 =; 6 *: <u>0</u>.

U: Press *4* for +.
C: *Displays result in table.*

The Total function is represented by the =. When this function is placed in a Cell it will add all the Subtotals in the cells directly above the Cell with the Total function in it.

VMS	**Reference Keystrokes**	**DOS**

U: Press *5* for Math.
C: *Prints* Math: 1 Calculate; 2 Formula; 3 Copy
Formula; 4 +; 5 =; 6 *: <u>0</u>.

U: Press *5* for =.
C: *Displays result in table.*

The Grand Total function is represented by the *. When this function is placed in a Cell it will add all the Totals in the cells directly above the Cell with the Grand Total function in it.

VMS	**Reference Keystrokes**	**DOS**

U: Press *5* for Math.
C: *Prints* Math: 1 Calculate; 2 Formula; 3 Copy
Formula; 4 +; 5 =; 6 *: <u>0</u>.

U: Press *6* for *.
C: *Displays result in table.*

Negative Numbers

Negative numbers may be placed into cells in your table and can be used in formulas.

Table Edit: Options

This option allows you to modify setting for all the table's cells.

VMS   **Reference Keystrokes**   **DOS**

U: Press *6* for Options.
C: *Displays Table Options Menu.*

Screen 6-10 displays the Table Options Menu.

Screen 6-10

```
┌─────────────────────────────────────────────────────────┐
│ Table Options                                            │
│                                                          │
│     1 - Spacing Between Text and Lines                   │
│             Left              0.083"                     │
│             Right             0.083"                     │
│             Top               0.1"                       │
│             Bottom            0"                         │
│                                                          │
│     2 - Display Negative Results      1                  │
│             1 = with minus signs                         │
│             2 = with parentheses                         │
│                                                          │
│     3 - Position of Table             Left               │
│                                                          │
│     4 - Gray Shading (% of black)     10%                │
│                                                          │
│                                                          │
│ Selection: 0                                             │
└─────────────────────────────────────────────────────────┘
```

Spacing Between Text and Lines allows you to change the amount of space between your text and the cell border. To change spacing do the following:

VMS   **Reference Keystrokes**   **DOS**

U: Press *1* for Spacing Between Text and Lines.
C: *Positions cursor to right of Left.*

U: Use *Down arrow key* to move to the Right, Top,
   or Bottom options.
C: *Positions cursor.*

U: Enter new value(s) and press the *Enter key*
   until you return to Selection.
C: *Echoes numbers.*

Display Negative Results allows you to change the way negative numbers are displayed in your table. You may display negative numbers either like -77 or (77). When you enter the negative number into the table you may use either format.

Position of the Table allows you to align your table in your document. To align your table do the following:

VMS	Reference Keystrokes	DOS

U: Press *3* for Position of Table.
C: *Prints* Table Position: 1 Left; 2 Right; 3 Center;
    4 Full; 5 Set Position: 0.

Table Position Left aligns the table against the left margin, Right aligns the table against the right margin, Center aligns the table between the left and right margins, Full aligns the table against both the left and right margins, and Set Position allows you to enter the offset from the left edge.

If you want to select an option between 1 and 4 do the following:

VMS	Reference Keystrokes	DOS

U: Select *1* for Left, *2* for Right, *3* for Center, or
    4 for Full.
C: *Echoes table position.*

Otherwise, if you want to select option 5 do the following:

VMS	Reference Keystrokes	DOS

U: Press *5* for Set Position.
C: *Prints* Enter offset from left edge: 0".

Gray Shading allows you to enter the percentage of shading you would like in a cell. If you choose 100% then the shading will be black.

Table Edit: Join

This option allows you to join multiple cells into one big cell. For example, in the table below, Table 6-5, you may join Cells B2 and C2 to produce one cell.

Table 6-5

	B2	C2	

To join the cells in this example, Table 6-5, you could perform the following steps:

VMS	Reference Keystrokes	DOS

U: Position your cursor in Cell B2.
C: *Positions cursor.*

VMS	**Reference Keystrokes**	**DOS**

| PF3,F10
OR
F20 | U: Press **Block**.
C: *Prints* Block on. | Alt-F4
OR
F12 |

U: Press the **Right arrow key** to highlight Cell C2.
C: *Blocks Cells B2 and C2.*

U: Press *7* for Join.
C: *Prints* Join cells? <u>N</u>o (Yes).

U: Press *Y* for Yes.
C: *Joins cells.*

The new table, Table 6-6, that contains the joined cells, is shown below:

Table 6-6

Any text that may have been located in the joined cells will be separated by tabs. If you joined two cells in the same column the text would be separated by hard returns.

Table Edit: Split

This option allows you to separate one cell into two or more rows or columns. For example, in the table below, Table 6-7, you may separate Cell A2 into two different rows.

Table 6-7

A2	B2	

In our example, Table 6-7, you could split a cell as follows:

VMS	**Reference Keystrokes**	**DOS**

U: Position your cursor in Cell A2.
C: *Positions cursor.*

U: Press *8* for Split.
C: *Prints* Split: 1 Rows; 2 Columns: <u>0</u>.

U: Press *1* for Rows.
C: *Prints* Number of Rows: <u>1</u>.

VMS   Reference Keystrokes   DOS

U: Enter in number and press the *Enter key.*
C: *Splits cell.*

The new table, Table 6-8, that contains the split cell, is shown below:

Table 6-8

	B2	

Also, in the table above you may separate Cell B2 into three different columns. You can split a cell as follows:

VMS   Reference Keystrokes   DOS

U: Position your cursor in Cell B2.
C: *Positions cursor.*

U: Press *8* for Split.
C: *Prints* Split: 1 Rows; 2 Columns: 0.

U: Press *2* for Columns.
C: *Prints* Number of Columns: 1.

U: Enter in number and press the *Enter key.*
C: *Splits cell.*

The new table, Table 6-9, that contains the split cell, is shown below:

Table 6-9

Exiting from the Table Edit Menu

To exit from the Table Edit Menu do the following:

VMS	**Reference Keystrokes**	**DOS**
F13	U: Press *Exit*. C: *Returns to Document*.	F7

Invoking the Table Edit Menu

When you are editing your document if you wish to return to the Table Edit Menu you may do the following if your cursor is located within the table:

VMS	**Reference Keystrokes**	**DOS**
PF3,F13	U: Press *Columns/Table*. C: *Displays Table Edit Menu*.	Alt-F7

If your cursor is not located within a table you may do the following:

VMS	**Reference Keystrokes**	**DOS**
PF3,F13	U: Press *Columns/Table*. C: *Prints* 1 Columns; 2 Tables; 3 Math: <u>0</u>. U: Press *2* for Tables. C: *Prints* Table: 1 Create; 2 Edit: <u>0</u>. U: Press *2* for Edit. C: *Displays Table Edit Menu*.	Alt-F7

WordPerfect will search from the current cursor position backward in the document to the top for the first table it can find. If a table is not found between the current cursor position and the top of the document then WordPerfect will search forward from the current cursor position to the bottom of the document for the first table.

Entering and Editing Text and Numbers in a Table

Entering and editing text and numbers in a table is almost identical to normal editing in WordPerfect. All you have to do is position your cursor (with your arrow keys) into the cell you want to enter text or a number into and start typing.

Cursor Movement

To move to a column to the right of your current column press the *Tab key*. To move to a column to the left of your current column press *<-Margin Release* (Shift-Tab).

When you press the Return Key while entering information into a cell you will move to the second line of the cell if you have multiple line cells.

Formatting Text

If you want to Bold some information you are entering into a cell you may press the *Bold key* and type in the text or if you want to change the font of the text you may also do that.

Inserting/Deleting Rows

To insert or delete a row you do not have to go into the Table Edit Menu, you may just press *Ctrl-Insert* to insert a row above the current row or press *Ctrl-Delete* to delete the current row your cursor is located in.

Creating a Table Macro

In this section, a macro will be written to create a Five Row by Four Column Table.

VMS	Keystroke Action	DOS
PF2,F18	1. U: Press *Macro Define.* C: *Prints* Define macro: _.	Ctrl-F10
	2. U: Type in <u>WAGES</u> and press the *Enter key.* C: *Prints* Description: _.	

	3. U: Type in <u>Creates an Employee Wage Table</u>
	    and press the *Enter key.*
	    C: *Prints* Macro Def.	

PF3,F13	4. U: Press *Columns/Table.* C: *Prints* 1 Columns; 2 Tables; 3 Math: <u>0</u>.	Alt-F7
	5. U: Press *2* for Tables. C: *Prints* Table: 1 Create; 2 Edit: <u>0</u>.	
	6. U: Press *1* for Create. C: *Prints* Number of Columns: <u>3</u>.	

	7. U: Type in *4* for four columns and press the
	    Enter key.
	    C: *Prints* Number of Rows: <u>1</u>.	

	8. U: Type in *8* for eight rows and press the
	    Enter key.
	    C: *Prints* Updating Table *and Displays the*
	    Table Edit Menu.	

	9. U: Press *4* for Header. C: *Prints* Number of header rows: <u>0</u>.	

| **VMS** | **Keystroke Action** | **DOS** |

10. U: Type in *1* and press the *Enter key.*
     C: *Displays the Table Edit Menu.*

11. U: Press *3* for Lines.
     C: *Prints* Lines: 1 Left; 2 Right; 3 Top;
         4 Bottom; 5 Inside; 6 Outside; 7 All;
         8 Shade: 0.

12. U: Press *4* for Bottom.
     C: *Prints* 1 None; 2 Single; 3 Double;
         4 Dashed; 5 Dotted; 6 Thick; 7 Extra
         Thick: 0.

13. U: Press *3* for Double.
     C: *Displays the Table Edit Menu.*

14. U: Press the *Right arrow key.*
     C: *Positions cursor in Cell B1.*

15. U: Press *3* for Lines.
     C: *Prints* Lines: 1 Left; 2 Right; 3 Top;
         4 Bottom; 5 Inside; 6 Outside; 7 All;
         8 Shade: 0.

16. U: Press *4* for Bottom.
     C: *Prints* 1 None; 2 Single; 3 Double;
         4 Dashed; 5 Dotted; 6 Thick; 7 Extra
         Thick: 0.

17. U: Press *3* for Double.
     C: *Displays the Table Edit Menu.*

18. U: Press the *Right arrow key.*
     C: *Positions cursor in Cell C1.*

19. U: Press *3* for Lines.
     C: *Prints* Lines: 1 Left; 2 Right; 3 Top;
         4 Bottom; 5 Inside; 6 Outside; 7 All;
         8 Shade: 0.

20. U: Press *4* for Bottom.
     C: *Prints* 1 None; 2 Single; 3 Double;
         4 Dashed; 5 Dotted; 6 Thick; 7 Extra
         Thick: 0.

21. U: Press *3* for Double.
     C: *Displays the Table Edit Menu.*

VMS   **Keystroke Action**   **DOS**

22. U: Press the *Right arrow key*.
    C: *Positions cursor in Cell D1.*

23. U: Press *3* for Lines.
    C: *Prints* Lines: 1 Left; 2 Right; 3 Top;
    4 Bottom; 5 Inside; 6 Outside; 7 All;
    8 Shade: <u>0</u>.

24. U: Press *4* for Bottom.
    C: *Prints* 1 None; 2 Single; 3 Double;
    4 Dashed; 5 Dotted; 6 Thick; 7 Extra
    Thick: <u>0</u>.

25. U: Press *3* for Double.
    C: *Displays the Table Edit Menu.*

26. U: Press the *Down arrow key*.
    C: *Positions cursor in Cell D2.*

27. U: Press *5* for Math.
    C: *Prints* Math: 1 Calculate; 2 Formula;
    3 Copy Formula; 4 +; 5 =; 6 *: <u>0</u>.

28. U: Press *2* for Formula.
    C: *Prints* Enter formula: <u> </u>.

29. U: Type in <u>B2*C2</u> and press the *Enter key*.
    C: *Displays the Table Edit Menu.*

30. U: Press *5* for Math.
    C: *Prints* Math: 1 Calculate; 2 Formula;
    3 Copy Formula; 4 +; 5 =; 6 *: <u>0</u>.

31. U: Press *3* for Copy Formula.
    C: *Prints* Copy Formula To: 1 Cell; 2 Down;
    3 Right: <u>0</u>.

32. U: Press *2* for Down.
    C: *Prints* Number of times to copy formula: <u>1</u>.

33. U: Type in *5* for five times (total of rows in
    table that will be used for employees) and
    press the *Enter key*.
    C: *Prints 0.00 in all of Column D's cells except
    the last cell and Displays the Table Edit
    Menu.*

VMS	**Keystroke Action**	**DOS**

PF2,PF4 34. U: Press *Goto*.   Ctrl-Home
        C: *Prints* Go to _.

       35. U: Type in <u>D8</u> and press the *Enter key*.
        C: *Positions cursor in Cell D8.*

       36. U: Press *5* for Math.
        C: *Prints* Math: 1 Calculate; 2 Formula; 3 Copy Formula; 4 +; 5 =; 6 *: <u>0</u>.

       37. U: Press *4* for +.
        C: *Prints 0.00 in Cell D8 and Displays the Table Edit Menu.*

PF2,PF4 38. U: Press *Goto*.   Ctrl-Home
        C: *Prints* Go to _.

       39. U: Type in <u>A1</u> and press the *Enter key*.
        C: *Positions cursor in Cell A1.*

F13   40. U: Press *Exit*.   F7
        C: *Returns to Document.*

       41. U: Type in <u>Employee</u>, press the *Enter key*, type in <u>Name</u>, and press the *Tab key*.
        C: *Echoes characters and Positions cursor in Cell B1.*

       42. U: Type in <u>Hourly</u>, press the *Enter key*, type in <u>Rate</u>, and press the *Tab* key.
        C: *Echoes characters and Positions cursor in Cell C1.*

       43. U: Type in <u>Hours</u>, press the *Enter key*, type in <u>Worked</u>, and press the *Tab key*.
        C: *Echoes characters and Positions cursor in Cell D1.*

       44. U: Type in <u>Gross</u>, press the *Enter key*, and type in <u>Wages</u>, and press the *Tab key*.
        C: *Echoes characters and Positions cursor in Cell A2.*

PF2,F18 45. U: Press *Macro Define* to finish defining the Ctrl-F10
          macro.
        C: *Saves macro.*

VMS	Keystroke Action	DOS

PF3,F13   46. U: Press *Columns/Table.*   Alt-F7
                     C: *Prints* 1 Columns; 2 Tables; 3 Math: <u>0</u>.

Applications of the Table Macro

The keystrokes contained in the "WAGES.WPM" macro are shown on Screen 6-11 or Screen 6-12.

Screen 6-11: VMS Users

```
Macro: Action

        File            WAGES.WPM

        Description     Creates an Employee Wage Table

        ┌─────────────────────────────────────────────────────┐
        │{DISPLAY OFF}{Columns/Tables}214{Enter}              │
        │8{Enter}                                             │
        │41{Enter}                                            │
        │343{Right}343{Right}343{Right}343{Down}52B2*C2{Enter}│
        │5325{Enter}                                          │
        │{Goto}D8{Enter}                                      │
        │54{Goto}A1{Enter}                                    │
        │{Exit}Employee{Enter}                                │
        │Name{Tab}Hourly{Enter}                               │
        │Rate{Tab}Hours{Enter}                                │
        │Worked{Tab}Gross{Enter}                              │
        │Wages{Tab}                                           │
        └─────────────────────────────────────────────────────┘

PF2,Prev Scr for macro commands;  Press Exit when done
```

Screen 6-12: DOS Users

```
Macro: Action

        File            WAGES.WPM

        Description     Creates an Employee Wage Table

        ┌─────────────────────────────────────────────────────┐
        │{DISPLAY OFF}{Columns/Tables}214{Enter}              │
        │8{Enter}                                             │
        │41{Enter}                                            │
        │343{Right}343{Right}343{Right}343{Down}52B2*C2{Enter}│
        │5325{Enter}                                          │
        │{Goto}D8{Enter}                                      │
        │54{Goto}A1{Enter}                                    │
        │{Exit}Employee{Enter}                                │
        │Name{Tab}Hourly{Enter}                               │
        │Rate{Tab}Hours{Enter}                                │
        │Worked{Tab}Gross{Enter}                              │
        │Wages{Tab}                                           │
        └─────────────────────────────────────────────────────┘

Ctrl-V to Insert next key as command;
Ctrl-PgUp for macro commands;  Press Exit when done
```

This macro is ready for immediate use. Remember to calculate your table when you have added in all of your data (See Chapter 6: Table Edit: Formulas or Using the Macro). It can be modified in the Macro Editor to fit your personal needs if you have more employees at your company or if you need different table definition.

Using the Macro

The initial conditions for this macro assume you are starting a new document or that you are currently editing a document to include this particular table.

To invoke this macro do the following:

VMS	**Keystroke Action**	**DOS**
PF3,F18	1. U: Press *Macro.* C: *Prints* Macro: _.	Alt-F10
	2. U: Type in <u>WAGES</u> and press the *Enter key.* C: *Macro invokes.*	

When invoking this macro you will see what is shown on Screen 6-13:

Screen 6-13

Employee Name	Hourly Rate	Hours Worked	Gross Wages
			0.00
			0.00
			0.00
			0.00
			0.00
			0.00
			0.00

Now you can add Employee Names, Hourly Rates, and Hours Worked into the table. When all the data is in the table you can calculate the table by doing the following:

VMS	**Keystroke Action**	**DOS**
PF3,F13	3. U: Press *Columns/Table.* C: *Prints* 1 Columns; 2 Tables; 3 Math: <u>0</u>.	Alt-F7

VMS   **Keystroke Action**   **DOS**

4. U: Press *5* for Math.
    C: *Prints* Math: 1 Calculate; 2 Formula; 3
        Copy Formula; 4 +; 5 =; 6 *: <u>0</u>.

5. U: Press *1* for Calculate.
    C: *Calculates formulas and displays new*
        calculation results in tables.

Then your screen will look similar to Screen 6-14:

Screen 6-14

Employee Name	Hourly Rate	Hours Worked	Gross Wages
Phil	9.00	7	63.00
John	9.00	5	45.00
Diane	7.00	10	70.00
Doug	7.00	10	70.00
Rich	5.00	7	35.00
Crystal	5.00	5	25.00
			308.00

GRAPHICS MACRO

Graphics Feature

Graphics pictures are easily inserted into any text using the WordPerfect 5.1 Graphics Feature. They are an excellent addition for newsletters, letterheads for the office, or even personal use.

In this chapter the basic graphic terminology of WordPerfect 5.1 will be discussed first. Then, as a graphics macro is created, the basic graphic terminology foundation will be expanded. The macro we create will contain a graphics image using a fictitious "Travel the World, Incorporated" company's letterhead.

A printer that supports graphics is required when printing any document that contains graphic images. Also note that a graphics card is required in your computer for graphics to be displayed on your screen.

Boxes

WordPerfect 5.1 allows graphic images to be imbedded in five different types of boxes. The types are: Figure, Table, Text, User, and Equation. Any of the five boxes may hold any type of text, data, or pictures. However, for practical purposes the Figure Box is used for graphic pictures, the Table Box is used for tabular data, the Text Box is used for actual text, the User Box is used for everything else, and the Equation Box is used for mathematical equations. You will notice in the following Screens 7-1 through 7-5 that the nine options common to each type of box have a different set of default settings. We will show how any default setting can be changed, within limits, by the user.

Screen 7-1: The Figure Box

```
Options:  Figure
    1 - Border Style
            Left                       Single
            Right                      Single
            Top                        Single
            Bottom                     Single
    2 - Outside Border Space
            Left                       0.167"
            Right                      0.167"
            Top                        0.167"
            Bottom                     0.167"
    3 - Inside Border Space
            Left                       0"
            Right                      0"
            Top                        0"
            Bottom                     0"
    4 - First Level Numbering Method   Numbers
    5 - Second Level Numbering Method  Off
    6 - Caption Number Style           [BOLD]Figure 1[bold]
    7 - Position of Caption            Below box, Outside borders
    8 - Minimum Offset from Paragraph  0"
    9 - Gray Shading (% of black)      0%
Selection: 0
```

Screen 7-2: The Table Box

```
Options:  Table
     1 - Border Style
               Left                              None
               Right                             None
               Top                               Thick
               Bottom                            Thick
     2 - Outside Border Space
               Left                              0.167"
               Right                             0.167"
               Top                               0.167"
               Bottom                            0.167"
     3 - Inside Border Space
               Left                              0.167"
               Right                             0.167"
               Top                               0.167"
               Bottom                            0.167"
     4 - First Level Numbering Method            Roman
     5 - Second Level Numbering Method           Off
     6 - Caption Number Style                    [BOLD]Table 1[bold]
     7 - Position of Caption                     Above box, Outside borders
     8 - Minimum Offset from Paragraph           0"
     9 - Gray Shading (% of black)               0%
Selection: 0
```

Screen 7-3: The Text Box

```
Options:  Text Box
     1 - Border Style
               Left                              None
               Right                             None
               Top                               Thick
               Bottom                            Thick
     2 - Outside Border Space
               Left                              0.167"
               Right                             0.167"
               Top                               0.167"
               Bottom                            0.167"
     3 - Inside Border Space
               Left                              0.167"
               Right                             0.167"
               Top                               0.167"
               Bottom                            0.167"
     4 - First Level Numbering Method            Numbers
     5 - Second Level Numbering Method           Off
     6 - Caption Number Style                    [BOLD]1[bold]
     7 - Position of Caption                     Below box, Outside borders
     8 - Minimum Offset from Paragraph           0"
     9 - Gray Shading (% of black)               10%
Selection: 0
```

Screen 7-4: The User Box

```
Options:  User Box
    1 - Border Style
            Left                    None
            Right                   None
            Top                     None
            Bottom                  None
    2 - Outside Border Space
            Left                    0.167"
            Right                   0.167"
            Top                     0.167"
            Bottom                  0.167"
    3 - Inside Border Space
            Left                    0"
            Right                   0"
            Top                     0"
            Bottom                  0"
    4 - First Level Numbering Method   Numbers
    5 - Second Level Numbering Method  Off
    6 - Caption Number Style           [BOLD]1[bold]
    7 - Position of Caption            Below box, Outside borders
    8 - Minimum Offset from Paragraph  0"
    9 - Gray Shading (% of black)      0%
Selection: 0
```

Screen 7-5: The Equation Box

```
Options:  Equation
    1 - Border Style
            Left                    None
            Right                   None
            Top                     None
            Bottom                  None
    2 - Outside Border Space
            Left                    0.083"
            Right                   0.083"
            Top                     0.083"
            Bottom                  0.083"
    3 - Inside Border Space
            Left                    0.083"
            Right                   0.083"
            Top                     0.083"
            Bottom                  0.083"
    4 - First Level Numbering Method   Numbers
    5 - Second Level Numbering Method  Off
    6 - Caption Number Style           [BOLD](1)[bold]
    7 - Position of Caption            Right side
    8 - Minimum Offset from Paragraph  0"
    9 - Gray Shading (% of black)      0%
Selection: 0
```

Options

Each option covers a range of choices that can be used to meet the special needs of any user.

Border Style: Allows the user to choose the border style preferred for the box contained in the document. There are seven different border styles:

None: No Border

Single   Double   Dashed

Dotted   Thick   Extra Thick

Outside Border Space: Lets the user choose the amount of blank space between each of the four borders of the box and the text outside of the box.

Inside Border Space: Lets the user choose the amount of blank space between each of the four borders of the box and whatever is contained in the box.

First Level Numbering Method: Allows the user to choose numbering for the boxes' first level, or section, of captions for each box's description. The user may choose either off, numbers, letters, or Roman numerals.

Second Level Numbering Method: Allows the user to choose numbering for the boxes' second level, or section, of captions to further enhance the first level numbering method and also differentiate between the two numbering methods the user uses for a box. The user may choose either off, numbers, letters, or Roman numerals.

Caption Number Style: Provides a choice of styles for the boxes' caption's text and numbers.

Position of Caption: Lets the user choose the position of each of the captions for the boxes.

Minimum Offset from Paragraph: Tells the user exactly how far a paragraph type graphics box may be moved into the paragraph before it is automatically moved to the next page.

Gray Shading (% of black): Allows the user to enter the percentage of shading for the specified graphics box. For example, 0% equals white while 100% equals black.

Graphics in Your Document

To insert a graphic image box in any document do the following:

VMS	**Reference Keystrokes**	**DOS**
PF3,F17	U: Press *Graphics*. C: *Displays Graphics Menu.*	Alt-F9

The computer will then display a screen like Screen 7-6 below.

Screen 7-6

```
1 Figure; 2 Table Box; 3 Text Box; 4 User Box; 5 Line; 6 Equation: 0
```

Select one of the five box types or the vertical/horizontal line draw option. Once a box type is selected a new menu will appear. If you select 1 for Figure, the menu for the Figure Box will appear as shown on Screen 7-7.

Screen 7-7

```
Figure: 1 Create; 2 Edit; 3 New Number; 4 Options: 0
```

The options in the Figure Box Menu, as well as the other Box Menus include create, edit, new number, and options.

Create: Enters the chosen graphics box into the document, header, footer, endnotes, or footnotes. Right after this option is selected the computer will advance into the Figure Definition Menu and assign the type of figure, table, text, user, or equation and a number to the box.

Edit: Asks the user for the figure, table, text, user, or equation number box that you wish to edit and then advances you directly into the Figure Definition Menu.

New Number: This option will renumber the graphic box's numbers following the box with the new number.

Options: Allows you to change the default options of the five different types of boxes.

At this point, we could select *1* to Create the Figure Box.

Box Definitions

After we select the Create option, your screen will display the Figure Menu for a Paragraph type box as shown on Screen 7-8.

Screen 7-8

```
Definition:  Figure

     1 - Filename

     2 - Contents             Empty

     3 - Caption

     4 - Anchor Type          Paragraph

     5 - Vertical Position    0"

     6 - Horizontal Position  Right

     7 - Size                 3.25" wide x 3.25" (high)

     8 - Wrap Text Around Box  Yes

     9 - Edit
Selection: 0
```

The nine different items contained in the Definition: Figure Menu are described as follows:

Filename: Contains the filename of the graphic image or text that you enter in as the filename. Whatever filename you enter will be displayed in the box that you are creating. Remember to include the correct file specification (VMS) OR pathname (DOS) for the file.

VMS Users: *The graphic images listed in Table 7-1 are the pictures that are included in your WordPerfect 5.1 software package for VMS that your System Manager should have installed on your computer system. Ask your System Manager for correct file specification or logical to use to locate the graphic images.*

DOS Users: *The graphic images listed in Table 7-2 are the pictures that are included in your WordPerfect 5.1 software package and are located on a disk that came with the software program.*

You can type in one of these filenames and that specific file's graphic image will be displayed in the box. Also, a graphic image may be imported from other specific graphic packages and inserted into the box. If you do not choose a filename then regular text can be entered into the box. To enter text into the box you must select the edit option and then type in the text and/or codes you want to appear in the box.

Table 7-1: VMS Users

ARROW-22.WPG	BALLOONS.WPG
BANNER-3.WPG	BICYCLE.WPG
BORDER.WPG	BULB.WPG
BURST-1.WPG	CALENDAR.WPG
CERTIF.WPG	CHKBOX-1.WPG
CLOCK.WPG	CNTRCT-2.WPG
DEVICE-2.WPG	DIPLOMA.WPG
FLOPPY-2.WPG	GAVEL.WPG
GLOBE2-M.WPG	HANDS-3.WPG
MAGNIF.WPG	MAILBAG.WPG
NEWS.WPG	PC-1.WPG
PRESNT-1.WPG	PRINTR-3.WPG
SCALE.WPG	TELPHONE.WPG
TROPHY.WPG	

Table 7-2: DOS Users

ARROW-22.WPG	BALLOONS.WPG
BANNER-3.WPG	BICYCLE.WPG
BKGRND-1.WPG	BORDER-8.WPG
BULB.WPG	BURST-1.WPG
BUTTRFLY.WPG	CALENDAR.WPG
CERTIF.WPG	CHKBOX-1.WPG
CLOCK.WPG	CNTRCT-2.WPG
DEVICE-2.WPG	DIPLOMA.WPG
FLOPPY-2.WPG	GAVEL.WPG
GLOBE2-M.WPG	HANDS-3.WPG
MAGNIF.WPG	MAILBAG.WPG
NEWS.WPG	PC-1.WPG
PRESNT-1.WPG	PRINTR-3.WPG

Table 7-2: DOS Users continued.

SCALE.WPG	STAR-5.WPG
TELPHONE.WPG	TROPHY.WPG

Caption: Puts the user into the Caption Editor Screen. In this editing screen the user may type in a legend or description for the box. However, if the graphic box appears in a header, footer, footnote, or endnote, a caption cannot be included.

Type: Offers three different types of graphic boxes which include the paragraph, page, and character box. (Screens 7-8, 7-9, and 7-11 respectively.)

Paragraph type: Allows the surrounding text to wrap around the box while the user is editing the document. The function code for the paragraph type is located in the document at the beginning of the paragraph in which the cursor is located. (See Screen 7-8.)

Page type: Positions the graphic box in a specific fixed location on the current page. To define this type the user must place the cursor at the beginning of the page that this type will be defined on or the user must enter the number of pages to skip. For example, if the cursor is located on page 1 and you would like the graphics box to be located on page 7 then enter 6 pages to skip. (See Screen 7-9.)

Character type: Allows the graphics box to represent a single character. Thus, when a character type box is contained in a line which begins to wrap around, the next character in the line will appear directly below the box. These character boxes are the only boxes that are able to be included in footnotes and endnotes. (See Screen 7-10.)

Screen 7-9: The Page Type

```
Definition:  Figure

    1 - Filename

    2 - Contents          Empty

    3 - Caption

    4 - Anchor Type        Page

    5 - Vertical Position   Top

    6 - Horizontal Position  Margin, Right

    7 - Size               3.25" wide x 3.25" (high)

    8 - Wrap Text Around Box  Yes

    9 - Edit
Selection: 0
```

Screen 7-10: The Character Type: VMS Users

```
Definition:  Figure

      1 - Filename

      2 - Contents           Empty

      3 - Caption

      4 - Anchor Type         Character

      5 - Vertical Position   Bottom

      6 - Horizontal Position

      7 - Size                1.54" wide x 1.54" (high)

      8 - Wrap Text Around Box Yes

      9 - Edit
Selection: 0
```

Screen 7-11: The Character Type: DOS Users

```
Definition:  Figure

      1 - Filename

      2 - Contents           Empty

      3 - Caption

      4 - Anchor Type         Character

      5 - Vertical Position   Bottom

      6 - Horizontal Position

      7 - Size                3.25" wide x 3.25" (high)

      8 - Wrap Text Around Box Yes

      9 - Edit
Selection: 0
```

Vertical Position: Depending on the type of graphics box chosen it affects the vertical location of the graphics box.

If the **paragraph graphic box** was selected the following would be displayed:

Offset from top of paragraph: 0"

The user can select an Offset from the top of paragraph. The 0 inches default means that the graphic box will be directly even with the first line of the paragraph. Every subsequent inch locates the graphic box on the line, at the specified inch setting, of the paragraph.

If the **page type graphic box** was selected the following would be displayed:

Vertical Position: 1 Full Page; 2 Top; 3 Center; 4 Bottom; 5 Set Position: 0

You can select the position of the box on the full page, top, center, bottom, or set the position manually.

If the **character type graphic box** was selected the following would be displayed:

Character Box Alignment: 1 Top; 2 Center; 3 Bottom; 4 Baseline: 0

You can select the box's location in order to align the text with the top, center, bottom, or the baseline of the box.

Horizontal Position: Depending on the type of graphics box chosen it affects the horizontal location of the graphics box.

If the **paragraph type graphic box** was selected the following would be displayed:

Horizontal Position: 1 Left; 2 Right; 3 Center; 4 Full: 0

You can select the position in the paragraph for the box. For example, the left edge, the right edge, center of paragraph, or full (both the left and right edge).

If the **page type graphic box** was selected the following would be displayed:

Horizontal Position: 1 Margins; 2 Columns; 3 Set Position: 0

You can select the position of the box with regards to the margins, columns, or set the position. With the margins option, you can choose the left, right, center, or full (both left and right margins). With the columns option, you can enter a single column or a range of columns and then the position left, right, center, or full (both the left and right margins). The Set Position option allows the user to manually enter the offset from the left of the page.

If the **character type graphic box** was selected a choice of position is not required.

Size: Four options allow you to change the size of the graphic box.

Set Width/Auto Height: Allows you to enter a width value and then WordPerfect 5.1 will select the height of the box in order to keep the graphic image preserved in its original form.

Set Height/Auto Width: Allows you to enter a height value and then WordPerfect 5.1 will select the width of the box in order to keep the graphic image preserved in its original form.

Set Both: Allows you to enter both the width and height value. Note that the original image is easily distorted when using this option.

Auto Both: Allows you to set the width and height value back to the original values for this image.

Wrap Text Around Box: The default value equals "yes" where "yes" means that the text will wrap around the graphic box. If you change this option to "no" then the graphics box will not appear in the document and WordPerfect 5.1 will act like it is not even in the Reveal Codes. Editing uses normal procedures.

Edit: If a box is empty or contains text then a blank editing screen will be displayed. If a box contains a graphic image a graphic editing screen will be displayed.

Editing Empty Boxes or Text Boxes

The Editing Screen for Empty or Text Boxes is shown below (See Screen 7-12).

Screen 7-12

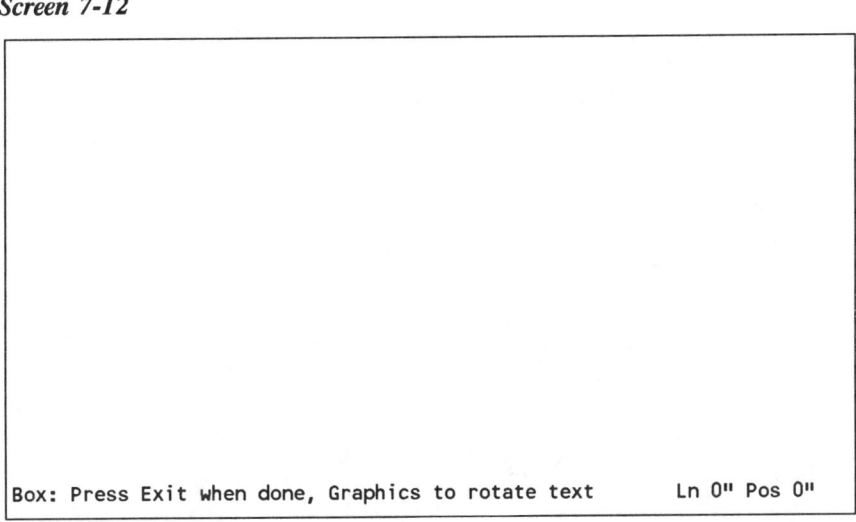

```
Box: Press Exit when done, Graphics to rotate text        Ln 0" Pos 0"
```

WordPerfect 5.1 allows the user to insert up to a page of a specified document or text into the box. However, if the box cannot hold all the text, then only part of the text will be put into the box. The text in the box can be edited in a normal manner. This text contained in the box also may be rotated by pressing Graphics PF3,F17 (VMS) or Alt-F9 (DOS). (See Screen 7-13.) A rotation of 0 degrees is the default. The rotated text will be adjusted to fit into the box. Some printers will not print rotated text, so if the user wants to use this option, the user should first verify whether or not their printer supports rotated text.

Screen 7-13

```
Rotate Text: 1 0°; 2 90°; 3 180°; 4 270°: 1
```

Editing Graphic Images

The Editing Screen for graphic images is shown on Screen 7-14.

Screen 7-14

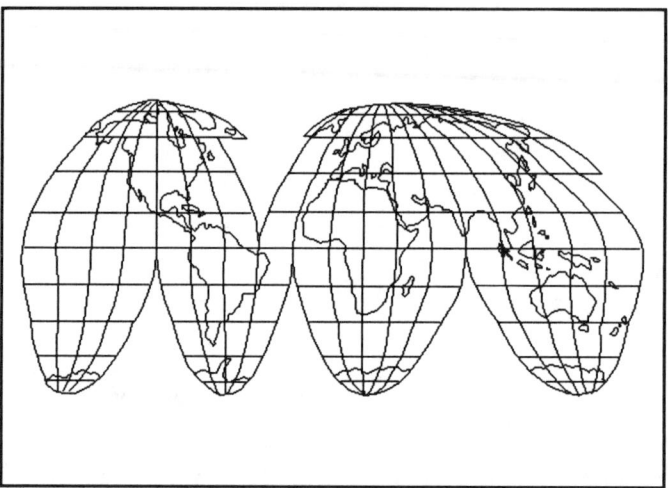

```
Arrow keys Move; PgUp/PgDn Scale; +/- Rotate; Ins % change; GoTo Reset
1 Move; 2 Scale; 3 Rotate; 4 Invert On; 5 Black & White: 0
```

The Edit Screen for graphic images offers the user several editing features to help modify the graphic image.

Arrow Keys: Allows you to move the image around within the box from left to right and top to bottom.

PgUp/PgDn Keys: Lets you change the scale of the image. PgDn will decrease the image's size, while PgUp will increase it.

+/- Keys: The "+" key will rotate the image clockwise, while the "-" key will rotate the image counterclockwise.

Ins Key: Provides a method of changing the percentage that the graphic editing keys discussed in this section will affect the moving, rotating, and scaling of the graphic image. Default is 10%. You can change it to 5, 1, or 25 percent. If you select 1% it will not rotate, etc., as much as if you had selected 25%.

Goto (Ctrl-Home): This option allows the user to reset all the changes that were previously made to the image. All the changes will be returned to their default value.

Move: Lets the user change the horizontal and vertical location of the image. For example, to move horizontally, -1 moves the image to the left and 1 moves the image to the right. To move vertically, -1 moves the image down and 1 moves the image up.

Scale: Allows you to either reduce or expand the image both horizontally and vertically.

Rotate: Lets the user determine the number of degrees (from 0 - 360) to rotate the graphic image. Also allows the user to rotate the image to obtain the mirror image of the graphic display.

Invert: This option works with paint-type bitmap images and allows the user to invert colors. For example, every black dot will change to white and every white dot will change to black.

Black & White: This option changes the print/display of the graphic image. The user can select a color display or a black & white display.

After editing your graphic image it can be saved for future use. To save the graphic image as a .WPG file type do the following:

VMS	Reference Keystrokes	DOS
F18	U: Press *Save.* C: *Prints* Document to be saved: _.	F10
	U: Enter file specification (VMS) or pathname (DOS) and the filename. The file will automatically be given a .WPG file type. Press the *Enter key.* C: *Saves file.*	

Creating a Graphics Macro

In this section we will create a macro that contains a graphics image in the "Travel the States, Incorporated" company's letterhead.

Before the next step please make sure your screen is cleared and make sure your cursor is located at the top of the cleared screen.

VMS	Keystroke Action	DOS
PF2,F18	1. U: Press *Macro Define.* C: *Prints* Define macro: _.	Ctrl-F10

2. U: Type in <u>TRAVEL</u> and press the *Enter key.*
     C: *Prints* Description: _.

3. U: Type in <u>Letterhead</u> and press the *Enter key.*
     C: *Prints* Macro Def.

4. U: Press the *Enter key* three times and the *Tab key* one time.
     C: *Inserts codes.*

5. U: Type in <u>Travel the World, Incorporated</u> and press the *Enter key.*
     C: *Echoes characters.*

6. U: Press the *Tab key.*
     C: *Inserts programming code.*

7. U: Type in <u>1 Ocean View Lane</u> and press the *Enter key.*
     C: *Echoes characters.*

8. U: Press the *Tab key.*
     C: *Inserts programming code.*

9. U: Type in <u>Figure Ten Island, NC 19979</u> and press the *Enter key.*
     C: *Echoes characters.*

10. U: Press the *Enter key.*
     C: *Inserts code.*

11. U: Press the *Tab key.*
     C: *Inserts programming code.*

12. U: Type in **President: Arielle Austin** and press the *Enter key.*
     C: *Echoes characters.*

13. U: Press the *Enter key* four more times.
     C: *Inserts codes.*

14. U: Press *Home, Home, Up keys.*
     C: *Positions cursor at top of document.*

VMS	**Keystroke Action**	**DOS**

15. U: Press *Down arrow key* two times so that the cursor is located at the left margin on the line above Travel the World, Incorporated.
    C: *Positions cursor.*

PF3,F17	16. U: Press *Graphics.*	Alt-F9

16. C: *Prints* 1 Figure; 2 Table Box; 3 Text Box; 4 User Box; 5 Line; 6 Equation: 0.

Let's establish a Figure box containing a picture of the World and place it on the screen just to the right of the Heading you just typed in.

VMS	**Keystroke Action**	**DOS**

17. U: Press *1* for Figure.
    C: *Prints* Figure: 1 Create; 2 Edit; 3 New Number; 4 Options: 0.

18. U: Press *4* for Options.
    C: *Displays Options: Figure Menu.*

19. U: Press *1* for Border Style.
    C: *Prints* 1 None; 2 Single; 3 Double; 4 Dashed; 5 Dotted; 6 Thick; 7 Extra Thick: 0.

20. U: Press *7* for Extra Thick four times until the cursor returns to the Command Line.
    C: *Prints* 1 None; 2 Single 3 Double; 4 Dashed; 5 Dotted; 6 Thick; 7 Extra Thick: 0 *and then Returns to Command Line.*

F13	21. U: Press *Exit.*	F7

21. C: *Returns to Document.*

PF3,F17	22. U: Press *Graphics.*	Alt-F9

22. C: *Prints* 1 Figure; 2 Table Box; 3 Text Box; 4 User Box; 5 Line; 6 Equation: 0.

23. U: Press *1* for Figure.
    C: *Prints* Figure: 1 Create; 2 Edit; 3 New Number; 4 Options: 0.

VMS	**Keystroke Action**	**DOS**
	24. U: Press *1* for Create. C: *Displays Definition: Figure Menu.*	
	25. U: Press *1* for Filename. C: *Prints* Enter filename: _.	
	26. U: Type in file specification (VMS) or pathname (DOS) of where your WordPerfect graphic files are located if necessary. Then type in the name of the file GLOBE2-M.WPG and press the *Enter key*. C: *Returns to Command Line.*	
	27. U: Type *3* for Caption. C: *Displays Caption Edit Screen and Prints* Figure 1.	
	28. U: Press the *Backspace key* once since we do not want a caption with the image on our screen. C: *Erases* Figure 1.	
F13	29. U: Press *Exit*. C: *Returns to Definition: Figure Menu.*	F7
	30. U: Press *7* for Size. C: *Prints* 1 Set Width/Auto Height; 2 Set Height/Auto Width; 3 Set Both; 4 Auto Both: 0.	
	31. U: Press *2* for Set Height/Auto Width. C: *Prints* Height = 3.25".	
	32. U: Press *1* for 1" and press the *Enter key*. C: *Returns to Command Line.*	
F13	33. U: Press *Exit*. C: *Returns to Document.*	F7
PF4,PF4, Down	34. U: Press the *Home, Home, Down keys.* C: *Positions cursor at bottom of document.*	Home, Home
PF2,F18	35. U: Press *Macro Define.* C: *Returns to Document.*	Ctrl-F10

Applications of the Graphics Macro

The keystrokes contained in the "TRAVEL.WPM" macro are shown on Screen 7-15 or Screen 7-16.

Screen 7-15: VMS Users

```
Macro: Action

       File           TRAVEL.WPM

       Description    Letterhead

    ┌─────────────────────────────────────────────────────────────┐
    │ {DISPLAY OFF}{Enter}                                          │
    │ {Enter}                                                       │
    │ {Enter}                                                       │
    │ {Tab}Travel•the•World,•Incorporated{Enter}                    │
    │ {Tab}1•Ocean•View•Lane{Enter}                                 │
    │ {Tab}Figure•Ten•Island,•NC•19979{Enter}                       │
    │ {Enter}                                                       │
    │ {Tab}President:••Arielle•Austin{Enter}                        │
    │ {Enter}                                                       │
    │ {Enter}                                                       │
    │ {Enter}                                                       │
    │ {Enter}                                                       │
    │ {Home}{Home}{Up}{Down}{Down}{Graphics}1417777{Exit}{Graphics} │
    │ 111GLOBE2-M.WPG{Enter}                                        │
    │ 3{Backspace}{Exit}721{Enter}                                  │
    │ {Exit}{Home}{Home}{Down}                                      │
    └─────────────────────────────────────────────────────────────┘

PF2,Prev Scr for macro commands;  Press Exit when done
```

Screen 7-16: DOS Users

```
Macro: Action

       File           TRAVEL.WPM

       Description    Letterhead

    ┌─────────────────────────────────────────────────────────────┐
    │ {DISPLAY OFF}{Enter}                                          │
    │ {Enter}                                                       │
    │ {Enter}                                                       │
    │ {Tab}Travel•the•World,•Incorporated{Enter}                    │
    │ {Tab}1•Ocean•View•Lane{Enter}                                 │
    │ {Tab}Figure•Ten•Island,•NC•19979{Enter}                       │
    │ {Enter}                                                       │
    │ {Tab}President:••Arielle•Austin{Enter}                        │
    │ {Enter}                                                       │
    │ {Enter}                                                       │
    │ {Enter}                                                       │
    │ {Enter}                                                       │
    │ {Home}{Home}{Up}{Down}{Down}{Graphics}1417777{Exit}{Graphics} │
    │ 111GLOBE2-M.WPG{Enter}                                        │
    │ 3{Backspace}{Exit}721{Enter}                                  │
    │ {Exit}{Home}{Home}{Down}                                      │
    └─────────────────────────────────────────────────────────────┘

Ctrl-V to Insert next key as command;
Ctrl-PgUp for macro commands;  Press Exit when done
```

This macro was used for tutorial purposes only. It can be modified in the Macro Editor to fit your personal needs.

Using the Macro

The initial condition for this macro assumes you want to insert the keystrokes in this macro at the top of some page where you need a letterhead.

To invoke this macro do the following:

VMS	**Keystroke Action**	**DOS**
PF3,F18	1. U: Press *Macro.* C: *Prints* Macro: _.	Alt-F10
	2. U: Type in <u>TRAVEL</u> and press the *Enter key.* C: *Macro invokes.*	

The graphics picture will not appear on the screen. It will appear either when you print or view the document. Your final screen will look like Screen 7-17 without the graphic picture.

Screen 7-17

```
Travel the World, Incorporated
1 Ocean View Lane
Figure Ten Island, NC 19979


President:  Arielle Austin
```

Once the macro is invoked you can type in any other information you would like to include in this letter and then print it.

CHAPTER 8

MATH MACRO

Math Feature

The math feature allows WordPerfect 5.1 to act as a calculator. This feature allows the user to enter text and numbers into documents and then perform mathematical calculations on those numbers. The calculations may be performed across the rows or down the columns. Math in WordPerfect 5.1 may be used for many different things including balancing a checking account, keeping an inventory list, billing clients, and recording student's grades.

It is important to note that WordPerfect 5.1 has a Tables feature which is more like an electronic spreadsheet than the Math feature.

Tab Settings

Before inserting math into your document you must define tab settings for each column you include in your document. Decide how many columns of data you will need and then set the appropriate tab settings in your WordPerfect document. Math allows you to use absolute and relative tabs. Change your Tab Settings to meet your needs.

Math Definition

We will start with math definition. Access WordPerfect 5.1's math definition menu as follows:

VMS	Reference Keystrokes	DOS
PF3,F13	U: Press *Columns/Table.* C: *Prints* 1 Columns; 2 Tables; 3 Math: <u>0</u>.	Alt-F7
	U: Press *3* for Math. C: *Prints* Math: 1 On; 2 Off; 3 Define; 4 Calculate: <u>0</u>.	
	U: Press *3* for Define. C: *Displays the Math Definition Menu.*	

The Math Definition menu is shown on Screen 8-1.

Screen 8-1

```
Math Definition            Use arrow keys to position cursor

Columns                    A B C D E F G H I J K L M N O P Q R S T U V W X

Type                       2 2 2 2 2 2 2 2 2 2 2 2 2 2 2 2 2 2 2 2 2 2 2 2

Negative Numbers           ( ( ( ( ( ( ( ( ( ( ( ( ( ( ( ( ( ( ( ( ( ( ( (

Number of Digits to        2 2 2 2 2 2 2 2 2 2 2 2 2 2 2 2 2 2 2 2 2 2 2 2
  the Right (0-4)

Calculation    1
  Formulas     2
               3
               4

Type of Column:
    0 = Calculation    1 = Text      2 = Numeric     3 = Total

Negative Numbers
    ( = Parentheses (50.00)        - = Minus Sign    -50.00

Press Exit when done
```

The different options in the Math Definition menu are as follows:

1.   **Column:** Shows the titles of all the possible columns. The columns are titled A to X, which adds up to a total of 24 columns available for use in a document. Column A represents the first tab stop from the left margin, not including the left margin and Column B is the second tab stop from the left margin, etc. Where Column X will then be the twenty-fourth tab stop from the left margin.

2.   **Type:** Allows you to define what the type of columns A to X will be. The four possible types of columns are: Calculation, Text, Numeric, and Total. The default column type is Numeric, represented by 2's on Screen 8-1.

     Calculation Columns: Symbolized by 0 and used when you want to make horizontal calculations using the column data on one line.

     Text Columns: Symbolized by 1 and used to insert a name or heading for a specific column or when you want to insert a number which will not be used in any mathematical calculations.

     Numeric Columns: Symbolized by 2, the default, and used when you want to perform some type of vertical calculation using the numbers in one column. Typically it is used to calculate subtotals, totals, and grand totals.

     Total Columns: Symbolized by 3 and used when you want the totals only, of the column to the left, shown.

3.   **Negative numbers:** Allows you to decide how you would like negative numbers to be displayed in the document. There are two ways to display

negative numbers: 1) with parentheses or 2) with a minus sign. For example, with parentheses negative 100.00 would look like (100.00), whereas positive 100.00 would look like 100.00. On the other hand, with the minus sign negative 100.00 would look like -100.00, whereas positive 100.00 would again look like 100.00. All the columns have the default value of using parentheses to display negative numbers.

4. **Number of Digits to the Right (0-4):** Allows the user to decide how many digits are needed to the right of the decimal point for each calculation. All the columns have the default value of 2 digits to the right of the decimal point. For example, 100.00 or 76.55. The user can choose anywhere from 0 to 4 digits. The calculated number will be rounded, if necessary, to fit into the format you have chosen. If the number is greater than or equal to 5 the number will be rounded up.

Math Definition Editing

To change any of the default values for Type, Negative Numbers, or Number of Digits to the Right (0-4) options use the *right, left, up* and *down arrow keys* to move the cursor to the desired option and then to the desired column. Then press the number or character you want to use to replace the default character.

Calculations Columns

When the cursor is positioned in the Type row, and the user enters a 0 for Calculation, the cursor will jump down to the Calculation Formulas section. If this is the first Calculation Formula in the Type row the cursor will be positioned to the right of Calculation Formula 1. The user should insert the calculation formula needed, see Screen 8-2.

Screen 8-2

```
Math Definition         Use arrow keys to position cursor

Columns                 A B C D E F G H I J K L M N O P Q R S T U V W X

Type                    2 2 2 2 2 2 2 2 2 2 2 2 2 2 2 2 2 2 2 2 2 2 2 2

Negative Numbers        ( ( ( ( ( ( ( ( ( ( ( ( ( ( ( ( ( ( ( ( ( ( ( (

Number of Digits to     2 2 2 2 2 2 2 2 2 2 2 2 2 2 2 2 2 2 2 2 2 2 2 2
  the Right (0-4)

Calculation    1    A
  Formulas     2
               3
               4

Type of Column:
     0 = Calculation    1 = Text     2 = Numeric     3 = Total

Negative Numbers
     ( = Parentheses (50.00)         - = Minus Sign    -50.00

Press Exit when done
```

A Calculation Formula consists of Column Letters, i.e., A, B, C, etc., and/or positive, negative, and fractional numbers along with any combination of the following operators. Calculation Formulas are limited to the use of four operators. These operators include:

Operations Performed	Symbol Used
1. Add	+
2. Subtract	-
3. Multiply	*
4. Divide	/

A negative number should be entered as -75 and a fraction as .25 or in parentheses as (1/4) instead of 1/4.

All the calculations are done from left to right. Thus, the operators do not have an order of precedence. The only way to alter the order of calculations is to include parentheses around calculations that should be performed first.

You can also insert four special formulas into the Calculation Formulas section. These include:

Formulas	Description
+	Across the numeric columns this will add numbers
+/	Across the numeric columns this will average numbers
=	Across the total columns this will add numbers
=/	Across the total columns this will average numbers

Each one of the special Calculations Formulas can only be used by itself.

Press the Enter key after the Calculation Formula has been typed in.

To edit any of the Calculation Formulas at a later time just use the arrow keys in the Math Definition menu and type a 0 over the last 0 to instruct the cursor to jump down to the Calculation Formulas section. Then edit the formula and press enter to go back to the main part of the Math Definition's menu.

Numeric and Total Columns

In the Numeric and Total Columns one of six types of operators may be used. To insert these operators just type the character with or without a number into the column of your document. The operators and the order in which they should be used are as shown in Table 8-1, except for the Negative Function, which may be used anywhere.

Table 8-1

Function	Operator	Description
Subtotal	+	Adds numbers in column above the "+" operator and below any other "+" operator.
Extra Subtotal	t	Allows insertions for extra subtotals into a column after the "t" operator and will be included in any future Total calculations. Type this character in before a number.

Table 8-1 continued.

Function	Operator	Description
Total	=	Adds only subtotals above the "=" operator and below any other "=" operator.
Extra Total	T	Allows insertions for extra totals into a column after it and will be included in any future Grand Total calculations. Type this character in before a number.
Grand Total	*	Adds all totals in column above the "*" operator and below any other "*" operator.
Negative	N	Uses the negative value of a number typed in after the "N" operator. This operator has no order ranking so it may be used anywhere in the document.

When you are located in the Math Definition Menu you can enter in all the necessary information and then to exit out of the Math Definition Menu do the following:

VMS	**Reference Keystrokes**	**DOS**
	U: Enter all the required information about your math document into the Math Definition Menu.	
	C: *Records the necessary math definitions.*	
F13	U: Press *Exit.*	F7
	C: *Prints* Math: 1 On; 2 Off; 3 Define; 4 Calculate: <u>0</u>.	

Turn Math On

With a newly created math definition you are ready to turn math on in your document. As you turn math on you will see a [Math On] code located in Reveal Codes, also, you will see Math located in the lower right-hand corner of your screen. To turn Math On do the following:

VMS	**Reference Keystrokes**	**DOS**
	U: Press *1* for Math On.	
	C: *Returns to Document.*	

Now you can enter all your data into your math document.

Press the Tab key to enter data in horizontal rows. When the cursor moves into a column designated as a calculation column an exclamation mark (!) will appear. WordPerfect

5.1 uses this insert to indicate where a calculation will take place.

Perform Mathematical Calculations

When you are done entering in all your data do the following to have WordPerfect perform the mathematical calculations

VMS	Reference Keystrokes	DOS
PF3,F13	U: Press *Columns/Table.*	Alt-F7
	C: *Prints* 1 Columns; 2 Tables; 3 Math: 0.	
	U: Press *3* for Math.	
	C: *Prints* Math: 1 On; 2 Off; 3 Define; 4 Calculate: 0.	
	U: Press *4* for Calculate.	
	C: *Everything in math document is calculated.*	

Turn Math Off

To turn the Math feature off and insert the [Math Off] code into Reveal Codes, do the following:

VMS	Reference Keystrokes	DOS
PF3,F13	U: Press *Columns/Table.*	Alt-F7
	C: *Prints* 1 Columns; 2 Tables; 3 Math: 0.	
	U: Press *3* for Math.	
	C: *Prints* Math: 1 On; 2 Off; 3 Define; 4 Calculate: 0.	
	U: Press *2* for Off.	
	C: *Turns math feature off.*	

Alignment and Separator Characters

Decimal/align character/thousands separator may be used to improve the appearance of the numbers in a document. This feature designates the period as the separator between a whole number and the decimal fraction segment of the number. For example, in the number 34.55, 34 is the whole number and .55 is the fraction segment. The comma designates the separation of the hundreds segment of a number from the thousands segment of a number. For example, in the number 1,999, 1 is the thousands segment of the number and 999 is the hundreds segment of the number.

To change these separators to a different character do the following:

VMS	**Reference Keystrokes**	**DOS**
	U: Locate the cursor at the position you wish these new separators to go into effect. C: *Positions the cursor.*	
PF1,F14	U: Press *Format.* C: *Displays the Format Menu.*	Shift-F8
	U: Press *4* for Other. C: *Displays the Format: Other Menu.*	
	U: Press *3* for Decimal/Align Character Thousands' Separator. C: *Positions the cursor to right of* Decimal/Align Character.	
	U: Enter the character to separate the whole number from its decimal fraction. C: *Inserts new character and moves to right of* Thousands' Separator.	
	U: Enter the character to separate the hundreds from the thousands. C: *Inserts new character and Returns to Command Line.*	
F13	U: Press *Exit.* C: *Returns to Document.*	F7

Creating a Math Macro

The macro in this section will calculate the total amount of purchases by consumers from "Computer Concepts, Incorporated".

VMS	**Keystroke Action**	**DOS**
PF2,F18	1. U: Press *Macro Define.* C: *Prints* Define macro: _.	Ctrl-F10
	2. U: Type in <u>PURCHASE</u> and press the *Enter key.* C: *Prints* Description _.	
	3. U: Type in <u>Calculates total amount of purchases</u> and press the *Enter key.* C: *Prints* Macro Def.	

VMS	Keystroke Action	DOS
	4. U: Press the *Enter key* twice. C: *Inserts code.*	
PF1,F12	5. U: Press *Center.* C: *Positions cursor.*	Shift-F6
	6. U: Type in <u>PURCHASE ORDER</u> and press the *Enter key* two times. C: *Echoes characters.*	
	7. U: Press the *Tab key.* C: *Inserts programming code.*	
	8. U: Type in <u>Item Ordered</u>. C: *Echoes characters.*	
VMS Users	9. U: Press the *Tab key* twice. U: Press the *Tab key* three times. C: *Inserts programming code.*	*DOS Users*
	10. U: Type in <u>Quantity</u>. C: *Echoes characters.*	
	11. U: Press the *Tab key* twice. C: *Inserts programming code.*	
	12. U: Type in <u>Price</u>. C: *Echoes characters.*	
	13. U: Press the *Tab key* twice. C: *Inserts programming code.*	
	14. U: Type in <u>Total Price</u>. C: *Echoes characters.*	
	15. U: Press the *Enter key* two times. C: *Inserts code.*	
PF3,F13	16. U: Press *Columns/Table.* C: *Prints* 1 Columns; 2 Tables; 3 Math: <u>0</u>.	Alt-F7
	17. U: Press *3* for Math. C: *Prints* Math: 1 On; 2 Off; 3 Define; 4 Calculate: <u>0</u>.	
	18. U: Press *3* for Define. C: *Displays Math Definition Menu.*	

VMS	**Keystroke Action**	**DOS**

19. U: Press *1* for Text since the first column will contain the items ordered.
    C: *Inserts a 1 under* Column A *and moves to the Type under Column B.*

20. U: Press ***Right arrow key*** two times to move the cursor to Column D since Column B should be numeric for the quantity and Column C should be numeric for the price of one item.
    C: *Positions cursor.*

21. U: Press *0* for Calculation since Column D will calculate the Total Price.
    C: *Inserts a D to right of* Calculation Formulas 1 *and the cursor is positioned to the right of the D.*

22. U: Type in <u>b*c</u>.
    C: *Echoes formula that will multiply Column B by Column C.*

F13   23. U: Press ***Exit.***   F7
             C: *Positions cursor under Column E in the Type line.*

F13   24. U: Press ***Exit.***   F7
             C: *Prints* Math: 1 On; 2 Off; 3 Define; 4 Calculate: <u>0</u>.

F13   25. U: Press ***Exit.***   F7
             C: *Returns to Document.*

PF1,F14   26. U: Press ***Format.***   Shift-F8
             C: *Displays Format Menu.*

             27. U: Press *1* for Line.
                 C: *Displays Format: Line Menu.*

             28. U: Press *8* for Tab Set.
                 C: *Displays Tab Menu.*

PF2   29. U: Press ***Ctrl*** (DOS users hold it down) and   Ctrl
             tap the ***End key.***
             C: *Deletes all tab settings.*

VMS	Keystroke Action	DOS
	30. U: Type in *0* and press the *Enter key*. C: *Echoes character and prints an L at position 0.*	
	31. U: Type in *0.5* and press the *Enter key*. C: *Echoes character and prints an L at position 0.5.*	
VMS Users *VMS Users*	32. U: Type in *3.0* and press the *Enter key*. U: Type in *2.9* and press the *Enter key*. C: *Echoes character and prints an L at position 3.0.* C: *Echoes character and prints an L at position 2.9.*	*DOS Users* *DOS Users*
VMS Users *VMS Users*	33. U: Type in *4.2* and press the *Enter key*. U: Type in *4.15* and press the *Enter key*. C: *Echoes character and prints an L at position 4.2.* C: *Echoes character and prints an L at position 4.15.*	*DOS Users* *DOS Users*
VMS Users *VMS Users*	34. U: Type in *6.2* and press the *Enter key*. U: Type in *5.55* and press the *Enter key*. C: *Echoes character and prints an L at position 6.2.* C: *Echoes character and prints an L at position 5.55.*	*DOS Users* *DOS Users*
F13	35. U: Press *Exit*. C: *Returns to Format: Line Menu.*	F7
F13	36. U: Press *Exit*. C: *Returns to Document.*	F7
PF3,F13	37. U: Press *Columns/Table*. C: *Prints* 1 Columns; 2 Tables; 3 Math: 0.	Alt-F7
	38. U: Press *3* for Math. C: *Prints* Math: 1 On; 2 Off; 3 Define; 4 Calculate: 0.	
	39. U: Press *1* for On. C: *Prints* Math.	
PF2,F18	40. U: Press *Macro Define*. C: *Saves macro.*	Ctrl-F10

Applications of the Math Macro

The keystrokes contained in the "PURCHASE.WPM" macro are shown on Screen 8-3 or Screen 8-4.

Screen 8-3: VMS Users

```
Macro: Action

        File            PURCHASE.WPM

        Description     Calculates total amount of purchases


     {DISPLAY OFF}{Enter}
     {Enter}
     {Center}PURCHASE•ORDER{Enter}
     {Enter}
     {Tab}Item•Ordered{Tab}{Tab}Quantity{Tab}{Tab}Price{Tab}
     {Tab}Total•Price
     {Enter}
     {Enter}
     {Columns/Tables}331{Right}{Right}0b*c{Exit}{Exit}{Exit}
     {Format}18{Del to EOL}0{Enter}
     0.5{Enter}
     3.0{Enter}
     4.2{Enter}
     6.2{Enter}
     {Exit}{Exit}{Columns/Tables}31

PF2,Prev Scr for macro commands;  Press Exit when done
```

Screen 8-4: DOS Users

```
Macro: Action

        File            PURCHASE.WPM

        Description     Calculates total amount of purchases


     {DISPLAY OFF}{Enter}
     {Enter}
     {Center}PURCHASE•ORDER{Enter}
     {Enter}
     {Tab}Item•Ordered{Tab}{Tab}{Tab}Quantity{Tab}{Tab}Price{Tab}
     {Tab}Total•Price
     {Enter}
     {Enter}
     {Columns/Tables}331{Right}{Right}0b*c{Exit}{Exit}{Exit}
     {Format}18{Del to EOL}0{Enter}
     0.5{Enter}
     2.9{Enter}
     4.15{Enter}
     5.55{Enter}
     {Exit}{Exit}{Columns/Tables}31

Ctrl-V to Insert next key as command;
Ctrl-PgUp for macro commands;  Press Exit when done
```

This macro was used for tutorial purposes only. It can be modified in the Macro Editor to fit your personal needs.

Using the Macro

The initial conditions for this macro assume you are starting a new document or that you are currently editing a document to include this particular math table.

To invoke this macro do the following:

VMS		**Keystroke Action**	**DOS**
PF3,F18	1.	U: Press *Macro*.	Alt-F10
		C: *Prints* Macro: _.	
	2.	U: Type in <u>PURCHASE</u> and press the *Enter key*.	
		C: *Macro invokes.*	

When invoking this macro you will see what is shown on Screen 8-5:

Screen 8-5

```
┌─────────────────────────────────────────────────────────────┐
│                                                               │
│                                                               │
│                        PURCHASE ORDER                         │
│                                                               │
│                                                               │
│      Item Ordered       Quantity     Price      Total Price   │
│                                                               │
│                                                               │
│                                                               │
│                                                               │
│                                                               │
│                                                               │
│                                                               │
│                                                               │
│                                                               │
│                                                               │
│                                                               │
│                                                               │
│                                                               │
└─────────────────────────────────────────────────────────────┘
```

After the macro is invoked you can add Items Ordered, Quantity, and Price into the columns.

Enter the data in Screen 8-6 to see how this macro works. Press the *Tab key* then type in Disks, etc. Remember to press the *Tab key* after each entry, including after the price so an "!" will appear below the "Total Price" column. When the *Tab key* is pressed the "!" will automatically be inserted by WordPerfect 5.1. If the "!" is excluded then no calculation will be performed.

Screen 8-6

```
                         PURCHASE ORDER

    Item Ordered       Quantity     Price      Total Price


    Disks                 200       $.50            !
    Desk                    1     $450.00           !
    3 1/2" Drive            1     $245.10           !
    Boxed Paper             5      $15.10           !
```

To calculate the Total Price do the following:

VMS	**Keystroke Action**	**DOS**
PF3,F13	1. U: Press *Columns/Table*. C: *Prints* 1 Columns; 2 Tables; 3 Math: <u>0</u>.	Alt-F7
	2. U: Press *3* for Math. C: *Prints* Math: 1 On; 2 Off; 3 Define; 4 Calculate: <u>0</u>.	
	3. U: Press *4* for Calculate. C: *Calculates Total Price*.	

The new screen with the calculated values of Total Price is shown on Screen 8-7.

Screen 8-7

```
                      PURCHASE ORDER


     Item Ordered      Quantity     Price      Total Price



     Disks               200        $.50          100.00!
     Desk                  1      $450.00         450.00!
     3 1/2" Drive          1      $245.10         245.00!
     Boxed Paper           5       $15.10          75.00!
```

CHAPTER 9

EQUATION MACRO

Equation Feature

The new equation feature is a great addition to WordPerfect 5.1. This feature enables the insertion of mathematical and scientific formulas into your WordPerfect documents, however it will not perform mathematical calculations like the Math feature. For example you can insert some of the following equations into your documents or create your own unique equations for your document.

$$\int_0^{10} x^2 \qquad y = \frac{\sqrt[5]{x}}{(x-5)} \qquad \begin{vmatrix} 5 & 7 & 9 \\ 5 & 9 & 9 \\ 7 & 5 & 7 \end{vmatrix}$$

$$x + \frac{y+2}{w-3} \qquad f'(x) \qquad 3\overline{)97}$$

Graphic Equation Box

WordPerfect 5.1's Equation feature is very simple to use. Equations are created in a graphic equation box. The default or initial values for the equation box are shown in Screen 9-1. For more information on the description of this graphic equation box refer to Chapter 7.

Screen 9-1

```
Options:  Equation
     1 - Border Style
             Left                          None
             Right                         None
             Top                           None
             Bottom                        None
     2 - Outside Border Space
             Left                          0.083"
             Right                         0.083"
             Top                           0.083"
             Bottom                        0.083"
     3 - Inside Border Space
             Left                          0.083"
             Right                         0.083"
             Top                           0.083"
             Bottom                        0.083"
     4 - First Level Numbering Method      Numbers
     5 - Second Level Numbering Method     Off
     6 - Caption Number Style              [BOLD](1)[bold]
     7 - Position of Caption               Right side
     8 - Minimum Offset from Paragraph     0"
     9 - Gray Shading (% of black)         0%
Selection: 0
```

Creating an Equation Box

Let's create an equation box:

VMS	Reference Keystrokes	DOS
PF3,F17	U: Press *Graphics.* C: *Displays Graphics Menu (See Screen 9-2).*	Alt-F9

The computer will display a menu screen like Screen 9-2:

Screen 9-2

```



















 1 Figure; 2 Table Box; 3 Text Box; 4 User Box; 5 Line; 6 Equation: 0
```

VMS   **Reference Keystrokes**   **DOS**

U: Press *6* for Equation.
C: *Displays Equation Menu.*

The menu for the Equation Box will appear as shown on Screen 9-3.

Screen 9-3

```
Equation: 1 Create; 2 Edit; 3 New Number; 4 Options: 0
```

The options in the Equation Menu, as well as the other Box Menus include create, edit, new number, and options.

Create: Enters the chosen graphics box into the document, header, footer, endnotes, or footnotes. Right after this option is selected the computer will advance into the Edit Menu.

Edit: Asks the user for the figure, table, text, user, or equation number box that you wish to edit and then advances you directly into the Edit Menu.

New Number: This option will renumber all the graphic boxes after the box that was given a new number.

Options: Allows you to change the default options of the five different types of boxes. See Screen 9-1.

VMS   **Reference Keystrokes**   **DOS**

U: Press *1* for Create.
C: *Displays Equation Definition Menu.*

The Equation Menu for a Paragraph type box is shown on Screen 9-4 or Screen 9-5.

Screen 9-4: VMS Users

```
Definition:  Equation
        1 - Filename
        2 - Contents           Equation
        3 - Caption
        4 - Anchor Type         Paragraph
        5 - Vertical Position   0"
        6 - Horizontal Position Full
        7 - Size                6.5" wide x 0.333" (high)
        8 - Wrap Text Around Box Yes
        9 - Edit
Selection: 0
```

Screen 9-5: DOS Users

```
Definition:  Equation
        1 - Filename
        2 - Contents           Equation
        3 - Caption
        4 - Anchor Type         Paragraph
        5 - Vertical Position   0"
        6 - Horizontal Position Full
        7 - Size                6.5" wide x 0.347" (high)
        8 - Wrap Text Around Box Yes
        9 - Edit
Selection: 0
```

The Equation Menu for a Page type box is shown on Screen 9-6 or 9-7.

Screen 9-6: VMS Users

```
Definition:  Equation

     1 - Filename

     2 - Contents          Equation

     3 - Caption

     4 - Anchor Type        Page

     5 - Vertical Position  Top

     6 - Horizontal Position  Margin, Full

     7 - Size               6.5" wide x 0.333" (high)

     8 - Wrap Text Around Box  Yes

     9 - Edit
Selection: 0
```

Screen 9-7: DOS Users

```
Definition:  Equation

     1 - Filename

     2 - Contents          Equation

     3 - Caption

     4 - Anchor Type        Page

     5 - Vertical Position  Top

     6 - Horizontal Position  Margin, Full

     7 - Size               6.5" wide x 0.347" (high)

     8 - Wrap Text Around Box  Yes

     9 - Edit
Selection: 0
```

The Equation Menu for a Character type box is shown on Screen 9-8 or Screen 9-9.

Screen 9-8: VMS Users

```
Definition:  Equation
     1 - Filename
     2 - Contents           Equation
     3 - Caption
     4 - Anchor Type        Character
     5 - Vertical Position  Bottom
     6 - Horizontal Position
     7 - Size               6.5" wide x 0.333" (high)
     8 - Wrap Text Around Box  Yes
     9 - Edit
Selection: 0
```

Screen 9-9: DOS Users

```
Definition:  Equation
     1 - Filename
     2 - Contents           Equation
     3 - Caption
     4 - Anchor Type        Character
     5 - Vertical Position  Bottom
     6 - Horizontal Position
     7 - Size               6.5" wide x 0.347" (high)
     8 - Wrap Text Around Box  Yes
     9 - Edit
Selection: 0
```

For specific information on the options on Screens 9-4 to 9-9 refer to Chapter 7: Graphics Macro.

VMS   Reference Keystrokes   DOS

U: Press *9* for Edit.
C: *Displays Equation Editor.*

The Equation Editor is shown on Screen 9-10.

Screen 9-10

```
                                        ┌─────────────┐
┌──────────────────────────────────────┤ Commands    │
│                                       │             │
│                                       │ OVER        │
│                                       │ SUP or  ^   │
│                                       │ SUB or  _   │
│                                       │ SORT        │
│                                       │ NROOT       │
│                                       │ FROM        │
│                                       │ TO          │
│                                       │ LEFT        │
│                                       │ RIGHT       │
│                                       │ STACK       │
│                                       │ STACKALIGN  │
│                                       │ MATRIX      │
│                                       │ FUNC        │
├───────────────────────────────────── │ UNDERLINE   │
│                                       │ OVERLINE    │
│  _                                    │ (           │
│                                       │ )           │
│                                       │ HORZ        │
│                                       │ VERT        │
│                                       └─────────────┘
└──────────────────────────────────────────────────────
 Screen Redisplay; List Commands; Switch Window; Setup Options    500%
```

The current window is the window with the double bar on its right-hand side.

The Equation Editor consists of three separate windows that include:

1.   **Editing Window:**   This window is where you enter in the commands which create your equation. Lower window.

2.   **Display Window:**   This window displays the equation you entered into the computer. Upper window.

3.   **Equation Palette:**   This window lists the available commands and symbols for your equation. Window on far right.

The Equation Editor's options include: Screen Redisplay, List Commands, Switch Window, and Setup Options.

Screen Redisplay

To rewrite/redraw the equation in the Display Window after you have entered an equation do the following:

VMS   Reference Keystrokes   DOS

PF2,F9   U: Press *Screen.*   Ctrl-F3
                 C: *Rewrites/redraws the equation.*

List Commands

To access the Equation Palette window do the following:

VMS	**Reference Keystrokes**	**DOS**
F11	U: Press *List*. C: *Places you into Equation Palette Window.*	F5

When you are in the Equation Palette window you can use the following keys to move around, select commands, and cancel out of this window:

Table 9-1

VMS Keystrokes	DOS Keystrokes	Description
Arrow keys	Arrow keys	Moves cursor to specified location in the current equation palette
KP3	PgDn	Moves down (forwards) across the eight different palettes that include: Commands, Large, Symbols, Greek, Arrows, Sets, Other, and Functions.
KP9	PgUp	Moves up (backwards) across the eight different palettes.
Enter	Enter	Selects the symbol or command in the current palette that the cursor is positioned on. Enter inserts the keyword (text) for the symbol or command if the character has a keyword representation.
PF2,Enter	Ctrl-Enter	Selects symbol or command in the current palette that the cursor is positioned on. Inserts the actual character representation.
Exit (F13)	Exit (F7)	No symbol or command is selected and you exit this window.
Cancel (F7)	Cancel (F1)	No symbol or command is selected and you cancel this window.

Switch Window

To rewrite/redraw your equation and move your cursor to the Display window do the following:

VMS	**Reference Keystrokes**	**DOS**
PF1,F9	U: Press *Switch*. C: *Moves cursor to Display Window.*	Ctrl-F3

In this window you can alter the location or size of your equation for viewing purposes only by using the keys listed in Table 9-2.

Table 9-2

VMS Keystrokes	DOS Keystrokes	Description
Arrow keys	Arrow keys	Relocates the equation in the equation box.
PgDn	PgDn	Decreases the size of the equation.
PgUp	PgUp	Increases the size of the equation.
GoTo (PF2,Home)	GoTo (Ctrl-Home)	All changes you made are canceled.

To return to the Editing window do the following:

VMS   Reference Keystrokes   DOS

PF1,F9   U: Press *Switch.*   Ctrl-F3
         C: *Moves cursor back to the Editing Window.*

Setup Options

To change any equation setup option while you are in the Equation Editor (Screen 9-10) do the following:

VMS   Reference Keystrokes   DOS

PF1,F7   U: Press *Setup.*   Shift-F1
         C: *Displays Equation: Options Menu.*

Screen 9-11 shows the Equation: Options Menu.

Screen 9-11

```
Equation: Options

    1 - Print as Graphics      Yes

    2 - Graphical Font Size     Default

    3 - Horizontal Alignment    Center

    4 - Vertical Alignment      Center




Selection:0
```

The equation options menu includes the following:

Print as Graphics: Defaults to Yes which means that all symbols in the equation will be printed as graphic characters.

Graphical Font Size: Defaults to the current base font and point size for all characters in the equation. You can change the point size.

Horizontal Alignment: Defaults to Center which means that the equation is located by default horizontally in the center of the equation box that surrounds it. You can change this to Left, Center, or Right.

Vertical Alignment: Defaults to Center which means that the equation is located by default vertically in the center of the equation box that surrounds it. You can change this to Top, Center, or Bottom.

Entering the Equation

The editing window is the window used for your equation. You can type in the equation using keywords or select the appropriate keywords or symbol from the equation palette window.

Equation Palettes

WordPerfect 5.1 includes the following eight palettes:

Commands: Commands that are represented as keywords to create a matrix, superscript, square roots, sets limits on an integral, etc. The user types in the keyword. See the WordPerfect Reference Manual for command descriptions.

Large: Keywords or symbols that contain operators in both small and large sizes.

Symbols: Keywords or symbols for many other mathematical or scientific equations.

Greek: Keywords or symbols that consist of Greek characters such as alpha, beta, delta, etc. The keyword can be typed in.

Arrows: The symbols contained in this palette include: arrows, triangles, stars, diamonds, circles, squares, and other similar items.

Sets: Some keywords or symbols include relational operators, set symbols, and other letters.

Other: Keywords or symbols that consist of diacritical marks and ellipses.

Functions: Keywords that are actual mathematical functions such as cos, sin, tan, etc. The keyword can be typed in.

Equation Syntax

Now you can actually start creating an equation in your equation box.

All you have to do is type in the correct commands for your equation or choose them from the equation palette.

For example, to type in an equation you could type in: z = x + y or include any other keywords or symbols from the eight equation palettes.

Creating an Equation Macro

This section will demonstrate the creation of a macro that inserts a mathematical/scientific formula into your document.

Before the next step please make sure your screen is cleared and make sure your cursor is located at the top of the cleared screen or that you are located in a place where an equation can be placed.

VMS	Keystroke Action	DOS
PF2,F18	1. U: Press *Macro Define.* C: *Prints* Define macro: _.	Ctrl-F10
	2. U: Type in <u>EQUAT</u> and press the *Enter key.* C: *Prints* Description: _.	
	3. U: Type in <u>Integral</u> and press the *Enter key.* C: *Prints* Macro Def.	
PF3,F17	4. U: Press *Graphics.* C: *Prints* 1 Figure; 2 Table Box; 3 Text Box; 4 User Box; 5 Line; 6 Equation: <u>0</u>.	Alt-F9
	5. U: Press *6* for Equation. C: *Displays Equation Menu.*	
	6. U: Press *1* for Create. C: *Prints* Equation: 1 Create; 2 Edit; 3 New Number; 4 Options: <u>0</u>.	
	7. U: Press *9* for Edit. C: *Displays Equation Editor.*	

VMS	Keystroke Action	DOS
	8. U: Type <u>INT u~du~=~uv~-~INT v~du</u>. INT is the keyword for Integral. The ~ will place a normal space between the items it is located between otherwise they will be placed next to each other. C: *Displays Equation Editor.*	
PF2,F9	9. U: Press *Screen.* C: *Displays equation in Display window.*	Ctrl-F3

VMS Users: *Depending on what type of terminal you have will depend on what you see on your screen. Print out the document then you will see the equation.*

VMS	Keystroke Action	DOS
F13	10. U: Press *Exit.* C: *Displays Equation Definition Menu.*	F7
F13	11. U: Press *Exit.* C: *Returns to Document.*	F7
PF2,F18	12. U: Press *Macro Define* to finish defining the macro. C: *Saves macro.*	Ctrl-F10

Applications of the Equation Macro

The keystrokes contained in the "EQUAT.WPM" macro are shown on Screen 9-12 or Screen 9-13.

Screen 9-12: VMS Users

```
Macro: Action

        File            EQUAT.WPM

        Description     Integral

    ┌────────────────────────────────────────────────────────┐
    │{DISPLAY OFF}{Graphics}619INT•u~du~=~uv~-~INT•v~du{Screen}│
    │{Exit}{Exit}                                             │
    │                                                         │
    │                                                         │
    │                                                         │
    │                                                         │
    └────────────────────────────────────────────────────────┘

PF2,Prev Scr for macro commands;  Press Exit when done
```

Screen 9-13: DOS Users

```
Macro: Action

        File            EQUAT.WPM

        Description     Integral

    ┌────────────────────────────────────────────────────────┐
    │{DISPLAY OFF}{Graphics}619INT•u~du~=~uv~-~INT•v~du{Screen}│
    │{Exit}{Exit}                                             │
    │                                                         │
    │                                                         │
    │                                                         │
    │                                                         │
    └────────────────────────────────────────────────────────┘

Ctrl-V to Insert next key as command;
Ctrl-PgUp for macro commands; Press Exit when done
```

This macro was used for tutorial purposes only. It can be modified in the Macro Editor to fit your personal needs.

Using the Macro

The initial conditions for this macro assume you are starting a new document or that you are currently editing a document to include this particular equation.

To invoke this macro do the following:

VMS	Keystroke Action	DOS
PF3,F18	1. U: Press *Macro.* C: *Prints* Macro: _.	Alt-F10

VMS   **Keystroke Action**   **DOS**

2.   U: Type in <u>EQUAT</u> and press the *Enter key.*
     C: *Macro invokes.*

The equation will not appear on the screen. It will appear either when you print or view the document. When you print or view the equation you will see what is shown on Screen 9-14.

Screen 9-14

$$\int u \ du \ = \ uv \ - \ \int v \ du$$

CHAPTER 10

MERGE MACRO

Merge Feature

The Merge Feature of WordPerfect merges two separate documents into one file. For example, the Merge Feature, also known as mail-merge, allows you to create one generic letter in WordPerfect and merge that letter with a document containing a list of addresses to produce one merged document. For example, if you had 10 addresses you wanted merged with one letter then the merged document will contain 10 copies of the original letter each with a different address.

Primary and secondary files are required for the merge process.

A **primary file** contains some type of text and a set of merge commands. An example of a primary file is a letter you wish to send out to a number of people whose names are contained in a mailing list.

The **secondary file,** in this example, contains the mailing list of addresses of the people who should receive the letter in the primary file. This **file** consists of data that makes up several fields which in turn make up a record. A **field** contains one type of data, for instance, a name or street address. A **record** consists of any number of fields, for instance, a record may be a complete mailing address that would include the name, street address, city, state, and zip of one person. Examine the two names shown below:

A File equals...

```
┌─────────────────────────────────────────────────────────────┐
│                ┌───────────────────────────────────────────┐ │
│                │ Field 1      Beverly Jensen               │ │
│   Record 1     │ Field 2      1717 East Lake Drive         │ │
│                │ Field 3      Chicago, IL 60009            │ │
│                └───────────────────────────────────────────┘ │
│                                                              │
│                ┌───────────────────────────────────────────┐ │
│                │ Field 1      Robert Nuteson               │ │
│   Record 2     │ Field 2      1991 South Park Ridge        │ │
│                │ Field 3      Santa Clara, CA 90007         │ │
│                └───────────────────────────────────────────┘ │
└─────────────────────────────────────────────────────────────┘
```

The file above contains two records. Each record contains the same three fields, for instance, Field 1 in Record 1 contains a name and Field 1 in Record 2 also contains a name. Also, both Field 2's contain the address and both Field 3's contain the city, state, and zip code. Thus, a file contains records and the records in turn are composed of identical fields.

The basic merge commands for WordPerfect 5.1 that can be inserted into primary files are listed in Table 10-1.

Table 10-1

Syntax:	{DATE}
Purpose:	This merge code inserts the current date into the document. The current date must have been entered when the user started the computer or the computer's internal system clock must have been set in order for this code to work.
Syntax:	{FIELD}n~
Purpose:	This merge code takes the information in the text field n in the secondary file which may be either a number or actual text and merges the information into the final merged file.

The basic merge commands for WordPerfect 5.1 that may be inserted into secondary files are listed in Table 10-2.

Table 10-2

Syntax:	{END FIELD}
Purpose:	This merge command is placed at the end of each field in the secondary file.
Syntax:	{END RECORD}
Purpose:	This merge code is placed at the end of each record in the secondary file.

Merge Programming

WordPerfect 5.1 merge features utilize many of the same programming commands that macros use. The very basic merge programming commands are contained in this chapter. For more information on the other merge programming commands refer to Appendix C: Merge Programming.

Creating a Merge Macro

Both the primary and secondary files must be created before a merge macro may be defined.

Please make sure that your screen is cleared and that the cursor is located at the top of the cleared screen before proceeding.

First, you can create the secondary file. In our example, we will have the following fields contained in our file:

Field Number	Description
1	First and Last Name
2	Street Address
3	City, State, and Zip Code

Type in the data on Screen 10-1. The *{END FIELD}* merge programming command can be inserted into the document by doing the following:

VMS	**Keystroke Action**	**DOS**
F17	U: Press *End Field*. C: *Inserts {END FIELD} merge programming command.*	F9

The *{END RECORD}* merge programming command can be inserted into the document by doing the following:

VMS	**Keystroke Action**	**DOS**
PF1,F17	U: Press *Merge Codes*. C: *Prints* 1 Field; 2 End Record; 3 Input; 4 Page Off; 5 Next Record; 6 More: <u>0</u>. U: Press *2* for End Record. C: *Inserts {END RECORD} merge programming command.*	Shift-F9

Screen 10-1

```
Steve Anderson{END FIELD}
1977  Shell Lane{END FIELD}
Jupiter, FL 32123{END RECORD}
========================================================================
Karen Jones{END FIELD}
1919 Lakeview Drive{END FIELD}
Chicago, IL 76457{END RECORD}
========================================================================
Warren Welles{END FIELD}
32 Main Street{END FIELD}
Rolling Meadows, TX 43212{END RECORD}
========================================================================
Dean Donnely{END FIELD}
23 Ocean View Circle{END FIELD}
Wilmington, NC 12345{END RECORD}
========================================================================
Leah Lewis{END FIELD}
1 SeaSide Drive{END FIELD}
Santa Barbara, CA 90123{END RECORD}
========================================================================
Kimberly Malcom{END FIELD}
1434 West Park Road{END FIELD}
Washington, D.C. 57914{END RECORD}
```

As we proceed to define the macro for the merge process, the secondary file must be saved. Save the secondary file as **SECOND.TXT** and then clear the screen.

Next, we will create the primary file.

VMS	Keystroke Action	DOS
	1. U: Press the *Enter key* three times. C: *Positions cursor.*	

PF1,F17	2. U: Press *Merge Codes.*
	    C: *Prints* 1 Field; 2 End Record; 3 Input;
	       4 Page Off; 5 Next Record; 6 More: <u>0</u>.
		Shift-F9

	3. U: Press *6* for More. C: *Displays Merge Programming Commands Menu.*	

	4. U: Use *Arrow keys* to highlight {DATE} and
	       press the *Enter key*.
	    C: *Highlights {DATE} and places merge programming command into your document.*	

The *{DATE}* merge programming command will insert the current date if you entered the current date when starting the computer or if your computer's internal clock is set.

VMS	Keystroke Action	DOS
	5. U: Press the *Enter key* two times. C: *Positions cursor.*	

PF1,F17	6. U: Press *Merge Codes.*
	    C: *Prints* 1 Field; 2 End Record; 3 Input;
	       4 Page Off; 5 Next Record; 6 More: <u>0</u>.
		Shift-F9

	7. U: Press *1* for Field. C: *Prints* Enter Field: <u> </u>.	

	8. U: Press *1* for the first field (This field contains
	       the first and last name of the people) and
	       press the *Enter key* two times.
	    C: *Inserts {FIELD}1~ merge programming command.*	

PF1,F17	9. U: Press *Merge Codes.*
	    C: *Prints* 1 Field; 2 End Record; 3 Input;
	       4 Page Off; 5 Next Record; 6 More: <u>0</u>.
		Shift-F9

	10. U: Press *1* for Field. C: *Prints* Enter Field: <u> </u>.	

VMS	Keystroke Action	DOS

11. U: Press *2* for the second field (This field contains the person's street address) and press the *Enter key* two times.
C: *Inserts {FIELD}2~ merge programming command.*

PF1,F17   12. U: Press *Merge Codes.*   Shift-F9
C: *Prints* 1 Field; 2 End Record; 3 Input; 4 Page Off; 5 Next Record; 6 More: 0.

13. U: Press *1* for Field.
C: *Prints* Enter Field: _.

14. U: Press *3* for the third field (This field contains the city, state, and zip) and press the *Enter key* two times.
C: *Inserts {FIELD}3~ merge programming command.*

15. U: Press the *Enter key* two times.
C: *Positions cursor.*

16. U: Type in <u>Dear</u> and a *space*.
C: *Echoes characters.*

PF1,F17   17. U: Press *Merge Codes.*   Shift-F9
C: *Prints* 1 Field; 2 End Record; 3 Input; 4 Page Off; 5 Next Record; 6 More: 0.

18. U: Press *3* for Input.
C: *Prints* Enter Message: 0.

19. U: Type in <u>Enter Personal Salutation</u> and press the *Enter key.*
C: *Inserts {INPUT}Enter Personal Salutation~ merge programming command.*

This *{INPUT}* merge programming command will pause the merge process temporarily while you enter in the correct personal salutation to address the person.

VMS	Keystroke Action	DOS

20. U: Press the *Enter key* two times.
C: *Positions cursor.*

Type in the information on Screen 10-2. As you type, the information can appear on your screen in different locations, depending on tab and margin settings, font selected, etc.

Screen 10-2

```
The office equipment you ordered from Office Supplies, Inc. is included
in this package(s) with your invoice of the products you purchased.

Please check your package(s) to make sure that all of the purchased
office equipment was included.  If you have any questions feel free
to call me at 1-800-312-345-3456.
```

Follow with Keystroke Actions 21-23 if you have created and want to include the "CLOSE.WPM" macro in Chapter 1: Macro Power Basics, otherwise type in what is on Screen 10-3 and then continue with Keystroke Action 24.

Screen 10-3

```
Thank you for purchasing all of your office equipment from
Office Supplies, Inc.  Please contact us if you need further
assistance.  Again, thank you for your patronage.

Sincerely,




Amanda A. Anderson
Manager
```

VMS	Keystroke Action	DOS
	21. U: Press the *Enter key* twice. C: *Positions cursor.*	
PF3,F18	22. U: Press *Macro.* C: *Prints* Define macro: _.	Alt-F10
	23. U: Type in <u>CLOSE</u> and press the *Enter key.* C: *Invokes close macro.*	

The final primary file should look like Screen 10-4.

Screen 10-4

```
{DATE}

{FIELD}1~
{FIELD}2~
{FIELD}3~


Dear {INPUT}Enter Personal Salutation~

The office equipment you ordered from Office Supplies, Inc. is included
in this package(s) with your invoice of the products you purchased.

Please check your package(s) to make sure that all of the purchased
office equipment was included.  If you have any questions feel free
to call me at 1-800-312-345-3456.

Thank you for purchasing all of your office equipment from
Office Supplies, Inc.  Please contact us if you need further
assistance.  Again, thank you for your patronage.

Sincerely,



Amanda A. Anderson
Manager
```

Since the primary file is complete you can save it with the file name of **PRIME.TXT** and then clear your screen.

Now we can define the actual merge macro:

VMS	Keystroke Action	DOS
PF2,F18	24. U: Press *Macro Define.* C: *Prints* Define macro: _.	Ctrl-F10
	25. U: Type in <u>MERGER</u> and press the *Enter key.* C: *Prints* Description: _.	
	26. U: Type in <u>Merges second with prime</u> and press the *Enter key.* C: *Prints* Macro Def.	
PF2,F17	27. U: Press *Merge/Sort.* C: *Prints* 1 Merge; 2 Sort; 3 Convert Old Merge Codes: <u>0</u>.	Ctrl-F9

VMS	Keystroke Action	DOS
	28. U: Press *1* for Merge. C: *Prints* Primary file: _.	
	29. U: Type in <u>PRIME.TXT</u> and press the ***Enter key.*** C: *Prints* Secondary file: _.	
	30. U: Type in <u>SECOND.TXT</u> and press the ***Enter key.*** C: *Starts performing merge action.*	
PF2,F18	31. U: Press ***Macro Define.*** C: *Saves macro.*	Ctrl-F10

When the merge process pauses the computer is expecting the user to enter the correct salutation. If the user normally greets the current person by first name, then the user would type in the first name for the salutation.

For example, when the macro pauses with the first person, Steve Anderson, do the following:

VMS	Keystroke Action	DOS
	32. U: Type in <u>Steve:</u>. C: *Echoes characters.*	
F17	33. U: Press ***End Field.*** C: *Inserts {END FIELD} merge programming command into document.*	F9

The macro will prompt you again for the next name. Type in the correct salutation as shown in Keystroke Action 32 and then perform Keystroke Action 33. You will perform these actions until you have entered all the personal salutations for each record in the secondary file second.

Applications of the Merge Macro

The keystrokes contained in the "MERGER.WPM" macro are shown on Screen 10-5 or Screen 10-6.

Screen 10-5: VMS Users

```
Macro: Action

      File              MERGER.WPM

      Description       Merges second with prime

    ┌────────────────────────────────────────────────────┐
    │ {Merge/Sort}1PRIME.TXT{Enter}                       │
    │ SECOND.TXT{Enter}                                   │
    │                                                     │
    │                                                     │
    │                                                     │
    │                                                     │
    └────────────────────────────────────────────────────┘

PF2,Prev Scr for macro commands;  Press Exit when done
```

Screen 10-6: DOS Users

```
Macro: Action

        File              MERGER.WPM

        Description       Merges second with prime

      ┌──────────────────────────────────────────────────┐
      │ {Merge/Sort}1PRIME.TXT{Enter}                     │
      │ SECOND.TXT{Enter}                                 │
      │                                                   │
      │                                                   │
      │                                                   │
      │                                                   │
      └──────────────────────────────────────────────────┘

Ctrl-V to Insert next key as command;
Ctrl-PgUp for macro commands; Press Exit when done
```

This macro is ready for immediate use.

Using the Macro

The initial condition for this macro assumes you have created a primary file, called **PRIME.TXT,** and a secondary document, called **SECOND.TXT,** and would like to merge the two documents together. Make sure your screen is cleared before invoking this macro.

To invoke this macro do the following:

VMS	**Keystroke Action**	**DOS**
PF3,F18	1. U: Press *Macro.* C: *Prints* Macro: _.	Alt-F10

VMS   Keystroke Action   DOS

2. U: Type in <u>MERGER</u> and press the *Enter key.*
   C: *Macro invokes.*

When invoking this macro you will see what is shown on Screen 10-7:

Screen 10-7

```
August 20, 1992

Steve Anderson
1977  Shell Lane
Jupiter, FL 32123


Dear _

The office equipment you ordered from Office Supplies, Inc. is included
in this package(s) with your invoice of the products you purchased.

Please check your package(s) to make sure that all of the purchased
office equipment was included.  If you have any questions feel free
to call me at 1-800-312-345-3456.

Thank you for purchasing all of your office equipment from
Office Supplies, Inc.  Please contact us if you need further
assistance.  Again, thank you for your patronage.

Sincerely,



Amanda A. Anderson
Manager
```

Remember: the macro will pause for each letter until you type in the correct salutation and press End Field (F17 for VMS or F9 for DOS).

Also, for every name you have contained in your secondary document you will receive a letter addressed to that particular person.

CHAPTER 11

SORT MACROS

Sort Feature

The Sort Feature of WordPerfect 5.1 allows the user to select and sort the following: lines, paragraphs, secondary merge records, or table rows.

Our sample list, below, will help clarify the definitions of several words that the user should be familiar with in order to completely understand the sort feature.

Sample list:

Name	Occupation	Telephone Number
Johnson, Chelsea	President	831-9090
Rainer, Sydney	Instructor	831-1561
Carlson, Gloria	Receptionist	831-2222
Beker, Scott	Programmer	831-9575
Richardson, Richard	Engineer	831-1541

A **record,** in the sample list above, is the complete line of a person's name, occupation, and telephone number. This list, therefore, includes five records.

Depending on the type of sort you are performing will depend on exactly what is used to designate the end of each record.

Sort Type	How Record Ends
Line Sort	Each line, or record, should end with either a *Hard Return* (*Return key* for VMS or *Enter key* for DOS) or *Soft Return* (Soft Return is when WordPerfect moves the rest of the current line to the next line automatically, also known as Word Wrap). A *Hard Return* inserts a [HRt] code into the document and a *Soft Return* moves the cursor to a new line.
Paragraph Sort	Each paragraph, or record, should end with at least two *Hard Returns.*
Secondary Merge Sort	Each record ends with the {*END RECORD*} Merge Code which inserts a double line into the document that represents a page break.
Table Sort	Each record is considered equivalent to a table's row.

A **field** contains some type of similar data that is found in each record. In the sample list there are three fields. The first field is a person's name; the second field is the person's occupation; the third field is the person's telephone number. Each of the records in our above

Sample List contains one of each of the three fields types. A record can contain any number of fields.

Depending on the type of sort you are performing will depend on exactly what each field must use to designate the end of the field.

Sort Type	How Field Ends
Line/Paragraph Sort	Fields are separated by either *Tabs* or *->Indents.*
Secondary Merge Sort	Fields are separated by {*END FIELD*} Merge Codes.
Table Sort	Each table cell is equivalent to a field.

Fields can be further broken down into a **word(s).** Within a field words are separated by the following:

1. Space
2. Forward Slash. (/)
3. Hard Hyphen. Press and hold the *Home key* and tap the *- (hyphen) key.*

The file that you want to sort is considered your **Input file,** whereas, the final sorted file is called your **Output file.** WordPerfect will ask for confirmation if you try to replace your Input file with your Output file.

To invoke the Sort Menu you must do the following (however, remember either you must have the file you want to sort shown on your screen or saved as a file):

VMS   Reference Keystrokes   DOS

PF2,F17

U: Press *Merge/Sort.*   Ctrl-F9
C: *Prints* 1 Merge; 2 Sort; 3 Convert Old Merge Codes: 0.

U: Press *2* for Sort.
C: *Prints* Input file to sort: (Screen).

U: Press the *Enter key* to accept the Screen as your input file or type in the name of your input file and press the *Enter key.*
C: *Prints* Output file for sort: (Screen).

U: Press the *Enter key* to accept the Screen as your output file or type in the name of your output file and press the *Enter key.*
C: *Displays Sort Menu.*

The Sort by Line Menu is shown on Screen 11-1 along with some data.

Screen 11-1

```
Delefield, Sandy        Account Executive        831-2414
Michaels, Rick          President                831-5555
Anderson, Michael       Programmer               831-4545

                                            Doc 2 Pg 1 Ln 1" Pos 1"


{▓▓▓▓▓▓▓▓▓▓▓▓▓▓▓▓▓▓▓▓▓▓▓▓▓▲▓▓▓▓▓▓▓▓▓▓▓▓▓▓▓▓▲▓▓▓▓▓▓▓▓▓▓▓▓}
------------------------- Sort by Line -----------------------------
Key Typ Field Word      Key Typ Field Word      Key Typ Field Word
 1   a    1    1         2                       3
 4                       5                       6
 7                       8                       9
Select

Action                  Direction               Type
Sort                    Ascending               Line sort

1 Perform Action; 2 View; 3 Keys; 4 Select; 5 Action; 6 Order 7 Type: 0
```

The command line at the bottom of the Screen 11-1 has seven options available to the user.

Perform Action: Starts the actual sorting or selecting.

View: Positions the cursor in the document shown on the top half of the screen. This allows the user to move through the document with the *arrow keys* or use the *Search* feature to search for an item(s) in the document.

Keys: Allows you to indicate which keys you want to use to sort the document. A **key** is defined as a word within a record's field and it can be either alphanumeric or numeric. **Alphanumeric keys** contain letters and/or numbers and are indicated with an **a.** The telephone numbers in the sample list are considered alphanumeric since they contain a -. Any actual numbers like zip codes must have the same number of characters if you want to designate them as alphanumeric keys. **Numeric keys** contain numbers, dollar signs, commas, and periods and they do not always have the same number of characters. You can have a maximum of 9 keys. An example of using keys is to use Key 1 to sort by Last Name first and Key 2 to sort by First Name second. Thus, if you have Smith, Terri and Smith, George then the sorted list would have Smith, George before Smith, Terri.

Select: Allows you to select certain records. For example, all the people with the same last name may be selected and then sorted. An example of this will be in the Section Creating a Selected Paragraph Sort Macro.

Action: When certain records are selected from a file this option is used. This will be explained further in the Section Creating a Selected Paragraph Sort Macro.

Order: Allows the user to sort the data in either Ascending (from A to Z and 0 to 9) or Descending (from Z to A and 9 to 0) Order.

Type: Defines the type of records the file contains. For example, line, paragraph, or secondary merge records.

Creating a Line Sort Macro

The macro you create in this section will sort a list of lines. In order for the macro to sort correctly, the list of items in the file must have the same format layout as the list on Screen 11-2. The format consists of each record being located on one line. A list must be created before the macro can be defined.

Before the next step please make sure that your screen is cleared and the cursor is placed at the top of the document.

Type in the following data which appears on Screen 11-2 below (Note: You must put *Tabs* or *->Indents* between the fields, otherwise shown as columns. When you set up the tab stops set the first one at the Left hand margin, the second tab stop where you want to type in the Job Title, and the third tab stop at the position where you want to type in the phone number. Do not include extra tab stops in the document).

Screen 11-2

```
Quarterman, Bob      Sales Executive      831-1111
Anderson, Tami       Advertising          831-3453
Mathews, Florence    Sales Manager        831-7645
Jones, Nancy         Sales Executive      831-4444
Anderson, Cindi      Manager              831-5656
Stevens, Sue         Vice-President       831-4242
Peters, Darryl       Programmer           831-5252
Zeke, Kevin          Advertising          831-1232
```

You can save the file as **LINE.TXT**. When you are finished with the file the macro to sort this list and any other similar lists by the last name first and the first name second can be defined.

VMS	**Keystroke Action**	**DOS**
PF2,F18	1. U: Press *Macro Define.* C: *Prints* Define macro: _.	Ctrl-F10
	2. U: Type in <u>LINESORT</u> and press the *Enter key.* C: *Prints* Description: _.	

VMS	**Keystroke Action**	**DOS**

3. U: Type in <u>Sorts a list of names in a line</u> and press the ***Enter key***.
   C: *Prints* Macro Def.

PF2,F17	4. U: Press ***Merge/Sort***.	Ctrl-F9

      C: *Prints* 1 Merge; 2 Sort; 3 Convert Old Merge Codes: <u>0</u>.

5. U: Press *2* for Sort.
   C: *Prints* Input file to sort: (Screen).

6. U: Press the ***Enter key*** in order to sort the document which appears on the screen.
   C: *Prints* Output file for sort: (Screen).

7. U: Press the ***Enter key*** to replace the current unsorted document on your screen with the sorted document.
   C: *Displays sort menu.*

In this tutorial example, the fields and records are defined as follows:

	Field 1	**Field 2**	**Field 3**
Record 1	Quarterman, Bob	Sales Executive	831-1111
Record 2	Anderson, Tami	Advertising	831-3453
Record 3	Mathews, Florence	Sales Manager	831-7645
Record 4	Jones, Nancy	Sales Executive	831-4444
Record 5	Anderson, Cindi	Manager	831-5656
Record 6	Stevens, Sue	Vice-President	831-4242
Record 7	Peters, Darryl	Programmer	831-5252
Record 8	Zeke, Kevin	Advertising	831-1232

      Key 1 is already correctly defined in the Sort Menu since we want to sort first by the person's last name. The key is defined as an alphanumeric key, in field one, and is the first word in the field.

      Key 2 must be defined, however, since if several people have the same last name WordPerfect 5.1 must then sort by the people's first names.

VMS	**Keystroke Action**	**DOS**

8. U: Press *7* for Type.
   C: *Prints* Type: 1 Merge; 2 Line; 3 Paragraph: <u>0</u>.

VMS	Keystroke Action	DOS

9. U: Press *2* for Line since each of our records
    are lines.
    C: *Prints* Line sort *under Type heading.*

Screen 11-3 shows the Line Sort Menu.

Screen 11-3

```
Quarterman, Bob        Sales Executive        831-1111
Anderson, Tami         Advertising            831-3453
Mathews, Florence      Sales Manager          831-7645
Jones, Nancy           Sales Executive        831-4444
Anderson, Cindi        Manager                831-5656
Stevens, Sue           Vice-President         831-4242

                                       Doc 2 Pg 1 Ln 1" Pos 1"
{                              ▲                    ▲              }
---------------------------- Sort by Line ----------------------------
Key Typ Field Word      Key Typ Field Word      Key Typ Field Word
 1   a    1    1         2                        3
 4                       5                        6
 7                       8                        9
Select

Action                  Direction               Type
Sort                    Ascending               Line sort

1 Perform Action; 2 View; 3 Keys; 4 Select; 5 Action; 6 Order 7 Type: 1
```

VMS	Keystroke Action	DOS

10. U: Press *3* for Keys.
    C: *Positions cursor on the Key 1 line and below*
    Typ.

11. U: Press *a* for alphanumeric.
    C: *Positions cursor on the Key 1 line and below*
    Field.

12. U: Press *1* and the **Right arrow key.**
    C: *Positions cursor on the Key 1 line and below*
    Word.

13. U: Press *1* and the **Right arrow key.**
    C: *Positions cursor on the Key 2 line and below*
    Typ.

14. U: Press *a* for alphanumeric.
    C: *Positions cursor on the Key 2 line and below*
    Field.

VMS	**Keystroke Action**	**DOS**
	15. U: Press *1* and the ***Right arrow key.*** C: *Positions cursor on the Key 2 line and below Word.*	
	16. U: Press *2* and the ***Right arrow key.*** C: *Changes the value on the Key 2 line and below Word to 2.*	
PF2,KP1	17. U: Press the ***Ctrl key*** (DOS users hold down) and tap the ***End key.*** C: *Deletes any other defined keys.*	Ctrl-End
F13	18. U: Press ***Exit.*** C: *Returns to Command Line.*	F7
	19. U: Press *4* for Select. C: *Positions cursor under the Select heading.*	
PF2,KP1	20. U: Press the ***Ctrl key*** (DOS users hold down) and tap the ***End key.*** C: *Deletes anything under Select.*	Ctrl-End
F13	21. U: Press ***Exit.*** C: *Returns to Command Line.*	F7
	22. U: Press *1* to Perform Action. C: *Performs the line sort and Returns to Document.*	
PF2,F18	23. U: Press ***Macro Define.*** C: *Saves macro.*	Ctrl-F10

On your screen all six names should appear in alphabetical order by last name first and then by first name as shown on Screen 11-4. Notice how even Cindi and Tami Anderson's names are sorted alphabetically by last and first name. However, if Tami's last name was Andersen instead, her name would appear before Cindi Anderson. Remember if you want to keep this document you must save it as a file.

Screen 11-4

```
Anderson, Cindi      Manager            831-5656
Anderson, Tami       Advertising        831-3453
Jones, Nancy         Sales Executive    831-4444
Mathews, Florence    Sales Manager      831-7645
Peters, Darryl       Programmer         831-5252
Quarterman, Robert   Sales Executive    831-1111
Stevens, Sue         Vice-President     831-4242
Zeke, Kevin          Advertising        831-1232
```

Applications of a Line Sort Macro

The keystrokes contained in the "LINESORT.WPM" macro are shown in the Macro Editor window on Screen 11-5 or Screen 11-6.

Screen 11-5: VMS Users

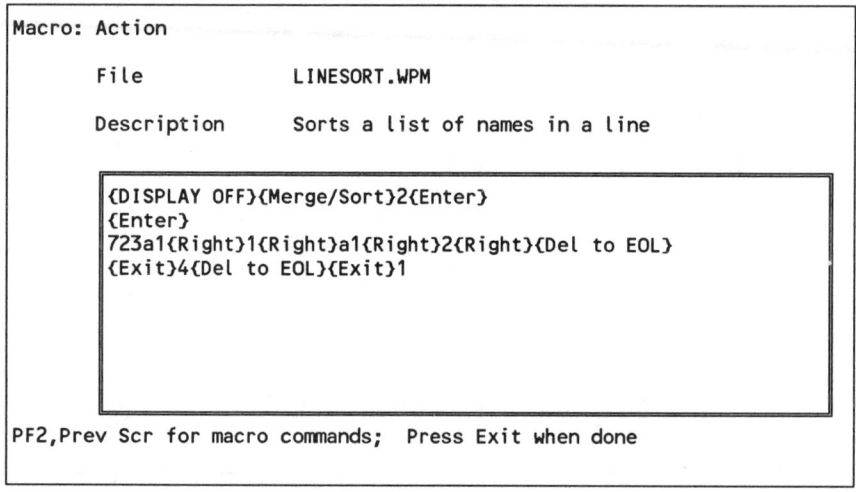

```
Macro: Action

        File            LINESORT.WPM

        Description     Sorts a list of names in a line

    ┌──────────────────────────────────────────────────────────┐
    │ {DISPLAY OFF}{Merge/Sort}2{Enter}                          │
    │ {Enter}                                                    │
    │ 723a1{Right}1{Right}a1{Right}2{Right}{Del to EOL}          │
    │ {Exit}4{Del to EOL}{Exit}1                                 │
    │                                                            │
    │                                                            │
    │                                                            │
    │                                                            │
    └──────────────────────────────────────────────────────────┘

PF2,Prev Scr for macro commands;   Press Exit when done
```

Screen 11-6: DOS Users

```
Macro: Action

       File              LINESORT.WPM

       Description       Sorts a list of names in a line

    ┌─────────────────────────────────────────────────────┐
    │ {DISPLAY OFF}{Merge/Sort}2{Enter}                    │
    │ {Enter}                                              │
    │ 723a1{Right}1{Right}a1{Right}2{Right}{Del to EOL}    │
    │ {Exit}4{Del to EOL}{Exit}1                           │
    │                                                      │
    │                                                      │
    │                                                      │
    └─────────────────────────────────────────────────────┘

Ctrl-V to Insert next key as command;
Ctrl-PgUp for macro commands;  Press Exit when done
```

To invoke this macro you need a list of line records as shown on Screen 11-2. This macro is ready for immediate use.

Using the Macro

The initial condition for this macro assumes you have a one per line list of items on your screen and you want to arrange them in alphabetical order. See Screen 11-7.

Screen 11-7

```
Mark, Jean
Young, Dot
Johnson, Debbie
Jones, Val
Stevenson, Eileen
Water, Mark
Osters, Lynne
Johnston, Morgan
Johnston, Matthew
Anders, Chris
Arthur, Tyler
Zyler, Joann
Harlin, Marsha
Andrews, Kara
Janson, Jodi
Bear, Joe
```

To invoke this macro do the following:

VMS	**Keystroke Action**	**DOS**
PF3,F18	1. U: Press *Macro.*	Alt-F10
	C: *Prints* Macro: _.	

VMS	Keystroke Action	DOS

2. U: Type in <u>LINESORT</u> and press the *Enter key.*
    C: *Macro invokes.*

When invoking this macro you will see what is shown on Screen 11-8. Note that the names are in alphabetical order.

Screen 11-8

```
Anders, Chris
Andrews, Kara
Arthur, Tyler
Bear, Joe
Harlin, Marsha
Janson, Jodi
Johnson, Debbie
Johnston, Matthew
Johnston, Morgan
Jones, Val
Mark, Jean
Osters, Lynne
Stevenson, Eileen
Water, Mark
Young, Dot
Zyler, Joann
```

Creating a Selected Paragraph Sort Macro

Before the next step please make sure that your screen is cleared and that the cursor is located at the top of the cleared screen.

In this section a selected paragraph sort macro will be defined. Remember that a paragraph sort is where each paragraph is a record and, therefore, must end with at least two hard returns.

Each line on Screen 11-9 ends with one hard return and each paragraph with two hard returns. Also, there is a space on each side of the hyphen in the telephone number. The space is needed since the macro will be defined to select only certain phone numbers that have the same first three digits. Remember these two conditions as you type in the data on Screen 11-9.

Screen 11-9

```
Barry Jones
786 - 9876

Corby Peterson
234 - 3232

Brian Rogers
453 - 9876

Randy Donnely
453 - 3212

Sam Meyers
231 - 9876

Mia Smithers
567 - 3423
```

In the selected paragraph sort macro the input file will be a saved file and the output file will be the screen. Thus, the file just typed in must be saved. Save the file and give it the name **PARA.TXT**, then clear your screen.

The macro may now be defined.

VMS	Keystroke Action	DOS
PF2,F18	1. U: Press *Macro Define.* C: *Prints* Define macro: _.	Ctrl-F10
	2. U: Type in <u>PARASORT</u> and press the *Enter key.* C: *Prints* Description: _.	
	3. U: Type in <u>Sorts a list of names in a paragraph</u> and press the *Enter key.* C: *Prints* Macro Def.	
PF2,F17	4. U: Press *Merge/Sort.* C: *Prints* 1 Merge; 2 Sort; 3 Convert Old Merge Codes: <u>0</u>.	Ctrl-F9
	5. U: Press *2* for Sort. C: *Prints* Input file to sort: (Screen).	
	6. U: Type in <u>PARA.TXT</u> for the input file to be sorted and press the *Enter key.* C: *Prints* Output file for sort: (Screen).	
	7. U: Press the *Enter key* for the screen to be the sorted output file. C: *Displays Sort Menu.*	

This selected paragraph sort macro will select the records containing telephone numbers beginning with 453 and then sort these selected records first by last name and then by first name.

VMS   Keystroke Action   DOS

8. U: Press *7* for Type.
   C: *Prints* Type: 1 Merge; 2 Line; 3 Paragraph: <u>0</u>.

9. U: Press *3* Paragraph since each of our records are in a paragraph.
   C: *Prints* Paragraph sort *under Type heading*.

Screen 11-10 shows the Paragraph Sort Menu.

Screen 11-10

```
Barry Jones
786 - 9876

Corby Peterson
234-3232

Brian Rogers
231 - 9876

Randy Donnely
453 - 3212
                                        Doc 2 Pg 1 Ln 1" Pos 1"
( ▲      ▲      ▲      ▲      ▲      ▲      ▲      ▲      ▲      ▲      )
---------------------- Sort by Paragraph ----------------------

Key Typ Line Field Word Key Typ Line Field Word Key Typ Line Field Word
 1   a    1     1    1   2                        3
 4                       5                        6
 7                       8                        9
Select

Action               Direction            Type
Sort                 Ascending            Paragraph sort

1 Perform Action; 2 View; 3 Keys; 4 Select; 5 Action; 6 Order 7 Type: 1
```

VMS   Keystroke Action   DOS

10. U: Press *3* for Keys.
    C: *Positions cursor on the Key 1 line and below Typ on a.*

11. U: Press *a* for alphanumeric.
    C: *Positions cursor on the Key 1 line and below Line.*

VMS	**Keystroke Action**	**DOS**

12. U: Press *1* and the ***Right arrow key.***
    C: *Positions cursor on the Key 1 line and below Field.*

13. U: Press *1* and the ***Right arrow key.***
    C: *Positions cursor on the Key 1 line and below Word.*

14. U: Press *2* and the ***Right arrow key.***
    C: *Changes the value on the Key 1 line and below Word to 2.*

15. U: Press *a* for alphanumeric.
    C: *Positions cursor on the Key 2 line and below Line.*

16. U: Press *1* and the ***Right arrow key.***
    C: *Positions cursor on the Key 2 line and below Field.*

17. U: Press *1* and the ***Right arrow key.***
    C: *Positions cursor on the Key 2 line and below Word.*

18. U: Press *1* and the ***Right arrow key.***
    C: *Positions cursor on the Key 3 line and below Typ.*

19. U: Press *n* for numeric.
    C: *Positions cursor on the Key 3 line and below Line.*

20. U: Press *2* and the ***Right arrow key.***
    C: *Positions cursor on the Key 3 line and below Field.*

21. U: Press *1* and the ***Right arrow key.***
    C: *Positions cursor on the Key 3 line and below Word.*

22. U: Press *1* and the ***Right arrow key.***
    C: *Changes the value on the Key 3 line and below Word to 1.*

PF2,KP1   23. U: Press the ***Ctrl key*** (DOS users hold down) and tap the ***End key.***   Ctrl-End
    C: *Deletes any other defined keys.*

VMS	**Keystroke Action**	**DOS**
F13	24. U: Press *Exit* since you do not want to change the next value. C: *Returns to Command Line.*	F7
	25. U: Press *4* for Select. C: *Positions cursor under the Select heading.*	
PF2,KP1	26. U: Press the *Ctrl key* (DOS users hold down) and tap the *End key.* C: *Deletes anything under Select.*	Ctrl-End

Eight logical symbols will appear on the command line. In Table 11-1 the symbols and an example of the symbols are shown.

Table 11-1

(1)	+(OR)	Purpose:	Selects the records that contain the same information of either key.
		Example:	key1=Johnson + key3=453 will select every Johnson or everyone with a telephone number beginning with 453.
(2)	*(AND)	Purpose:	Selects the records that contain the same information of both keys.
		Example:	key1=Anderson * key3=453 will select every record for all the Anderson's with a telephone number beginning with 453.
(3)	=	Purpose:	Selects the records that contain the same exact information of the key.
		Example:	key1=Johnson will select every record that contains Johnson in key1.
(4)	<>	Purpose:	Selects the records that do not contain the same information of the key.
		Example:	key1<>Johnson will select every record that does not contain Johnson in key1.
(5)	>	Purpose:	Selects the records that contain information greater than this key. Greater than is used in the alphabetical sense that B is after A and C is after B, etc. Greater than is used in the numerical sense that 999 is greater than 444.
		Example:	key1>Johnson will select every record that is greater than Johnson, or in other words that start with an alphabetical letter that is after J.

Table 11-1 continued.

(6)	>=	Purpose:	Selects the records that contain information greater than or equal to this key.
		Example:	key3>=453 will select every record that is greater than or equal to 453.
(7)	<	Purpose:	Selects the records that contain information less than this key. Less than is used in the alphabetical sense that A is before B and B is before C, etc. Less than is used in the numerical sense that 444 is less than 999.
		Example:	key1<Johnson will select every record that is less than Johnson, or in other words that start with an alphabetical letter that is before J.
(8)	<=	Purpose:	Selects the records that contain information less than or equal to this key.
		Example:	key3<=453 will select every record that is less than or equal to 453.

Note that selection is from left to right unless you use parentheses to rearrange the order.

Also, a global select, that selects all the records that contain the key, is defined by keyg=Johnson. Every record that contains Johnson will then be selected.

VMS	**Keystroke Action**	**DOS**
	27. U: Type in <u>key3=453</u>. C: *Prints Select and sort under Action heading.*	
F13	28. U: Press *Exit.* C: *Returns to Command Line.*	F7
	29. U: Press *1* to Perform Action. C: *Performs the selected paragraph sort and Returns to Document.*	
PF2,F18	30. U: Press *Macro* Define to finish defining the macro. C: *Saves macro.*	Ctrl-F10

On your screen the two names Brian Rogers and Randy Donnely should appear in last name alphabetical order as shown on Screen 11-11. Notice that each of the first three digits in their telephone number equals 453.

Screen 11-11

```
Randy Donnely
453 - 3212

Brian Rogers
453 - 9876
```

Applications of the Selected Paragraph Sort Macro

The keystrokes contained in the "PARASORT.WPM" macro are shown on Screen 11-12 or Screen 11-13.

Screen 11-12: VMS Users

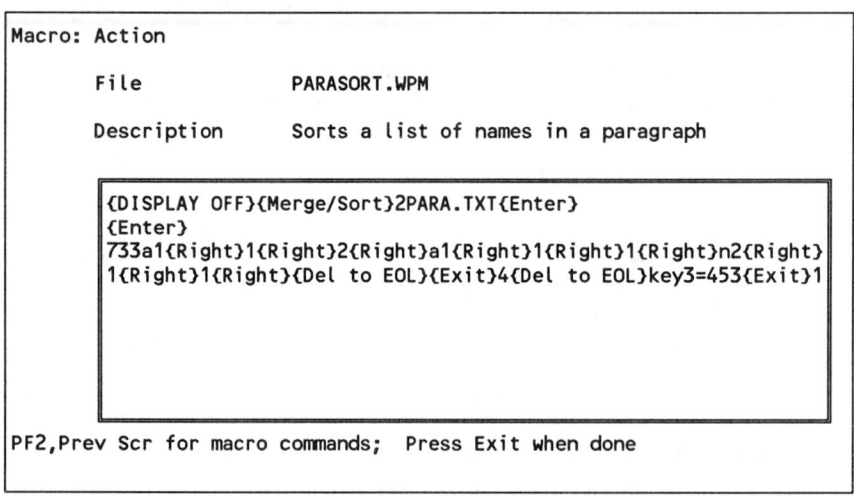

```
Macro: Action

        File            PARASORT.WPM

        Description     Sorts a list of names in a paragraph

     {DISPLAY OFF}{Merge/Sort}2PARA.TXT{Enter}
     {Enter}
     733a1{Right}1{Right}2{Right}a1{Right}1{Right}1{Right}n2{Right}
     1{Right}1{Right}{Del to EOL}{Exit}4{Del to EOL}key3=453{Exit}1

PF2,Prev Scr for macro commands;  Press Exit when done
```

Screen 11-13: DOS Users

```
Macro: Action

        File            PARASORT.WPM

        Description     Sorts a list of names in a paragraph

   ┌──────────────────────────────────────────────────────────┐
   │ {DISPLAY OFF}{Merge/Sort}2PARA.TXT{Enter}                 │
   │ {Enter}                                                   │
   │ 733a1{Right}1{Right}2{Right}a1{Right}1{Right}1{Right}n2{Right}│
   │ 1{Right}1{Right}{Del to EOL}{Exit}4{Del to EOL}key3=453{Exit}1│
   │                                                          │
   │                                                          │
   │                                                          │
   │                                                          │
   └──────────────────────────────────────────────────────────┘

Ctrl-V to Insert next key as command;
Ctrl-PgUp for macro commands;  Press Exit when done
```

This macro was used for tutorial purposes only. It can be modified in the Macro Editor to fit your personal needs.

Using the Macro

The initial condition for this macro assumes you have a list of records or paragraphs and you would like to make a separate list of the records that have a telephone number beginning with 453. This list must be a saved file called **PARA.TXT**. Your screen should be clear. See Screen 11-14.

Screen 11-14

```
Tiffany Sanders
234 - 4354

Tommy Catson
453 - 7979

Ashley Anders
343 - 5454

Randy Rathers
477 - 3467

Brian Johnson
571 - 7967

Missy Ball
453 - 9090
```

Remember that each line on Screen 11-9 must end with one hard return and each paragraph with two hard returns. Also, remember the space that is located on each side of the hyphen in the telephone number.

To invoke this macro do the following:

VMS	Keystroke Action	DOS
PF3,F18	1. U: Press *Macro.* C: *Prints* Macro: _.	Alt-F10
	2. U: Type in <u>PARASORT</u> and press the *Enter key.* C: *Macro invokes.*	

When invoking this macro you will see what is shown on Screen 11-15. Note that the records selected contain 453 as the beginning portion of the telephone number.

Screen 11-15

```
Missy Ball
453 - 9090

Tommy Catson
453 - 7979
```

Creating a Secondary Merge Records Sort Macro

In this section a macro will be defined to perform a secondary merge sort. Remember that in a secondary merge each record must end with the {*END RECORD*} Merge Code.

Before the next step please make sure that your screen is cleared and that the cursor is located at the top of the cleared screen.

Each field on Screen 11-16 ends with the {*END FIELD*} Merge Code. To place this merge code into your document do the following in all necessary locations:

VMS	Keystroke Action	DOS
F17	U: Press *Merge R.* C: *Prints* {END FIELD}.	F9

Each record, or complete address, ends with the {**END RECORD**} Merge Code. To place this merge code into your document do the following in each required location:

VMS	**Keystroke Action**	**DOS**

PF1,F17

U: Press *Merge Codes.*
C: *Prints* 1 Field; 2 End Record; 3 Input; 4 Page
Off; 5 Next Record; 6 More: 0.

U: Press *2* for End Record.
C: *Prints* {END RECORD} *and inserts a Hard
Page into your document automatically. The
Hard Page consists of a double dotted line.*

Shift-F9

Type in the data on Screen 11-16.

Screen 11-16

```
Carole Lane{END FIELD}
567 Shell Lane{END FIELD}
Long Beach, CA 99998{END RECORD}
=====================================================================
Gayle Andersen{END FIELD}
67 Bayberry Road{END FIELD}
New Orleans, LA 67787{END RECORD}
=====================================================================
Dave Rogers{END FIELD}
78 Main Street{END FIELD}
Las Vegas, NV 34543{END RECORD}
=====================================================================
Mike Shore{END FIELD}
77 Highway 1{END FIELD}
Santa Anna, CA 99797{END RECORD}
=====================================================================
```

In the secondary merge records sort macro the input file will be a saved file and the output file will be the screen. Thus, the file just typed in must be saved. Save the file and give it the name **MERG.TXT,** then clear your screen.

The macro for the secondary merge records sort may now be defined.

VMS	**Keystroke Action**	**DOS**

PF2,F18

1. U: Press *Macro Define.*
   C: *Prints* Define macro: _.

2. U: Type in MERGSORT and press the *Enter
   key.*
   C: *Prints* Description: _.

3. U: Type in Sorts merge records and press the
   Enter key.
   C: *Prints* Macro Def.

Ctrl-F10

VMS	Keystroke Action	DOS
PF2,F17	4. U: Press *Merge/Sort.* C: *Prints* 1 Merge; 2 Sort; 3 Convert Old Merge Codes: 0.	Ctrl-F9
	5. U: Press *2* for Sort. C: *Prints* Input file to sort: (Screen).	
	6. U: Type in <u>MERG.TXT</u> for the input file to be sorted and press the *Enter key.* C: *Prints* Output file for sort: (Screen).	
	7. U: Press the *Enter key* for the screen to be the sorted output file. C: *Displays Sort Menu.*	

This secondary merge sort will sort the records first by last name and then by first name.

VMS	Keystroke Action	DOS
	8. U: Press *7* for Type. C: *Prints* Type: 1 Merge; 2 Line; 3 Paragraph: 0.	
	9. U: Press *1* for Merge since each of our records are secondary merge addresses. C: *Prints* Merge sort *under Type heading.*	

Screen 11-17 shows the Merge Sort Menu.

Screen 11-17

```
Carole Lane{END FIELD}
567 Shell Lane{END FIELD}
Long Beach, CA 99998{END RECORD}
============================================================================
Gayle Andersen{END FIELD}
67 Bayberry Road{END FIELD}
New Orleans, LA 67787{END RECORD}
============================================================================
Dave Rogers{END FIELD}
                                         Doc 2 Pg 1 Ln 1" Pos 1"
⟨    ▲      ▲       ▲       ▲       ▲       ▲       ▲       ▲      ⟩
-------------------- Sort Secondary Merge File ----------------------

Key Typ Field Line Word Key Typ Field Line Word Key Typ Field Line Word
 1   a     1    1    1    2                       3
 4                        5                       6
 7                        8                       9
 Select

 Action                 Direction               Type
 Sort                   Ascending               Merge sort

1 Perform Action; 2 View; 3 Keys; 4 Select; 5 Action; 6 Order 7 Type: 1
```

VMS	**Keystroke Action**	**DOS**

10. U: Press *3* for Keys.
    C: *Positions cursor on the Key 1 line and below Typ.*

11. U: Press *a* for alphanumeric.
    C: *Positions cursor on the Key 1 line and below Field.*

12. U: Press *1* and the ***Right arrow key.***
    C: *Positions cursor on the Key 1 line and below Line.*

13. U: Press *1* and the ***Right arrow key.***
    C: *Positions cursor on the Key 1 line and below Word.*

14. U: Press *2* and the ***Right arrow key.***
    C: *Positions cursor on the Key 2 line and below Typ.*

15. U: Press *a* for alphanumeric.
    C: *Positions cursor on the Key 2 line and below Field.*

16. U: Press *1* and the ***Right arrow key.***
    C: *Positions cursor on the Key 2 line and below Line.*

VMS	Keystroke Action	DOS
	17. U: Press *1* and the ***Right arrow key.*** C: *Positions cursor on the Key 2 line and below Word.*	
	18. U: Press *1* and the ***Right arrow key.*** C: *Changes the value on the Key 2 line and below Word to 1 and positions cursor on Key 3 line and below Typ.*	
PF2	19. U: Press the ***Ctrl key*** (DOS users hold down) and tap the ***End key.*** C: *Deletes extra keys.*	Ctrl
F13	20. U: Press ***Exit.*** C: *Returns to Command Line.*	F7
	21. U: Press *4* for Select. C: *Positions cursor under the Select heading.*	
PF2,KP1	22. U: Press the ***Ctrl key*** (DOS users hold down) and tap the ***End key.*** C: *Deletes anything under Select.*	Ctrl-End
F13	23. U: Press ***Exit.*** C: *Returns to Command Line.*	F7
	24. U: Press *1* to Perform Action. C: *Performs the selected paragraph sort and Returns to Document.*	
PF2,F18	25. U: Press ***Macro Define*** to finish defining the macro. C: *Saves macro.*	Ctrl-F10

On your screen all four names should appear in alphabetical order by last name first and then by first name as shown on Screen 11-18.

Screen 11-18

```
Gayle Andersen{END FIELD}
67 Bayberry Road{END FIELD}
New Orleans, LA 67787{END RECORD}
========================================================================
Carole Lane{END FIELD}
567 Shell Lane{END FIELD}
Long Beach, CA 99998{END RECORD}
========================================================================
Dave Rogers{END FIELD}
78 Main Street{END FIELD}
Las Vegas, NV 34543{END RECORD}
========================================================================
Mike Shore{END FIELD}
77 Highway 1{END FIELD}
Santa Anna, CA 99797{END RECORD}
========================================================================
```

Applications of the Secondary Merge Records Sort Macro

The keystrokes contained in the "MERGSORT.WPM" macro are shown on Screen 11-19 or Screen 11-20.

Screen 11-19: VMS Users

```
Macro: Action

        File            MERGSORT.WPM

        Description     Sorts merge records.


    {DISPLAY OFF}{Merge/Sort}2MERG.TXT{Enter}
    {Enter}
    713a1{Right}1{Right}2{Right}a1{Right}1{Right}1{Right}
    {Del to EOL}{Exit}4{Del to EOL}{Exit}1




PF2,Prev Scr for macro commands;  Press Exit when done
```

Screen 11-20: DOS Users

```
Macro: Action

        File            MERGSORT.WPM

        Description     Sorts merge records.

    ┌─────────────────────────────────────────────────────────┐
    │{DISPLAY OFF}{Merge/Sort}2MERG.TXT{Enter}                  │
    │{Enter}                                                    │
    │713a1{Right}1{Right}2{Right}a1{Right}1{Right}1{Right}      │
    │{Del to EOL}{Exit}4{Del to EOL}{Exit}1                     │
    │                                                           │
    │                                                           │
    │                                                           │
    │                                                           │
    └─────────────────────────────────────────────────────────┘

Ctrl-V to Insert next key as command;
Ctrl-PgUp for macro commands;  Press Exit when done
```

To invoke this macro you need a list of secondary merge records as shown on Screen 11-16. This macro is ready for immediate use.

Using the Macro

The initial condition for this macro assumes you have a list of records or paragraphs that you would like to arrange in alphabetical order. This list must be a saved file called **MERG.TXT.** Your screen should be clear. See Screen 11-21.

Screen 11-21

```
Carl Peters{END FIELD}
557 Bluebird Way{END FIELD}
Jupiter, FL 34565{END RECORD}
===========================================================================
Robert Roberts{END FIELD}
79 Pelican Drive{END FIELD}
Naples, FL 34425{END RECORD}
===========================================================================
Ruth Michaels{END FIELD}
57 Ocean View{END FIELD}
Coral Beach, FL 34532{END RECORD}
===========================================================================
Christian Brandon{END FIELD}
277 Robin Way{END FIELD}
Coral Beach, FL 34532{END RECORD}
===========================================================================
Susan Steffen{END FIELD}
795 Shell Lane{END FIELD}
Shell Beach, FL 34555{END RECORD}
===========================================================================
```

Remember that each field on Screen 11-9 must end *{END FIELD}* and each record must end with *{END RECORD}*.

To invoke this macro do the following:

VMS	**Keystroke Action**	**DOS**

PF3,F18   1. U: Press *Macro.*   Alt-F10
                          C: *Prints* Macro: _.

                2. U: Type in <u>MERGSORT</u> and press the *Enter key.*
                          C: *Macro invokes.*

When invoking this macro you will see what is shown on Screen 11-22. Note that the names are in alphabetical order.

Screen 11-22

```
Christian Brandon{END FIELD}
277 Robin Way{END FIELD}
Coral Beach, FL 34532{END RECORD}
======================================================================
Ruth Michaels{END FIELD}
57 Ocean View{END FIELD}
Coral Beach, FL 34532{END RECORD}
======================================================================
Carl Peters{END FIELD}
557 Bluebird Way{END FIELD}
Jupiter, FL 34565{END RECORD}
======================================================================
Robert Roberts{END FIELD}
79 Pelican Drive{END FIELD}
Naples, FL 34425{END RECORD}
======================================================================
Susan Steffen{END FIELD}
795 Shell Lane{END FIELD}
Shell Beach, FL 34555{END RECORD}
======================================================================
```

CHAPTER 12

STYLE MACROS

Styles Feature

The style feature of WordPerfect 5.1 is very powerful. Styles are the different formats or document appearances you design to help you format your document to meet your needs. You can insert a style into a document or use it for the complete document. Styles should be used for formatting keystrokes that will be used numerous times in your document.

Styles are similar to macros because they execute packages of repetitive keystrokes at your command, however, styles are used for creating special formats for your documents.

For example, a style can be created to format identical subheadings, indent paragraphs in a special way, or set up special tab settings several times in a document. Also, they can set up the format for a memo, agenda minutes, or another type of unique document.

A specific example of a style for identical subheadings in a document can include the font point size change for each subheading in the document. Thus, you can place this defined style into your document every time you have a subheading. The subheading will automatically be formatted for you. The greatest advantage of styles is its capability of changing numerous locations with one change of style. For example, if you want to change the font size all you have to change is the style. WordPerfect 5.1 will then automatically change the font size in all the style locations. If you did not use a style you would have to find all the subheading's font size changes, erase them, and insert a new font size. However, if styles are used, you just have to edit the style and WordPerfect 5.1 will do the rest of the work for you. Thus, styles save the user a lot of time whereas macros in the same situation would have forced you to edit all occurrences.

Styles are always saved with the document they are contained in. However, they may also be saved as a file in order to be used in similar documents, at some other time.

Styles Menu

To access the Styles Menu do the following:

VMS	Reference Keystrokes	DOS
PF3,F14	U: Press *Style*. C: *Displays Styles Menu.*	Alt-F8

WordPerfect 5.1's styles are shown on Screen 12-1.

Screen 12-1

```
Styles

  Name          Type         Description

  Bibliogrphy   Paired       Bibliography
  Doc Init      Paired       Initialize Document Style
  Document      Outline      Document Style
  Pleading      Open         Header for numbered pleading paper
  Right Par     Outline      Right-Aligned Paragraph Numbers
  Tech Init     Open         Initialize Technical Style
  Technical     Outline      Technical Document Style

1 On; 2 Off; 3 Create; 4 Edit; 5 Delete; 6 Save; 7 Retrieve; 8 Update: 1
```

The Styles Menu is blank when you create a new WordPerfect 5.1 document unless you have chosen a style library file in *Setup* (See Addition B: Template Reference).

The Styles Menu contains eight options that are explained as follows:

On:	Turns the highlighted style on.
Off:	Turns the highlighted style off.
Create:	Places the user in the Styles: Edit Menu where a style can be created.
Edit:	The user can edit a previously created style that is highlighted.
Delete:	The user can delete the style that is highlighted.
Save:	Lets the user save the styles listed in the Styles menu as a separate document other than the one currently on the editing screen. This allows easy transfer of styles between documents.
Retrieve:	Permits the user to retrieve a file which contains only styles.
Update:	Allows the user to retrieve and update a style library if one was previously defined.

Creating a Style

A style must be created before it can be used. To create a style do the following:

VMS	**Reference Keystrokes**	**DOS**

U: Press *3* for Create.
C: *Displays the Styles: Edit Menu.*

The WordPerfect 5.1 Styles: Edit Menu contains the five items shown on Screen 12-2.

Screen 12-2

```
Styles: Edit

    1 - Name

    2 - Type           Paired

    3 - Description

    4 - Codes

    5 - Enter           HRt






Selection: 0
```

The five items are defined as follows:

1. Name: The title of the style is used for identification purposes. It can include up to 12 characters counting spaces and other characters.

2. Type: There are three possible style types. They are open, paired, and outline.

  Open: The open style turns on a feature. For instance it can be used for spacing, margin, and tab settings. This type is usually used for the entire document and is never turned off. The features are reset, if necessary, and only contain a beginning style code.

  Paired: The paired style turns a feature on and off. For instance consider bold and underline. This style is used, usually, for very small sections of the document. These features are always turned off and contain both a beginning and an ending style code.

  Outline: Allows the definition of styles for WordPerfect 5.1's Outline and Paragraph Number features. Thus, if you need to use a particular outline and paragraph numbering format you can create a style that contains the specific codes like bold, outline, etc., in your outline.

3. Description: Contains a brief explanation, 54 characters or less including spaces, of the style's purpose.

4. Codes: Displays the editing screen so WordPerfect 5.1's formatting and text keystrokes may be entered into the specified named style.

5. Enter: Tells the *Enter key's* function when the cursor is positioned in a paired style. The functions that the *Enter key* can have are the following:

a. Hrt Inserts a Hard Return
b. Off Turns a style off
c. Off/On Turns a style off then back on

The next step in the creation of a style follows:

VMS	Reference Keystrokes	DOS

U: Press *1* for Name.
C: *Positions cursor to right of Name.*

U: Type in the name for the style and press the *Enter key.*
C: *Echoes characters and Returns to Command Line.*

U: Press *2* for Type.
C: *Prints* Type: 1 Paired; 2 Open; 3 Outline: <u>0</u>.

The three available style types are discussed below.

1. Paired

The Style Code's Edit Screen for a paired style type is shown on Screen 12-3.

Screen 12-3

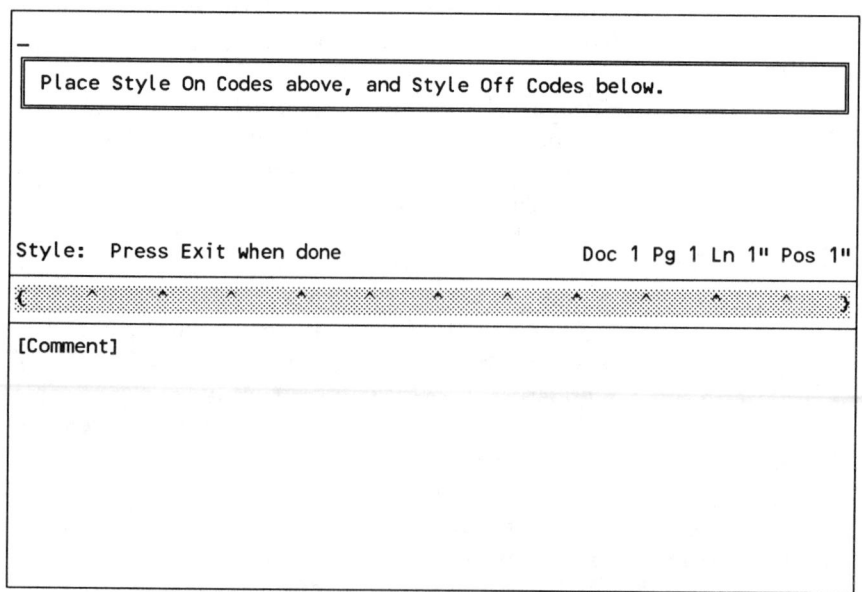

```
─

┌─────────────────────────────────────────────────────────────┐
│ Place Style On Codes above, and Style Off Codes below.       │
└─────────────────────────────────────────────────────────────┘




Style:  Press Exit when done              Doc 1 Pg 1 Ln 1" Pos 1"
( ░░^░░░░^░░░░^░░░░^░░░░^░░░░^░░░░^░░░░^░░░░^░░░░^░░░ )
[Comment]
```

If you have selected a paired style type a [Comment] code appears on the screen. Type in the format and/or text keystrokes that you want in your document when the style is turned on ahead of comment, above the double-lined boxed, and the format and/or text keystrokes that you want in your document when the style is turned off after the comment.

For example, on Screen 12-4 the Bold, Underline, and Italic appearance codes will be inserted into the document when the style is turned on and Bold, Underline, and Italic appearance will be turned off when the style is turned off.

Screen 12-4

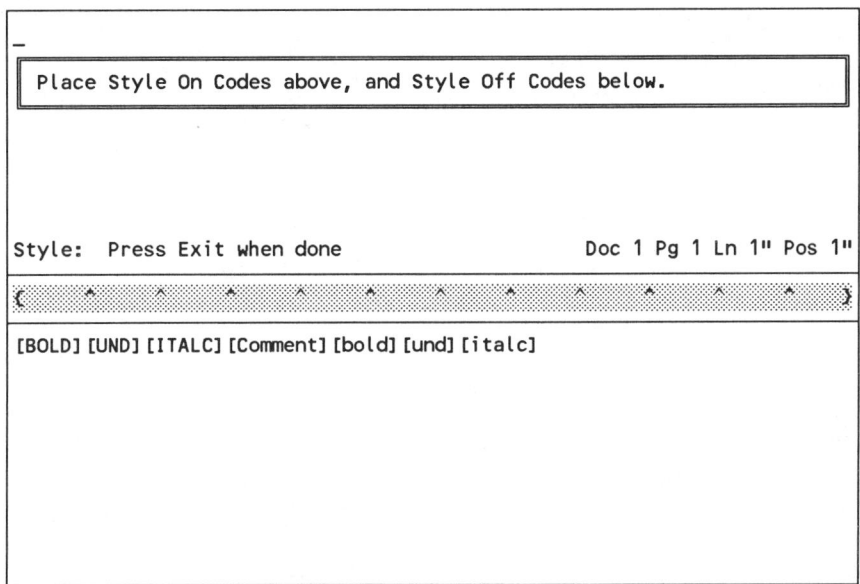

2. Open

If you selected an open style then any format code you place in this style will be turned on and used for the entire document unless you override the format code with another one. Codes placed in this style are usually codes that you would want to place in your document to initialize it.

For example the Style Code's Edit Screen for an open style type, on Screen 12-5 contains the Top/Bottom margin setting, Left/Right margins setting, and the line spacing. These are set initially for the complete document.

Screen 12-5

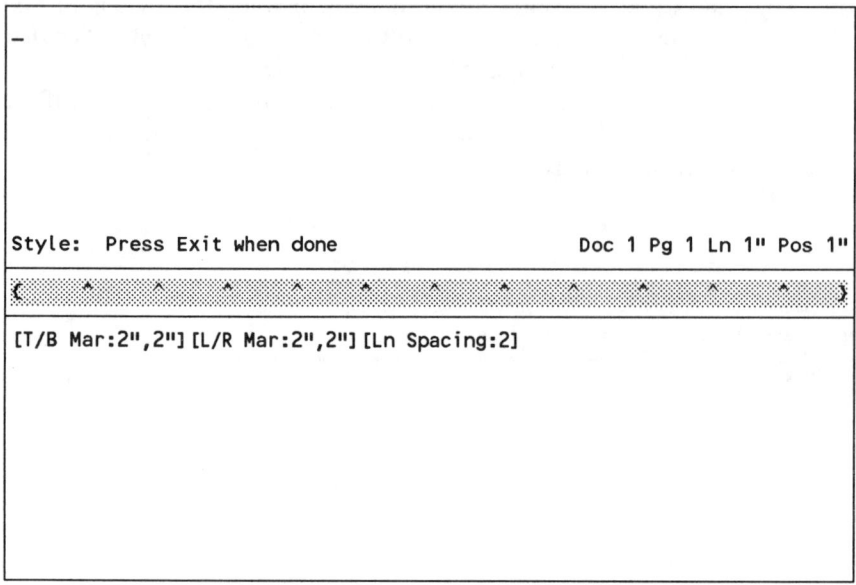

3. Outline

The Outline Type style menu is shown on Screen 12-6.
Details are associated with Screen 12-9.

Screen 12-6

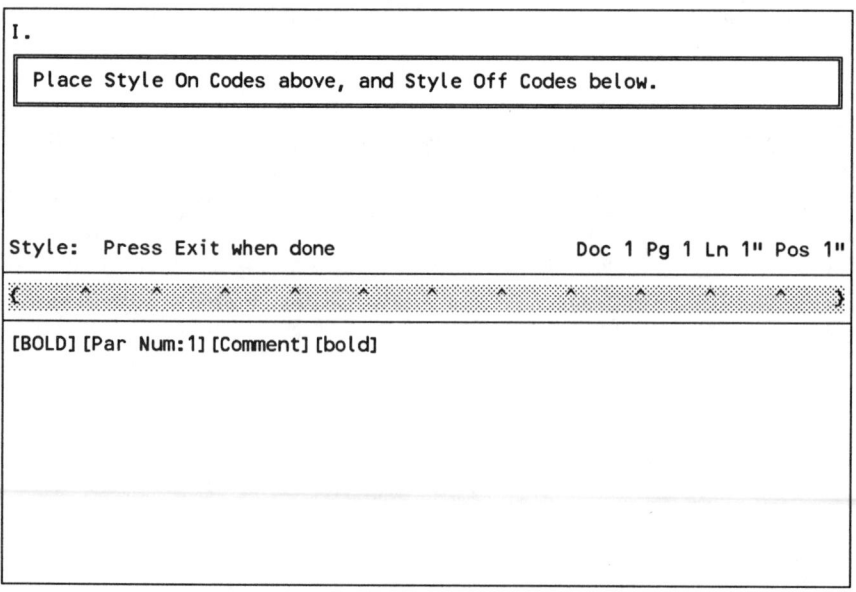

VMS   **Reference Keystrokes**   **DOS**

U: Select a Type.
C: *Prints selected type to right of Type in Styles: Edit menu.*

If you selected the Outline style type refer to the corresponding information in the section titled Details for Creating Outline Styles, beginning with Screen 12-9.

Details for Creating Open or Paired Styles

Let's continue with the creation of your Open or Paired style. If you selected one of those types, do the following:

VMS   **Reference Keystrokes**   **DOS**

U: Press *3* for Description.
C: *Positions cursor to right of Description.*

U: Type in a Description for the style and press the ***Enter key.***
C: *Echoes characters and Returns to Command Line.*

U: Press *4* for Codes.
C: *Displays Code's Edit Screen.*

Choice of a Paired style type will provide the display shown on Screen 12-7.

Screen 12-7

```
─

┌────────────────────────────────────────────────────────────┐
│  Place Style On Codes above, and Style Off Codes below.     │
└────────────────────────────────────────────────────────────┘




Style:   Press Exit when done                 Doc 1 Pg 1 Ln 1" Pos 1"
────────────────────────────────────────────────────────────────────
{   ^      ^      ^      ^      ^      ^      ^      ^      ^      }

[Comment]
```

Generally, the WordPerfect codes to the left of the [Comment] will be turned on when the style is turned on, while the codes to the right of the [Comment] will be turned on when the Style is turned off.

There are some deviations on the above statement. Any code to the left of the [Comment] will return to its original value before the style was even turned on, this applies even if there is a corresponding code to the right of the [Comment] which would normally, but not this time, be turned on when the style is turned off. What these codes do not include are the options on the *Format Menu* (PF1,F14 for VMS or Shift-F8 for DOS).

When you chose an Open style type you will see what is shown on Screen 12-8.

Screen 12-8

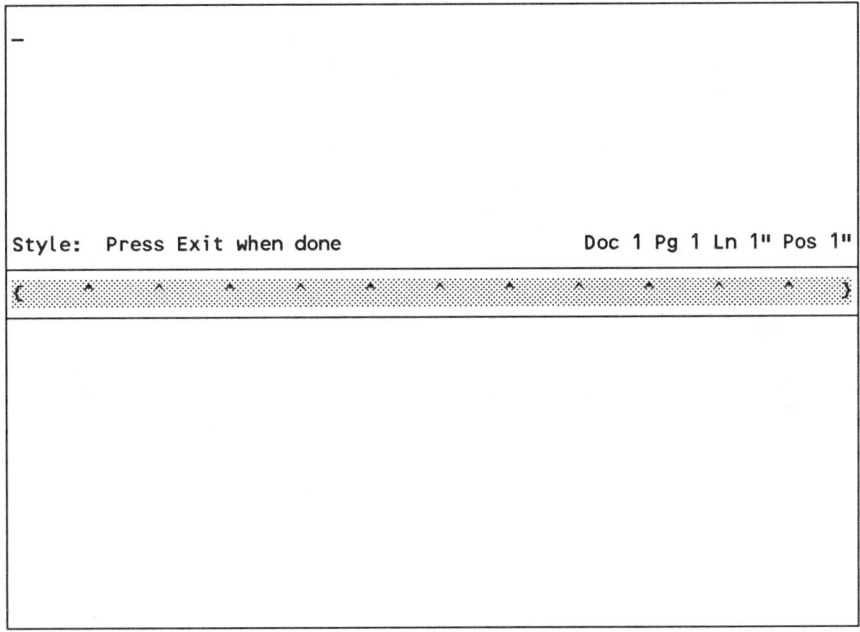

The Open style does not have the [Comment] marker. Type in the codes you want to set in your style.

VMS	**Reference Keystrokes**	**DOS**
	U: Enter appropriate codes.	
	C: *Displays codes.*	
F13	U: Press *Exit.*	F7
	C: *Displays the Styles: Edit menu.*	
	U: Press *5* for Enter.	
	C: *Prints* Enter: 1 Hrt; 2 Off; 3 Off/On: 0.	
	U: Press the appropriate number.	
	C: *Prints selected type to right of Enter in Styles: Edit menu.*	
F13	U: Press *Exit.*	F7
	C: *Displays Style Menu.*	
F13	U: Press *Exit.*	F7
	C: *Returns to Document.*	

Details for Creating Outline Styles

The details of creating an outline style are discussed in this section.

Screen 12-9 shows the screen you will see if you select the Outline style type.

Screen 12-9

```
Styles: Edit

     1 - Name            Test

     2 - Type            Paired

     3 - Description

     4 - Codes

     5 - Enter           HRt




Name:Test
```

VMS   Reference Keystrokes   DOS

U: Press the *Enter key* to confirm the name for the
   style.
C: *Displays the Styles: Edit menu and Prints* Level
   Number (1-8): _.

Screen 12-10 prompts you to determine the number of the Levels you will have in your
style.

Screen 12-10

```
Styles: Edit

    1 - Name            Test

    2 - Type            Paired

    3 - Description

    4 - Codes

    5 - Enter           HRt




Level Number (1-8): _
```

The Level Number is the total amount of different levels you need in your outline. An example outline is shown below:

Sales Report

    I.   Computers Sold
        A.   Units
            1. Microcomputers
            2. Minicomputers
            3. Mainframe
        B.   Dollar Amount
            1. Microcomputers
            2. Minicomputers
            3. Mainframe

    II.   Software Sold
        A.   Units
            1. Word Processing
            2. Spreadsheets
            3. Databases
        B.   Dollar Amount
            1. Word Processing
            2. Spreadsheets
            3. Databases

The following characters as defaulted by WordPerfect indicate the corresponding level shown below:

I	Level One
A	Level Two
1	Level Three
a	Level Four
(1)	Level Five
(a)	Level Six
i)	Level Seven
a)	Level Eight

In the above example three levels were used.

Outline styles allow you to format each Level with bold, font, center, etc., codes. For example you could format your outline so that all Level One items are underlined and Level Two items are bolded and this will be done automatically for you when you use the style. See below.

I.   <u>Computers Sold</u>
    A.   **Units**
         1. Microcomputers
         2. Minicomputers
         3. Mainframe
    B.   **Dollar Amount**
         1. Microcomputers
         2. Minicomputers
         3. Mainframe

II.   <u>Software Sold</u>
    A.   **Units**
         1. Word Processing
         2. Spreadsheets
         3. Databases
    B.   **Dollar Amount**
         1. Word Processing
         2. Spreadsheets
         3. Databases

If you have selected the Outline style type do the following:

VMS   **Reference Keystrokes**   **DOS**

U: Enter in the number of levels you will need.
C: *Displays the Outline Styles: Edit menu.*

Following the example shown above note Level 1 is underlined and Level 2 is bolded. Therefore, the only levels you need to format in your style would be Level 1 and 2. You could have selected 2 for the Level Number and then on the Outline Styles: Edit menu you would notice that Level 2 is different from the rest. The type of Level 2 is paired and states that the ***Enter key's*** function is a Hard Return.

Screen 12-11: VMS Users

```
Outline Styles: Edit

  Name:            Test

  Description:


  Level   Type       Return

    1     Open
    2     Paired     HRt
    3     Open
    4     Open
    5     Open
    6     Open
    7     Open
    8     Open



1 Name; 2 Description; 3 Type; 4 Return; 5 Codes: 0
```

Screen 12-12: DOS Users

```
Outline Styles: Edit

  Name:            Test

  Description:


  Level   Type       Enter

    1     Open
    2     Paired     HRt
    3     Open
    4     Open
    5     Open
    6     Open
    7     Open
    8     Open



1 Name; 2 Description; 3 Type; 4 Enter; 5 Codes: 0
```

The following options are listed in the Outline Style: Edit menu:

1. Name: The title of the style is used for identification purposes. It can include up to 12 characters counting spaces and other characters. This option should have been defined previously, however, you can change the name.

2. Description: Contains a brief explanation 54 characters or less including spaces, of the style's purpose.

3. **Type:**   Allows you to change the Level's Type. Choices include either Paired or Open style types.

4. **Return/Enter:**   Tells the *Enter key's* function when the cursor is positioned in a paired style. The following functions can be assigned to the *Enter key:*

          a.   Hrt   Inserts a Hard Return
          b.   Off   Turns a style off
          c.   Off/On   Turns a style off then back on

5. **Codes:**   Displays the editing screen so WordPerfect 5.1's formatting and text keystrokes may be entered into the specified named style.

VMS   Reference Keystrokes   DOS

U: Press *2* for Description.
C: *Positions cursor to right of Description.*

U: Type in a Description for the style and press the *Enter key.*
C: *Echoes characters and Returns to Command Line.*

NOTE 1:   *If you have many levels you must repeat the steps below until you reach the Note 2. These steps will be repeated for every level.*

VMS   Reference Keystrokes   DOS

U: Highlight a Level Number to determine the Level Number's Type, Enter key function, and codes.
C: *Highlights a Level Number.*

U: Press *3* for Type.
C: *Prints* Type: 1 Paired; 2 Open: 0.

U: Select a Type.
C: *Prints selected type to right of Type in Styles: Edit menu.*

U: Press *5* for Codes.
C: *Displays Code's Edit Screen.*

U: Enter appropriate codes.
C: *Displays codes.*

VMS	**Reference Keystrokes**	**DOS**
F13	U: Press *Exit.* C: *Displays Outline Styles: Edit menu.*	F7
VMS Users	U: Press *4* for Enter if it is a paired style. C: *Prints* Return: 1 Hrt; 2 Off; 3 Off/On: <u>0</u>. C: *Prints* Enter: 1 Hrt; 2 Off; 3 Off/On: <u>0</u>.	*DOS Users*
	U: Press the appropriate number. C: *Prints selected type below Enter in Outline Styles: Edit menu.*	

NOTE 2: **If you have more level numbers then go back up to NOTE 1 above until you are done.**

VMS	**Reference Keystrokes**	**DOS**
F13	U: Press *Exit.* C: *Displays Style menu.*	F7
F13	U: Press *Exit.* C: *Returns to Document.*	F7

Turning Styles On or Off

You may want to use a Style only in certain parts of your document.

VMS	**Reference Keystrokes**	**DOS**
PF3,F14	U: Press *Style.* C: *Displays Style Menu.*	Alt-F8
	U: Highlight the style you want to turn on in your document. C: *Highlights style.*	
	U: Press *1* for Select On to turn the style on. C: *Turns style on.*	
	U: Type in the text. C: *Echoes characters.*	

If the style is a paired style, you must also turn it off. To turn the style off use one of the following three methods:

VMS	Reference Keystrokes	DOS
PF3,F14	U: Press *Style.* C: *Displays Style Menu.*	Alt-F8
	U: Press **2** for Select Off to turn the style off. C: *Turns style off.*	

or

VMS	Reference Keystrokes	DOS
	U: Press the **Right arrow key** one time to move cursor past the Style Off code in the document. C: *Positions cursor after the Style Off code.*	

or

If the Enter key has been defined to turn the style off or off and on do the following:

VMS	Reference Keystrokes	DOS
	U: Press the **Enter key.** C: *Turns style off.*	

To turn a style on for a block of text that is already typed into the document do the following:

VMS	Reference Keystrokes	DOS
PF3,F10 OR F20	U: Press **Block.** C: *Prints* Block on.	Alt-F4 OR F12
	U: Highlight the block of text you want to be styled. C: *Block text highlighted.*	
PF3,F14	U: Press *Style.* C: *Displays Style Menu.*	Alt-F8
	U: Highlight the style you want to turn on in your document. C: *Highlights style.*	
	U: Press **1** for Select On to turn the style on. C: *Turns style on for the block.*	

Library

A style library or file of different formats, or styles is provided with WordPerfect 5.1. You can create your own style library by using the Save option in the Style's menu.

To have WordPerfect 5.1 automatically retrieve a style library whenever a document is created or when a document that is retrieved does not contain any styles do the following:

VMS	Reference Keystrokes	DOS
PF1,F7	U: Press **Setup**. C: *Displays Setup Menu.*	Shift-F1
	U: Press *6* for Location of Files. C: *Displays Setup: Location of Files Menu.*	
VMS Users	U: Press *5* for Style Files. U: Press *5* for Style File/Library Filename.	*DOS Users*
VMS Users	C: *Prints* Location of Style Files: _. C: *Positions cursor to right of Style File.*	*DOS Users*
VMS Users	U: Type in file specification for location of Style Files and press the **Enter key.** The file specification usually is WPCORP$WP51LRNDIR. U: Type in pathname for location of Style Files and press the **Enter key.** The pathname usually is c:\wp51\learn.	*DOS Users*
VMS Users	C: *Prints* Style Library Filename: _. C: *Positions cursor to right of Library Filename.*	*DOS Users*

VMS Users: *Ask your system manager if you need help with the file specification since it might be different for your specific environment.*

VMS	Reference Keystrokes	DOS
	U: Type in the correct file specification/pathname and the Style Library Filename. For WordPerfect 5.1's style library type in <u>LIBRARY.STY</u> for yours type in the correct name and press the **Enter key.** C: *Returns to Command Line.*	
F13 *VMS Users*	U: Press **Exit**. C: *Returns to Setup Menu.* C: *Returns to Document.*	F7 *DOS Users*

VMS Users: **Perform the following Reference Keystroke Action.**

DOS Users: **Do NOT perform the following Reference Keystroke Action.**

VMS	Reference Keystrokes	DOS
F13	U: Press *Exit.* C: *Returns to Document.*	F7

Next time you invoke Style you will see WordPerfect's or your own style library.

Creating a Style Macro

The macro created in this section will make turning styles on simpler.

VMS	Keystroke Action	DOS
PF2,F18	1. U: Press *Macro Define.* C: *Prints* Define macro: _.	Ctrl-F10
	2. U: Type in <u>STYON</u> and press the *Enter key.* C: *Prints* Description: _.	
	3. U: Type in <u>Turn style on</u> and press the *Enter key.* C: *Prints* Macro Def.	
PF3,F14	4. U: Press *Style.* C: *Displays Style Menu.*	Alt-F8
	5. U: Press *n* for Name Search, type in as many characters of the style as you need to distinguish it from the other available styles and press the *Enter key.* For example, you could type in <u>Init Tech</u>. C: *Highlights style.*	
	6. U: Press *1* for Select On to turn the style on. C: *Turns style on and Returns to Document.*	
PF2,F18	7. U: Press *Macro Def.* C: *Saves macro.*	Ctrl-F10

In this example if you used the style name of Init Tech then this style is now turned on as indicated by the **Outline** prompt in the lower left-hand corner of your screen. Remember to turn it off by following the steps under the section titled Turning Styles On or Off above.

Applications of the Style Macro

The keystrokes contained in the "STYON.WPM" macro are shown on Screen 12-13 or Screen 12-14.

Screen 12-13: VMS Users

```
Macro: Action

        File            STYON.WPM

        Description     Turn style on

     ┌────────────────────────────────────────────────┐
     │ {DISPLAY OFF}{Style}nTech•Init{Enter}           │
     │ 1                                                │
     │                                                  │
     │                                                  │
     │                                                  │
     │                                                  │
     │                                                  │
     └────────────────────────────────────────────────┘

PF2,Prev Scr for macro commands;   Press Exit when done
```

Screen 12-14: DOS Users

```
Macro: Action

        File            STYON.WPM

        Description     Turn style on

     ┌────────────────────────────────────────────────┐
     │ {DISPLAY OFF}{Style}nTech•Init{Enter}           │
     │ 1                                                │
     │                                                  │
     │                                                  │
     │                                                  │
     │                                                  │
     └────────────────────────────────────────────────┘

Ctrl-V to Insert next key as command;
Ctrl-PgUp for macro commands;   Press Exit when done
```

This macro is ready for immediate use.

Using the Macro

The initial conditions for this macro assume you are starting a new document or that you are currently editing a document to include a style.

To invoke this macro do the following:

VMS	Keystroke Action	DOS

PF3,F18

1. U: Press *Macro.*
   C: *Prints* Macro: _.

2. U: Type in <u>STYON</u> and press the *Enter key.*
   C: *Macro invokes.*

Alt-F10

When invoking this macro you will see what is shown on Screen 12-15 if you are in *Reveal Codes.*

Screen 12-15

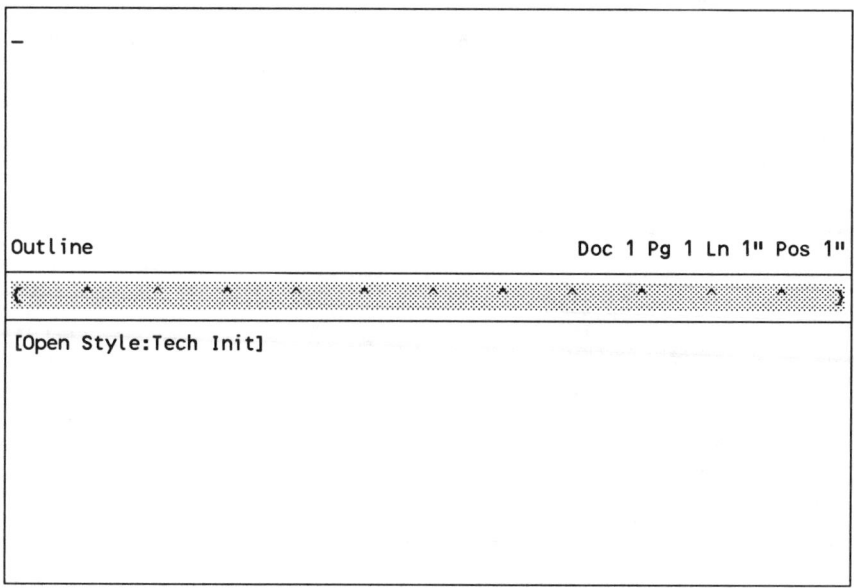

Now you can use this particular style and enter in the necessary data.

SECTION III:

ADVANCED PROGRAMMED MACROS

CHAPTER 13

DESK-TOP PUBLISHING

The Concept of Desk-Top Publishing

Desk-Top Publishing is an important "art" of the business world today. Companies print monthly newsletters for employees, send weekly advertisements to clients, and print many other items that need graphics incorporated in the document and are formatted in a specific and attractive style.   WordPerfect 5.1 has three great advanced features that are imperative to the achievement of a high quality newsletter. These features are columns, fonts, and graphics.

Most newsletters contain two to three columns, many different types and sizes of fonts, and, of course, graphic pictures. These features are essential when creating any Desk-Top Publishing document.

Each of these features has been discussed thoroughly in three separate chapters in the Advanced Features of WordPerfect 5.1: Using Macros Section of this book.

This Desk-Top Publishing chapter brings all three of these features together by using them in four effective macros that will provide macro power speed, effectiveness, and ease when creating any desk-top publishing item.

Desk-Top Publishing Macros

In this section, four macros will be shown. These macros will assist the user in creating Desk-Top Publishing documents. Each macro has a unique document layout. (See Table 13-1.)

Table 13-1

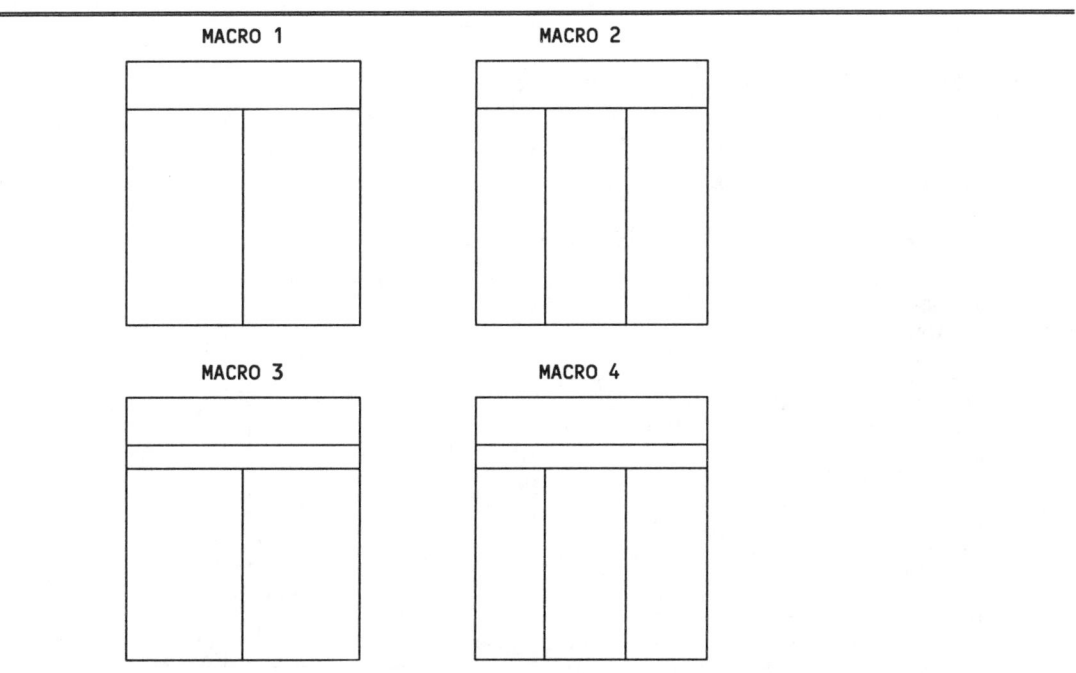

You can choose the macro for the layout desired, type in the given code in the Macro Editor or define the macro interactively, and then invoke it. After the macro is invoked the user can enter the text and graphic pictures into the Desk-Top Publishing document.

Macro 1

The keystrokes that are contained in the "DTP1" macro are shown on Screen 13-1 or Screen 13-2.

Screen 13-1: VMS Users

```
Macro: Action

       File           DTP1

       Description    Desk-Top Publishing Layout 1

       ┌──────────────────────────────────────────────┐
       │{DISPLAY OFF}                                  │
       │{Enter}                                        │
       │{Enter}                                        │
       │{Enter}                                        │
       │{Graphics}514.1{Enter}                         │
       │{Exit}{Enter}                                  │
       │{Enter}                                        │
       │{Columns/Tables}13                             │
       │{Exit}1{Graphics}5213{Enter}                   │
       │251.6{Enter}                                   │
       │4.1{Enter}                                     │
       │{Exit}                                         │
       └──────────────────────────────────────────────┘

PF2,Prev Scr for macro commands;   Press Exit when done
```

Screen 13-2: DOS Users

```
Macro: Action

       File           DTP1.WPM

       Description    Desk-Top Publishing Layout 1

       ┌──────────────────────────────────────────────┐
       │{DISPLAY OFF}{Enter}                           │
       │{Enter}                                        │
       │{Enter}                                        │
       │{Enter}                                        │
       │{Graphics}514.1{Enter}                         │
       │{Exit}{Enter}                                  │
       │{Enter}                                        │
       │{Columns/Tables}13                             │
       │{Exit}1{Graphics}5213{Enter}                   │
       │251.83{Enter}                                  │
       │4.1{Enter}                                     │
       │{Exit}                                         │
       └──────────────────────────────────────────────┘

Ctrl-V to Insert next key as command;
Ctrl-PgUp for macro commands;   Press Exit when done
```

Macro 2

The keystrokes that are contained in the "DTP2" macro are shown on Screen 13-3 or Screen 13-4.

Screen 13-3: VMS Users

```
Macro: Action

       File            DTP2

       Description     Desk-Top Publishing Layout 2

       ┌─────────────────────────────────────────────────────┐
       │ {DISPLAY OFF}                                        │
       │ {Enter}                                              │
       │ {Enter}                                              │
       │ {Enter}                                              │
       │ {Graphics}514.1{Enter}                              │
       │ {Exit}{Enter}                                        │
       │ {Enter}                                              │
       │ {Columns/Tables}1323{Enter}                         │
       │ {Exit}1{Graphics}5213{Enter}                        │
       │ 251.6{Enter}                                        │
       │ 4.1{Enter}                                          │
       │ {Exit}                                              │
       │ {Graphics}52132{Enter}251.6{Enter}4.1{Enter}{Exit}  │
       └─────────────────────────────────────────────────────┘

PF2,Prev Scr for macro commands;  Press Exit when done
```

Screen 13-4: DOS Users

```
Macro: Action

       File            DTP2.WPM

       Description     Desk-Top Publishing Layout 2

       ┌─────────────────────────────────────────────────────┐
       │ {DISPLAY OFF}{Enter}                                │
       │ {Enter}                                              │
       │ {Enter}                                              │
       │ {Enter}                                              │
       │ {Graphics}514.1{Enter}                              │
       │ {Exit}{Enter}                                        │
       │ {Enter}                                              │
       │ {Columns/Tables}1323{Enter}                         │
       │ {Exit}1{Graphics}5213{Enter}                        │
       │ 251.83{Enter}                                       │
       │ 4.1{Enter}                                          │
       │ {Exit}                                              │
       │ {Graphics}52132{Enter}251.83{Enter}4.1{Enter}{Exit} │
       └─────────────────────────────────────────────────────┘

Ctrl-V to Insert next key as command;
Ctrl-PgUp for macro commands;  Press Exit when done
```

Macro 3

The keystrokes that are contained in the "DTP3" macro are shown on Screen 13-5 or Screen 13-6.

Screen 13-5: VMS Users

```
Macro: Action

       File            DTP3

       Description     Desk-Top Publishing Layout 3

    ┌─────────────────────────────────────────────────────┐
    │ {DISPLAY OFF}                                        │
    │ {Enter}                                             │
    │ {Enter}                                             │
    │ {Enter}                                             │
    │ {Graphics}514.1{Enter}                             │
    │ {Exit}                                             │
    │ {Enter}                                             │
    │ {Enter}                                             │
    │ {Graphics}514.1{Enter}                             │
    │ {Exit}{Enter}                                      │
    │ {Enter}                                             │
    │ {Columns/Tables}13{Exit}1{Graphics}5213{Enter}    │
    │ 251.77{Enter}                                      │
    │ 4.1{Enter}                                         │
    │ {Exit}                                             │
    └─────────────────────────────────────────────────────┘
 PF2,Prev Scr for macro commands;   Press Exit when done
```

Screen 13-6: DOS Users

```
Macro: Action

       File            DTP3.WPM

       Description     Desk-Top Publishing Layout 3

    ┌─────────────────────────────────────────────────────┐
    │ {DISPLAY OFF}{Enter}                                │
    │ {Enter}                                             │
    │ {Enter}                                             │
    │ {Enter}                                             │
    │ {Graphics}514.1{Enter}                             │
    │ {Exit}{Enter}                                      │
    │ {Enter}                                             │
    │ {Enter}                                             │
    │ {Graphics}514.1{Enter}                             │
    │ {Exit}{Enter}                                      │
    │ {Enter}                                             │
    │ {Columns/Tables}13{Exit}1{Graphics}5213{Enter}    │
    │ 252.29{Enter}                                      │
    │ 4.1{Enter}                                         │
    │ {Exit}                                             │
    └─────────────────────────────────────────────────────┘
 Ctrl-V to Insert next key as command;
 Ctrl-PgUp for macro commands;   Press Exit when done
```

Macro 4

The keystrokes that are contained in the "DTP4" macro are shown on Screen 13-7 or Screen 13-8.

Screen 13-7: VMS Users

```
Macro: Action

        File            DTP4

        Description     Desk-Top Publishing Layout 4

        ┌─────────────────────────────────────────────────────────┐
        │{DISPLAY OFF}                                             │
        │{Enter}                                                   │
        │{Enter}                                                   │
        │{Enter}                                                   │
        │{Graphics}514.1{Enter}                                   │
        │{Exit}                                                    │
        │{Enter}                                                   │
        │{Enter}                                                   │
        │{Graphics}514.1{Enter}                                   │
        │{Exit}{Enter}                                             │
        │{Enter}                                                   │
        │{Columns/Tables}1323{Enter}                              │
        │{Exit}1{Graphics}5213{Enter}                             │
        │251.77{Enter}                                            │
        │4.1{Enter}                                               │
        │{Exit}{Graphics}52132{Enter}251.77{Enter}4.1{Enter}{Exit}│
        └─────────────────────────────────────────────────────────┘

PF2,Prev Scr for macro commands;   Press Exit when done
```

Screen 13-8: DOS Users

```
Macro: Action

        File            DTP4.WPM

        Description     Desk-Top Publishing Layout 4

        ┌─────────────────────────────────────────────────────────┐
        │{DISPLAY OFF}{Enter}                                     │
        │{Enter}                                                   │
        │{Enter}                                                   │
        │{Enter}                                                   │
        │{Graphics}514.1{Enter}                                   │
        │{Exit}{Enter}                                             │
        │{Enter}                                                   │
        │{Enter}                                                   │
        │{Graphics}514.1{Enter}                                   │
        │{Exit}{Enter}                                             │
        │{Enter}                                                   │
        │{Columns/Tables}1323{Enter}                              │
        │{Exit}1{Graphics}5213{Enter}                             │
        │252.29{Enter}                                            │
        │4.1{Enter}                                               │
        │{Exit}{Graphics}52132{Enter}252.29{Enter}4.1{Enter}{Exit}│
        └─────────────────────────────────────────────────────────┘

Ctrl-V to Insert next key as command;
Ctrl-PgUp for macro commands;   Press Exit when done
```

These macros are ready for immediate use. They may have to be slightly adjusted depending on your exact Desk-Top Publishing needs. For instance, if you create a newsletter every month, then you could add the heading of the newsletter. Also, you can specify different fonts that you want to use in different locations.

CHAPTER 14

MACRO POWER LIBRARY

The power of the macro is demonstrated in the following library of alternate and programmed macros. These powerful macros make complicated tasks easy and show you how to let Macro Power work for you.

PF/Alternate A to Z Macros

This section contains twenty-six PF/Alternate Macros, one for each letter of the alphabet.

VMS Users: *PF Macros are VMS Macros. PF represents either the PF1 or PF3 key macros. In WordPerfect for VMS it is possible to have 26 PF1 macros along with 26 different PF3 macros. When you press the PF1 key and then a letter of the alphabet the macro will be given the filename of PF1Letter.WPM where Letter is an alphabetic character from A to Z. When you press the PF3 key and then a letter of the alphabet the macro will be given the filename of ALTLetter.WPM where Letter is an alphabetic character from A to Z. PF3 is really the TRUE alternate key.*

    NOTE: When you press the PF1 key to create a PF macro you must press PF1 to also invoke the macro; you cannot then press PF3 to invoke the macro, likewise with PF3.

    NOTE: This chapter will assume the use of the PF3 key for all of screens containing PF macros.

DOS Users: *When you press the Alt key and then a letter of the alphabet the macro will be given the filename and extension of ALTLetter.WPM where Letter is an alphabetic character from A to Z.*

For the A to Z PF/Alternate macros, follow the Keystroke Actions below each PF-? (VMS) or Alt-? (DOS), where ? represents some letter between A and Z. Make sure you define the macro at the same time that you actually want to do the specified action because the macros invoke as they are being created or create a test document to use when you define these macros. To invoke the macros press the *PF* (VMS) or *Alt* (DOS) key.

VMS Users: *You can press the PF key then lift your hand up since it is not necessary to hold down the PF key when you press the corresponding alphabetic character.*

DOS Users: *You must hold down the Alt key and tap the corresponding letter, then lift your hand up.*

The PF/Alternate A to Z Macros

VMS	DOS	Letter	Description
PF	Alt	A	Appearance Attributes Menu displayed
PF	Alt	B	Bolds a word
PF	Alt	C	Copies a paragraph
PF	Alt	D	Deletes a paragraph
PF	Alt	E	End of document cursor relocated
PF	Alt	F	Font (Base Font) Directory displayed
PF	Alt	G	Go to VMS or DOS prompt
PF	Alt	H	Header A Menu displayed
PF	Alt	I	Inserts current date into document
PF	Alt	J	Joins two normally separated words by a hard space
PF	Alt	K	Keyboard Layout Menu displayed
PF	Alt	L	Locks a document
PF	Alt	M	Moves a paragraph
PF	Alt	N	Numbers document pages
PF	Alt	O	One window displayed
PF	Alt	P	Prints a document after it spell checks and saves document
PF	Alt	Q	Quits WordPerfect after it saves your document
PF	Alt	R	Reports the printer status
PF	Alt	S	Spell checks and saves your document
PF	Alt	T	Top of document cursor relocated
PF	Alt	U	Unlocks a document
PF	Alt	V	View your document
PF	Alt	W	Windows, Two
PF	Alt	X	Exits WordPerfect without saving your document
PF	Alt	Y	Yanks back deletion mistakes
PF	Alt	Z	Zaps a page by deleting the page

PF/Alt - A

This macro will quickly display the Appearance Attributes Menu so you can change the appearance of your text.

VMS	Keystroke Action	DOS
PF2,F18	1. U: Press *Macro Define*. C: *Prints* Define Macro: _.	Ctrl-F10
VMS Users	2. U: Press the *PF3 key* and press the *A key*. U: Press the *Alt key* and hold it down while pressing the *A key*. C: *Prints* Description: _.	*DOS Users*
	3. U: Type in <u>Displays Attribute Menu</u> and press the *Enter key*. C: *Prints* Macro Def.	

VMS	Keystroke Action	DOS
PF2,F14	4. U: Press *Font*. C: *Prints* 1 Size; 2 Appearance; 3 Normal; 4 Base Font; 5 Print Color: 0.	Ctrl-F8
	5. U: Press *2* for Appearance attributes. C: *Prints* 1 Bold 2 Undln 3 Dbl Und 4 Italc 5 Outln 6 Shadw 7 Sm Cap 8 Redln 9 Stkout: 0.	
PF2,F18	6. U: Press *Macro Define*. C: *Saves macro*.	Ctrl-F10
F13	7. U: Press *Exit*. C: *Returns to Document*.	F7

The keystrokes that are contained in the "ALTA.WPM" macro are shown on Screens 14-1 or 14-2.

Screen 14-1: VMS Users

```
Macro: Action

        File            ALTA.WPM

        Description     Displays Attribute Menu

        ┌─────────────────────────────────────────┐
        │ {Font}2                                  │
        │                                          │
        │                                          │
        │                                          │
        │                                          │
        │                                          │
        └─────────────────────────────────────────┘
PF2,Prev Scr for macro commands;   Press Exit when done
```

Screen 14-2: DOS Users

```
Macro: Action

       File            ALTA.WPM

       Description     Displays Attribute Menu

      ┌──────────────────────────────────────────────┐
      │ {Font}2                                        │
      │                                                │
      │                                                │
      │                                                │
      │                                                │
      │                                                │
      │                                                │
      └──────────────────────────────────────────────┘

Ctrl-V to Insert next key as command;
Ctrl-PgUp for macro commands;  Press Exit when done
```

PF/Alt - B

This macro will bold the word on which your cursor is currently positioned (the cursor can be on any character in the word).

VMS	Keystroke Action	DOS
PF2,F18	1. U: Press *Macro Define*. C: *Prints* Define Macro: _.	Ctrl-F10
VMS Users	2. U: Press the *PF3 key* and press the *B key*. U: Press the *Alt key* and hold it down while pressing the *B key*. C: *Prints* Description: _.	*DOS Users*
	3. U: Type in <u>Bolds a Word</u> and press the *Enter key*. C: *Prints* Macro Def.	
PF2,Right arrow key	4. U: Press *Word Right*. C: *Positions cursor on the next word to the right of the cursor.*	Ctrl-Right arrow key
PF3,F10 OR F20	5. U: Press *Block*. C: *Displays Format Menu.*	Alt-F4 OR F12
PF2,Left arrow key	6. U: Press *Word Left*. C: *Positions cursor on the next word to the right of the cursor.*	Ctrl-Left arrow key

VMS	**Keystroke Action**	**DOS**

7. U: Press *Left arrow key.*
    C: *Positions cursor one position before the next word.*

F12   8. U: Press *Bold.*   **F6**
    C: *Bolds word.*

PF2,F18   9. U: Press *Macro Define.*   **Ctrl-F10**
    C: *Saves macro.*

The keystrokes that are contained in the "ALTB.WPM" macro are shown on Screen 14-3 or 14-4.

Screen 14-3: VMS Users

```
Macro: Action

        File            ALTB.WPM

        Description     Bolds a Word

    ┌──────────────────────────────────────────────────────────┐
    │ {DISPLAY OFF}{Word Right}{Block}{Word Left}{Left}{Bold}    │
    │                                                            │
    │                                                            │
    │                                                            │
    │                                                            │
    └──────────────────────────────────────────────────────────┘

PF2,Prev Scr for macro commands;  Press Exit when done
```

Screen 14-4: DOS Users

```
Macro: Action

        File            ALTB.WPM

        Description     Bolds a Word

    ┌──────────────────────────────────────────────────────────┐
    │ {DISPLAY OFF}{Word Right}{Block}{Word Left}{Left}{Bold}    │
    │                                                            │
    │                                                            │
    │                                                            │
    │                                                            │
    └──────────────────────────────────────────────────────────┘

Ctrl-V to Insert next key as command;
Ctrl-PgUp for macro commands;  Press Exit when done
```

PF/Alt - C

This macro will copy a paragraph. Place the cursor at the beginning of the paragraph you want to copy before you define this macro.

VMS	Keystroke Action	DOS
PF2,F18	1. U: Press *Macro Define*. C: *Prints* Define macro: _.	Ctrl-F10
VMS Users	2. U: Press the *PF3 key* and press the *C* key. U: Press the *Alt key* and hold it down while pressing the *C* key. C: *Prints* Description: _.	*DOS Users*
	3. U: Type in <u>Copy a paragraph</u> and press the *Enter key*. C: *Prints* Macro Def.	
PF2,F10	4. U: Press *Move*. C: *Prints* Move: 1 Sentence; 2 Paragraph; 3 Page; 4 Retrieve: 0.	Ctrl-F4
	5. U: Press *2* for Paragraph. C: *Prints* 1 Move; 2 Copy; 3 Delete; 4 Append: 0.	
VMS Users	6. U: Press *2* for Copy. C: *Prints* Move cursor; press Return to retrieve. C: *Prints* Move cursor; press Enter to retrieve.	*DOS Users*
PF2,F18	7. U: Press *Macro Define*. C: *Saves macro*.	Ctrl-F10
	8. U: Move cursor to new location and press the *Enter* key. C: *Retrieves paragraph copied*.	

The keystrokes that are contained in the "ALTC.WPM" macro are shown on Screen 14-5 or 14-6.

Screen 14-5: VMS Users

```
Macro: Action

       File              ALTC.WPM

       Description       Copy a paragraph

      ┌─────────────────────────────────────────────────┐
      │ {DISPLAY OFF}{Move}22                            │
      │                                                  │
      │                                                  │
      │                                                  │
      │                                                  │
      │                                                  │
      │                                                  │
      │                                                  │
      └─────────────────────────────────────────────────┘

PF2,Prev Scr for macro commands;   Press Exit when done
```

Screen 14-6: DOS Users

```
Macro: Action

       File              ALTC.WPM

       Description       Copy a paragraph

      ┌─────────────────────────────────────────────────┐
      │ {DISPLAY OFF}{Move}22                            │
      │                                                  │
      │                                                  │
      │                                                  │
      │                                                  │
      │                                                  │
      │                                                  │
      │                                                  │
      └─────────────────────────────────────────────────┘

Ctrl-V to Insert next key as command;
Ctrl-PgUp for macro commands;   Press Exit when done
```

PF/Alt - D

This macro will delete a paragraph. Place the cursor at the beginning of a paragraph you want to delete before you define this macro.

VMS	Keystroke Action	DOS
PF2,F18	1. U: Press *Macro Define*. C: *Prints* Define macro: _.	Ctrl-F10

VMS Users	2. U: Press the *PF3 key* and press the *D key*.
	     U: Press the *Alt key* and hold it down while pressing the *D key*.
	     C: *Prints* Description: _.
		DOS Users

VMS	**Keystroke Action**	**DOS**
	3. U: Type in <u>Deletes a paragraph</u> and press the ***Enter key.*** C: *Prints* Macro Def.	
PF2,F10	4. U: Press ***Move.*** C: *Prints* Move: 1 Sentence; 2 Paragraph; 3 Page; 4 Retrieve: <u>0</u>.	Ctrl-F4
	5. U: Press **2** for Paragraph. C: *Prints* 1 Move; 2 Copy; 3 Delete; 4 Append: <u>0</u>.	
	6. U: Press **3** for Delete. C: *Deletes paragraph and Returns to Document.*	
PF2,F18	7. U: Press ***Macro Define.*** C: *Saves macro.*	Ctrl-F10

The keystrokes that are contained in the "ALTD.WPM" macro are shown on Screen 14-7 or 14-8.

Screen 14-7: VMS Users

```
┌──────────────────────────────────────────────────────────────┐
│ Macro: Action                                                  │
│                                                                │
│         File            ALTD.WPM                               │
│                                                                │
│         Description     Deletes a paragraph                    │
│       ┌──────────────────────────────────────────────────┐    │
│       │ {DISPLAY OFF}{Move}23                            │    │
│       │                                                  │    │
│       │                                                  │    │
│       │                                                  │    │
│       │                                                  │    │
│       │                                                  │    │
│       └──────────────────────────────────────────────────┘    │
│                                                                │
│ PF2,Prev Scr for macro commands;   Press Exit when done        │
└──────────────────────────────────────────────────────────────┘
```

Screen 14-8: DOS Users

```
Macro: Action

        File              ALTD.WPM

        Description       Deletes a paragraph

    ┌─────────────────────────────────────────────┐
    │ {DISPLAY OFF}{Move}23                         │
    │                                               │
    │                                               │
    │                                               │
    │                                               │
    │                                               │
    └─────────────────────────────────────────────┘

Ctrl-V to Insert next key as command;
Ctrl-PgUp for macro commands;  Press Exit when done
```

PF/Alt - E

This macro positions the cursor at the end of the document.

VMS	**Keystroke Action**	**DOS**
PF2,F18	1. U: Press *Macro Define*. C: *Prints* Define macro: _.	Ctrl-F10
VMS Users	2. U: Press the *PF3 key* and press the *E key*. U: Press the *Alt key* and hold it down while pressing the *E key*. C: *Prints* Description: _.	*DOS Users*
	3. U: Type in <u>Moves cursor to end of document</u> and press the *Enter key*. C: *Prints* Macro Def.	
	4. U: Press the *Home, Home,* and *Down arrow keys*. C: *Positions cursor at end of Document*.	
PF2,F18	5. U: Press *Macro Define*. C: *Saves macro*.	Ctrl-F10

The keystrokes that are contained in the "ALTE.WPM" macro are shown on Screen 14-9 or 14-10.

Screen 14-9: VMS Users

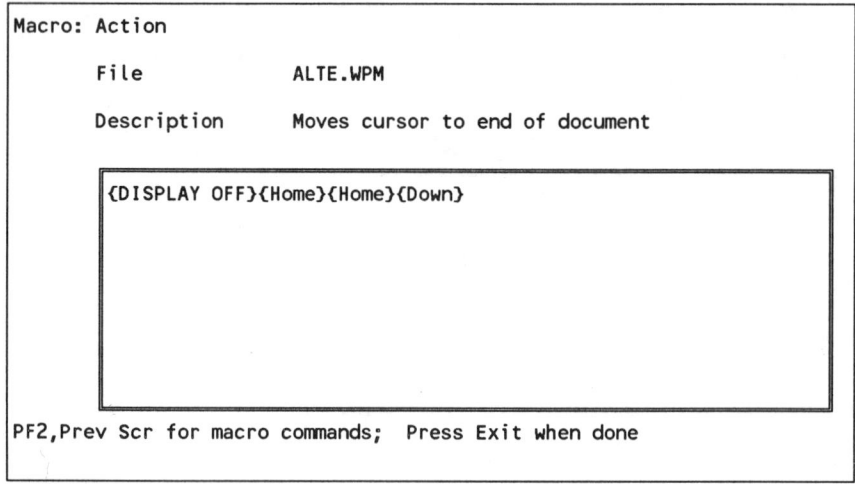

```
Macro: Action

     File           ALTE.WPM

     Description    Moves cursor to end of document

     ┌──────────────────────────────────────────────────────┐
     │{DISPLAY OFF}{Home}{Home}{Down}                       │
     │                                                      │
     │                                                      │
     │                                                      │
     │                                                      │
     │                                                      │
     │                                                      │
     └──────────────────────────────────────────────────────┘

PF2,Prev Scr for macro commands;  Press Exit when done
```

Screen 14-10:   DOS Users

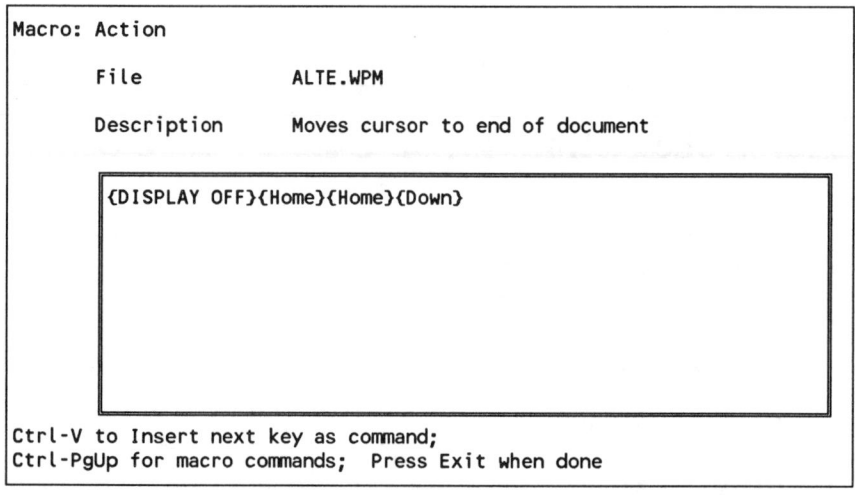

```
Macro: Action

     File           ALTE.WPM

     Description    Moves cursor to end of document

     ┌──────────────────────────────────────────────────────┐
     │{DISPLAY OFF}{Home}{Home}{Down}                       │
     │                                                      │
     │                                                      │
     │                                                      │
     │                                                      │
     │                                                      │
     └──────────────────────────────────────────────────────┘

Ctrl-V to Insert next key as command;
Ctrl-PgUp for macro commands;  Press Exit when done
```

PF/Alt - F

This macro will display the Base Font Directory.

VMS	Keystroke Action	DOS
PF2,F18	1. U: Press *Macro Define*. C: *Prints* Define macro: _.	Ctrl-F10

VMS Users	2. U: Press the *PF3 key* and press the *F key*.
	    U: Press the *Alt key* and hold it down while pressing the *F key*.
	    C: *Prints* Description: _.
		DOS Users

VMS	**Keystroke Action**	**DOS**

3. U: Type in <u>Displays base font directory</u> and
        press the ***Enter key***.
    C: *Prints* Macro Def.

PF2,F14   4.   U: Press ***Font***.   **Ctrl-F8**
                                     C: *Prints* 1 Size; 2 Appearance; 3 Normal;
                                           4 Base Font; 5 Print Color: <u>0</u>.

5. U: Press *4* for Base Font.
    C: *Displays Base Font Menu.*

PF2,F18   6.   U: Press ***Macro Define***.   **Ctrl-F10**
                                           C: *Saves macro.*

F13   7.   U: Press ***Exit***.   **F7**
                                           C: *Returns to Document.*

The keystrokes that are contained in the "ALTF.WPM" macro are shown on
Screen 14-11 or 14-12.

Screen 14-11:   ***VMS Users***

```
┌───────────────────────────────────────────────────────────────┐
│ Macro: Action                                                  │
│                                                                │
│         File          ALTF.WPM                                 │
│                                                                │
│         Description   Displays base font directory             │
│                                                                │
│      ┌─────────────────────────────────────────────────────┐  │
│      │ {Font}4                                              │  │
│      │                                                      │  │
│      │                                                      │  │
│      │                                                      │  │
│      │                                                      │  │
│      │                                                      │  │
│      └─────────────────────────────────────────────────────┘  │
│                                                                │
│ PF2,Prev Scr for macro commands;  Press Exit when done         │
│                                                                │
└───────────────────────────────────────────────────────────────┘
```

Screen 14-12:   DOS Users

```
Macro: Action

       File          ALTF.WPM

       Description   Displays base font directory

      ┌─────────────────────────────────────────────┐
      │ {Font}4                                      │
      │                                              │
      │                                              │
      │                                              │
      │                                              │
      │                                              │
      │                                              │
      └─────────────────────────────────────────────┘

Ctrl-V to Insert next key as command;
Ctrl-PgUp for macro commands;   Press Exit when done
```

PF/Alt - G

This macro will use the VMS/DOS shell feature of WordPerfect 5.1.

VMS	Keystroke Action	DOS
PF2,F18	1. U: Press **Macro Define**. C: *Prints* Define macro: _.	Ctrl-F10
VMS Users	2. U: Press the **PF3 key** and press the **G key**. U: Press the **Alt key** and hold it down while pressing the **G key**. C: *Prints* Description: _.	*DOS Users*
VMS Users	3. U: Type in <u>Go to VMS shell</u> and press the **Enter key**. U: Type in <u>Go to DOS shell</u> and press the **Enter key**. C: *Prints* Macro Def.	*DOS Users*
PF2,F7 *VMS Users*	4. U: Press **Shell**. C: *Prints* DCL: 1 Go to; 2 Command; 3 Command (Without pause); Clipboard: 4 Save; 5 Append; 6 Retrieve: <u>0</u>. C: *Prints* 1 Go to DOS; 2 DOS Command: <u>0</u>.	Ctrl-F1 *DOS Users*

VMS	**Keystroke Action**	**DOS**

VMS Users	5. U: Press *1* for Go to.	
	U: Press *1* for Go to DOS.	*DOS Users*
VMS Users	C: *Goes to VMS shell and displays the VMS shell prompt (WPCORP_$).*	
	C: *Goes to DOS shell and displays the DOS shell prompt (C:\WP51).*	*DOS Users*
VMS Users	6. U: Type in <u>logout</u> and press the ***Enter key*** to return to WordPerfect.	
	U: Type in <u>exit</u> and press the ***Enter key*** to return to WordPerfect.	*DOS Users*
	C: *Returns to WordPerfect.*	
PF2,F18	7. U: Press **Macro Define**.	Ctrl-F10
	C: *Saves macro.*	

The keystrokes that are contained in the "ALTG.WPM" macro are shown on Screen 14-13 or 14-14.

Screen 14-13:   VMS Users

```
Macro: Action

     File           ALTG.WPM

     Description    Go to VMS shell

     ┌─────────────────────────────────────────────────┐
     │ {DISPLAY OFF}{Shell}1                           │
     │                                                 │
     │                                                 │
     │                                                 │
     │                                                 │
     │                                                 │
     └─────────────────────────────────────────────────┘

PF2,Prev Scr for macro commands;  Press Exit when done
```

Screen 14-14:   **DOS Users**

```
Macro: Action

      File            ALTG.WPM

      Description     Go to DOS shell

   ┌──────────────────────────────────────────────┐
   │ {DISPLAY OFF}{Shell}1                          │
   │                                                │
   │                                                │
   │                                                │
   │                                                │
   │                                                │
   │                                                │
   │                                                │
   └──────────────────────────────────────────────┘

Ctrl-V to Insert next key as command;
Ctrl-PgUp for macro commands;  Press Exit when done
```

PF/Alt - H

This macro will display WordPerfect 5.1's Header A Menu.

VMS	Keystroke Action	DOS
PF2,F18	1. U: Press *Macro Define*. C: *Prints* Define macro: _.	Ctrl-F10
VMS Users	2. U: Press the *PF3 key* and press the *H key*. U: Press the *Alt key* and hold it down while pressing the *H key*. C: *Prints* Description: _.	*DOS Users*
	3. U: Type in <u>Displays Header A Menu</u> and press the *Enter key.* C: *Prints* Macro Def.	
PF1,F14	4. U: Press *Format*. C: *Displays Format Menu.*	Shift-F8
	5. U: Press *2* for Page. C: *Displays Format: Page Menu.*	
	6. U: Press *3* for Headers. C: *Prints* 1 Header A; 2 Header B: <u>0</u>.	
	7. U: Press *1* for Header A. C: *Prints* 1 Discontinue; 2 Every Page; 3 Odd Pages; 4 Even Pages; 5 Edit: <u>0</u>.	

VMS	**Keystroke Action**	**DOS**
PF2,F18	8. U: Press **Macro Define**. C: *Saves macro.*	Ctrl-F10
F13	9. U: Press **Exit**. C: *Returns to Document.*	F7

The keystrokes that are contained in the "ALTH.WPM" macro are shown on Screen 14-15 or 14-16.

Screen 14-15:   *VMS Users*

```
Macro: Action

     File            ALTH.WPM

     Description     Displays Header A Menu

     ┌─────────────────────────────────────────────┐
     │ {Format}231                                 │
     │                                             │
     │                                             │
     │                                             │
     │                                             │
     │                                             │
     └─────────────────────────────────────────────┘

PF2,Prev Scr for macro commands;  Press Exit when done
```

Screen 14-16:   *DOS Users*

```
Macro: Action

     File            ALTH.WPM

     Description     Displays Header A Menu

     ┌─────────────────────────────────────────────┐
     │ {Format}231                                 │
     │                                             │
     │                                             │
     │                                             │
     │                                             │
     │                                             │
     └─────────────────────────────────────────────┘

Ctrl-V to Insert next key as command;
Ctrl-PgUp for macro commands;  Press Exit when done
```

PF/Alt - I

This macro will insert the current date into your document. In order for this macro to work you must set the current date initially on your computer.

VMS	Keystroke Action	DOS
PF2,F18	1. U: Press *Macro Define*. C: *Prints* Define macro: _.	Ctrl-F10
VMS Users	2. U: Press the *PF3 key* and press the *I key*. U: Press the *Alt key* and hold it down while pressing the *I key*. C: *Prints* Description: _.	*DOS Users*
	3. U: Type in <u>Inserts current date into document</u> and press the *Enter* key. C: *Prints* Macro Def.	
PF1,F11	4. U: Press *Date/Outline*. C: *Prints* 1 Date Text; 2 Date Code; 3 Date Format; 4 Outline; 5 Para Num; 6 Define: <u>0</u>.	Shift-F5
	5. U: Press *1* for Date Text. C: *Inserts Current Date into Document.*	
PF2,F18	6. U: Press *Macro Define*. C: *Saves macro.*	Ctrl-F10

The keystrokes that are contained in the "ALTI.WPM" macro are shown on Screen 14-17 or 14-18.

Screen 14-17:   VMS Users

```
Macro: Action

        File              ALTI.WPM

        Description       Inserts current date into document

   ┌──────────────────────────────────────────────────────────┐
   │ {DISPLAY OFF}{Date/Outline}1                              │
   │                                                          │
   │                                                          │
   │                                                          │
   │                                                          │
   │                                                          │
   │                                                          │
   │                                                          │
   └──────────────────────────────────────────────────────────┘

PF2,Prev Scr for macro commands;   Press Exit when done
```

Screen 14-18:   DOS Users

```
Macro: Action

        File              ALTI.WPM

        Description       Inserts current date into document

   ┌──────────────────────────────────────────────────────────┐
   │ {DISPLAY OFF}{Date/Outline}1                              │
   │                                                          │
   │                                                          │
   │                                                          │
   │                                                          │
   │                                                          │
   │                                                          │
   └──────────────────────────────────────────────────────────┘

Ctrl-V to Insert next key as command;
Ctrl-PgUp for macro commands;   Press Exit when done
```

PF/Alt - J

This macro will join two normally separated words with a hard space. Thus, these two words will never be separated onto two different lines. Place cursor between two words and create the macro. These two words must only be separated by one space. When you invoke it also place the cursor between two words so it works properly.

VMS	Keystroke Action	DOS
PF2,F18	1. U: Press *Macro Define*. C: *Prints* Define macro: _.	Ctrl-F10

VMS	Keystroke Action	DOS
VMS Users	2. U: Press the *PF3 key* and press the *J key*.	
	U: Press the *Alt key* and hold it down while pressing the *J key*.	*DOS Users*
	C: *Prints* Description: _.	
	3. U: Type in <u>Joins words</u> and press the *Enter key*.	
	C: *Prints* Macro Def.	
	4. U: Press the *Delete key* to delete current normal space.	
	C: *Deletes space*.	
PF4	5. U: Press *Home* and *space bar*.	
	C: *Inserts hard space between words*.	
PF2,F18	6. U: Press *Macro Define*.	Ctrl-F10
	C: *Saves macro*.	

The keystrokes that are contained in the "ALTJ.WPM" macro are shown on Screen 14-19 or 14-20.

Screen 14-19:   *VMS Users*

```
Macro: Action

      File            ALTJ.WPM

      Description     Joins words

      ┌─────────────────────────────────────────────┐
      │ {DISPLAY OFF}{Del}{Home}•                    │
      │                                              │
      │                                              │
      │                                              │
      │                                              │
      │                                              │
      │                                              │
      └─────────────────────────────────────────────┘

PF2,Prev Scr for macro commands;  Press Exit when done
```

Screen 14-20:   DOS Users

```
Macro: Action

     File          ALTJ.WPM

     Description   Joins words

    ┌─────────────────────────────────────────────────┐
    │ {DISPLAY OFF}{Del}{Home}•                        │
    │                                                  │
    │                                                  │
    │                                                  │
    │                                                  │
    │                                                  │
    │                                                  │
    └─────────────────────────────────────────────────┘

Ctrl-V to Insert next key as command;
Ctrl-PgUp for macro commands;  Press Exit when done
```

PF/Alt - K

This macro will display the Keyboard Layout Menu.

VMS		Keystroke Action	DOS
PF2,F18	1.	U: Press *Macro Define*. C: *Prints* Define macro: _.	Ctrl-F10
VMS Users	2.	U: Press the *PF3 key* and press the *K key*. U: Press the *Alt key* and hold it down while pressing the *K key*. C: *Prints* Description: _.	*DOS Users*
	3.	U: Type in <u>Keyboard Layout Menu displayed</u> and press the *Enter key*. C: *Prints* Macro Def.	
PF1,F7	4.	U: Press *Setup*. C: *Displays Setup Menu.*	Shift-F1
	5.	U: Press *5* for Keyboard Layout. C: *Displays Setup: Keyboard Layout Menu.*	
PF2,F18	6.	U: Press *Macro Define*. C: *Saves macro.*	Ctrl-F10

The keystrokes that are contained in the "ALTK.WPM" macro are shown on Screen 14-21 or 14-22.

Screen 14-21:   VMS Users

```
Macro: Action

        File           ALTK.WPM

        Description    Keyboard Layout Menu displayed

        ┌─────────────────────────────────────────────────┐
        │ {Setup}5                                         │
        │                                                  │
        │                                                  │
        │                                                  │
        │                                                  │
        │                                                  │
        │                                                  │
        │                                                  │
        └─────────────────────────────────────────────────┘

PF2,Prev Scr for macro commands;   Press Exit when done
```

Screen 14-22:   DOS Users

```
Macro: Action

        File           ALTK.WPM

        Description    Keyboard Layout Menu displayed

        ┌─────────────────────────────────────────────────┐
        │ {Setup}5                                         │
        │                                                  │
        │                                                  │
        │                                                  │
        │                                                  │
        │                                                  │
        │                                                  │
        │                                                  │
        └─────────────────────────────────────────────────┘

Ctrl-V to Insert next key as command;
Ctrl-PgUp for macro commands;   Press Exit when done
```

PF/Alt - L

This macro will lock a document after you define or invoke the macro and save the document. Locking means that a password will be saved with the document and every time you want to retrieve, print, look, etc. at that document you must enter the correct password you had typed in for the document. This feature offers security for your files. Whenever you invoke this macro it will prompt you for a password to assign to your document and prompt you also to Re-Enter the password for verification, thus you can enter different passwords into all of your documents.

VMS	Keystroke Action	DOS
PF2,F18	1. U: Press *Macro Define*. C: *Prints* Define macro: _.	Ctrl-F10

VMS	**Keystroke Action**	**DOS**

VMS Users
2. U: Press the *PF3 key* and press the *L key*.
   U: Press the *Alt key* and hold it down while pressing the *L key*.   *DOS Users*
   C: *Prints* Description: _.

3. U: Type in <u>Lock a document</u> and press the *Enter* key.
   C: *Prints* Macro Def.

PF2,F11
VMS Users
4. U: Press *Text In/Out*.   Ctrl-F5
   C: *Prints* 1 ASCII Text; 2 Password; 3 Save As; 4 Comment; 5 Spreadsheet; 6 Read Only: <u>0</u>.
   C: *Prints* 1 DOS Text; 2 Password; 3 Save As;   *DOS Users*
   4 Comment; 5 Spreadsheet: <u>0</u>.

5. U: Press *2* for Password.
   C: *Prints* Password: 1 Add/Change; 2 Remove: <u>0</u>.

6. U: Press *1* for Add/Change.
   C: *Prints* Enter Password: _.

7. U: Type *password* where password is some password you would like to use and press the *Enter key.* Passwords can contain a maximum of 24 characters and can include any character in the WordPerfect character sets. (See WordPerfect Reference Manual.)
   C: *Prints* Re-Enter Password: _.

8. U: Type in *password* again to verify that you can type it in correctly twice.
   C: *Inserts password into your document. You must save your document to keep password in your document.*

PF2,F18
9. U: Press *Macro Define*.   Ctrl-F10
   C: *Saves macro.*

The keystrokes that are contained in the "ALTL.WPM" macro are shown on Screen 14-23 or 14-24.

Screen 14-23:   *VMS Users*

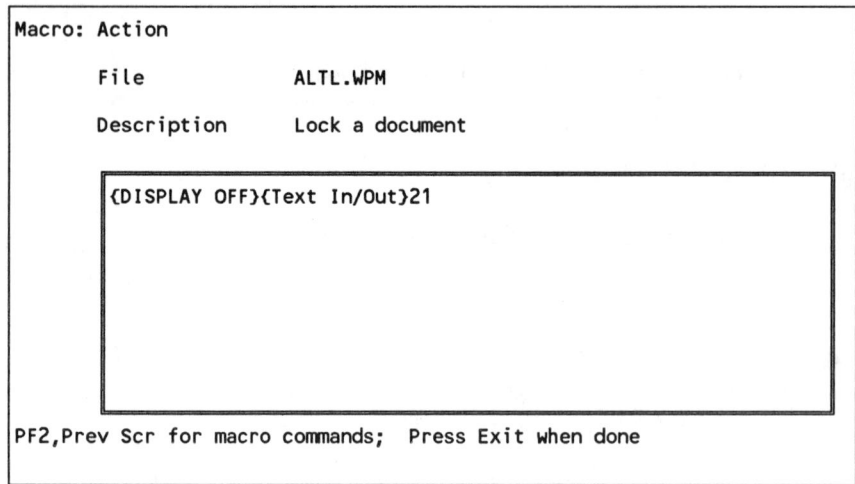

```
Macro: Action

       File            ALTL.WPM

       Description     Lock a document


       ┌─────────────────────────────────────────────────────────┐
       │ {DISPLAY OFF}{Text In/Out}21                             │
       │                                                         │
       │                                                         │
       │                                                         │
       │                                                         │
       │                                                         │
       └─────────────────────────────────────────────────────────┘

PF2,Prev Scr for macro commands;   Press Exit when done
```

Screen 14-24:   *DOS Users*

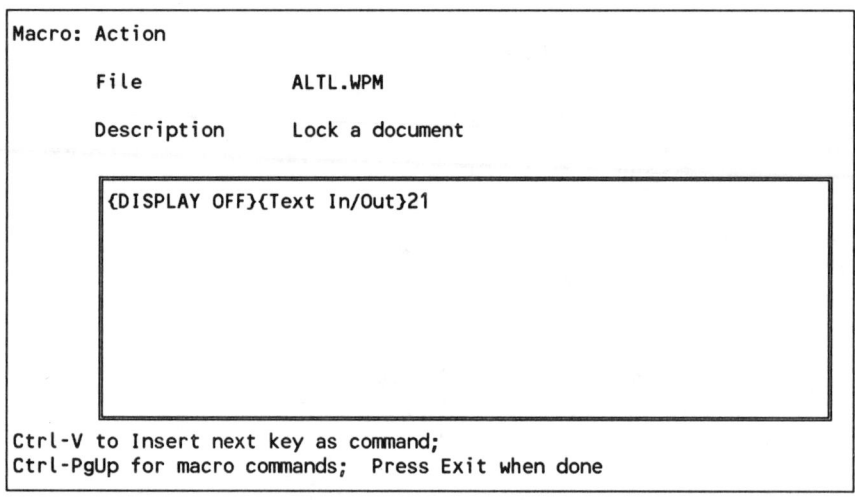

```
Macro: Action

       File            ALTL.WPM

       Description     Lock a document


       ┌─────────────────────────────────────────────────────────┐
       │ {DISPLAY OFF}{Text In/Out}21                             │
       │                                                         │
       │                                                         │
       │                                                         │
       │                                                         │
       │                                                         │
       └─────────────────────────────────────────────────────────┘

Ctrl-V to Insert next key as command;
Ctrl-PgUp for macro commands;   Press Exit when done
```

PF/Alt - M

This macro will move a paragraph.

VMS	Keystroke Action	DOS
PF2,F18	1. U: Press *Macro Define*. C: *Prints* Define macro: _.	Ctrl-F10

VMS Users	2. U: Press the *PF3 key* and press the *M key*.
	     U: Press the *Alt key* and hold it down while pressing the *M key*.
	     C: *Prints* Description: _.
		DOS Users

VMS	Keystroke Action	DOS

	3. U: Type in <u>Move a paragraph</u> and press the ***Enter key.***	
	C: *Prints* Macro Def.	
PF2,F10	4. U: Press ***Move.***	Ctrl-F4
	C: *Prints* Move: 1 Sentence; 2 Paragraph; 3 Page; 4 Retrieve: <u>0</u>.	
	5. U: Press ***2*** for Paragraph.	
	C: *Prints* 1 Move; 2 Copy; 3 Delete; 4 Append: <u>0</u>.	
	6. U: Press ***1*** for Move.	
VMS Users	C: *Prints* Move cursor; press Return to retrieve.	
	C: *Prints* Move cursor; press Enter to retrieve.	***DOS Users***
PF2,F18	7. U: Press ***Macro Define.***	Ctrl-F10
	C: *Saves macro.*	
	8. U: Move cursor and press the ***Enter key.*** The step was not included in the macro because you will want to retrieve the paragraph into different locations for every document.	
	C: *Retrieves paragraph.*	

The keystrokes that are contained in the "ALTM.WPM" macro are shown on Screen 14-25 or 14-26.

Screen 14-25:   VMS Users

```
Macro: Action

      File           ALTM.WPM

      Description    Move a paragraph

    ┌──────────────────────────────────────────────┐
    │ {DISPLAY OFF}{Move}21                         │
    │                                               │
    │                                               │
    │                                               │
    │                                               │
    │                                               │
    └──────────────────────────────────────────────┘

PF2,Prev Scr for macro commands;   Press Exit when done
```

Screen 14-26:   DOS Users

```
Macro: Action

      File          ALTM.WPM

      Description   Move a paragraph


   ┌────────────────────────────────────────────────────┐
   │ {DISPLAY OFF}{Move}21                               │
   │                                                     │
   │                                                     │
   │                                                     │
   │                                                     │
   │                                                     │
   │                                                     │
   └────────────────────────────────────────────────────┘

Ctrl-V to Insert next key as command;
Ctrl-PgUp for macro commands;   Press Exit when done
```

PF/Alt - N

This macro defines consecutive numbering of pages for your document. Invoke this macro at the top of the document. To see the page numbers you must either View or Print your document.

VMS	Keystroke Action	DOS
PF2,F18	1. U: Press *Macro Define*. C: *Prints* Define macro: _.	Ctrl-F10
VMS Users	2. U: Press the *PF3 key* and press the *N key*. U: Press the *Alt key* and hold it down while pressing the *N key*. C: *Prints* Description: _.	*DOS Users*
	3. U: Type in <u>Numbers pages</u> and press the *Enter key.* C: *Prints* Macro Def.	
PF1,F14	4. U: Press *Format*. C: *Displays Format Menu.*	Shift-F8
	5. U: Press *2* for Page Menu. C: *Displays Format: Page Menu.*	
	6. U: Press *6* for Page Numbering. C: *Displays Format: Page Numbering Menu.*	

VMS	**Keystroke Action**	**DOS**

7. U: Press *4* for Page Number Position.
    C: *Displays Format: Page Number Position Menu.*

8. U: Press *6* for Every Page Bottom Center Position for all page numbers.
    C: *Prints* Bottom Center *to right of Page Number Position.*

F13	9. U: Press *Exit*. C: *Returns to Document.*	F7
PF2,F18	10. U: Press *Macro Define*. C: *Saves macro.*	Ctrl-F10

The keystrokes that are contained in the "ALTN.WPM" macro are shown on Screen 14-27 or 14-28.

Screen 14-27:   VMS Users

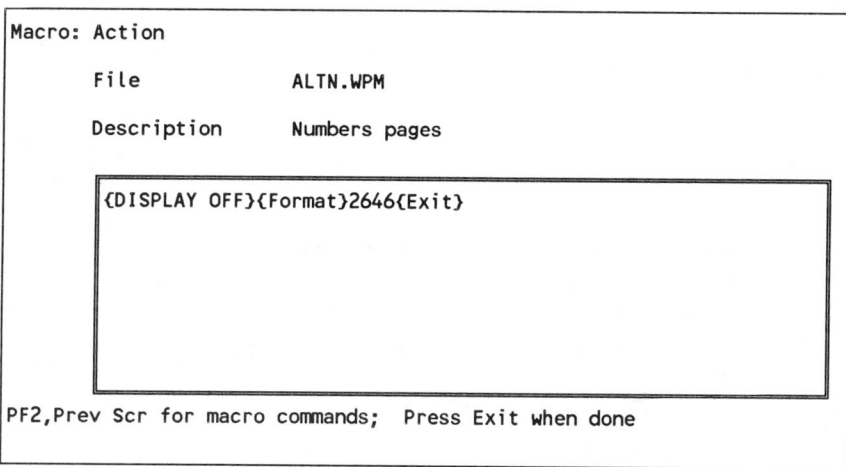

```
Macro: Action

        File            ALTN.WPM

        Description     Numbers pages

        ┌──────────────────────────────────────────────────┐
        │ {DISPLAY OFF}{Format}2646{Exit}                  │
        │                                                  │
        │                                                  │
        │                                                  │
        │                                                  │
        │                                                  │
        └──────────────────────────────────────────────────┘

PF2,Prev Scr for macro commands;   Press Exit when done
```

Screen 14-28: *DOS Users*

```
Macro: Action

       File            ALTN.WPM

       Description     Numbers pages

    ┌──────────────────────────────────────────────────┐
    │ {DISPLAY OFF}{Format}2646{Exit}                  │
    │                                                  │
    │                                                  │
    │                                                  │
    │                                                  │
    │                                                  │
    └──────────────────────────────────────────────────┘

Ctrl-V to Insert next key as command;
Ctrl-PgUp for macro commands;  Press Exit when done
```

PF/Alt - O

This macro changes your two window screens back into one normal window. Define the Alt-W macro first to set up the two windows on your screen. The window feature or two document editing screen must be active before this macro is defined.

VMS	Keystroke Action	DOS
PF2,F18	1. U: Press *Macro Define*. C: *Prints* Define macro: _.	Ctrl-F10
VMS Users	2. U: Press the *PF3 key* and press the *O key*. U: Press the *Alt key* and hold it down while pressing the *O key*. C: *Prints* Description: _.	*DOS Users*
	3. U: Type in <u>One window</u> and press the *Enter key*. C: *Prints* Macro Def.	
PF2,F9 *VMS Users*	4. U: Press *Screen*. C: *Prints* 1 Window; 2 Line Draw; 3 Rewrite; 4 Screen Size: <u>3</u>. C: *Prints* 1 Window; 2 Line Draw; 3 Rewrite: <u>3</u>.	Ctrl-F3 *DOS Users*
	5. U: Press *1* for Window. C: *Prints* Number of lines in this window: <u>12</u>.	

VMS	Keystroke Action	DOS

	6.	U: Press *0* for zero lines and press the *Enter key*. C: *Returns to Original Document with Full Screen Editing Features.*	
PF2,F18	7.	U: Press *Macro Define*. C: *Saves macro.*	Ctrl-F10

The keystrokes that are contained in the "ALTO.WPM" macro are shown on Screen 14-29 or 14-30.

Screen 14-29: **VMS Users**

```
Macro: Action

    File           ALTO.WPM

    Description    One window

    ┌─────────────────────────────────────────────────────┐
    │ {DISPLAY OFF}{Screen}10{Enter}                      │
    │                                                     │
    │                                                     │
    │                                                     │
    │                                                     │
    │                                                     │
    │                                                     │
    └─────────────────────────────────────────────────────┘

PF2,Prev Scr for macro commands;  Press Exit when done
```

Screen 14-30: **DOS Users**

```
Macro: Action

    File           ALTO.WPM

    Description    One window

    ┌─────────────────────────────────────────────────────┐
    │ {DISPLAY OFF}{Screen}10{Enter}                      │
    │                                                     │
    │                                                     │
    │                                                     │
    │                                                     │
    │                                                     │
    └─────────────────────────────────────────────────────┘

Ctrl-V to Insert next key as command;
Ctrl-PgUp for macro commands;  Press Exit when done
```

PF/Alt - P

This macro spell checks, saves, and prints a named file (where a named file is a document that has been previously saved). Before this macro is defined make sure that the file shown on your screen is a previously saved file. Also, verify that a printer has been selected.

VMS	Keystroke Action	DOS
PF2,F18	1. U: Press *Macro Define*. C: *Prints* Define macro: _.	Ctrl-F10
VMS Users	2. U: Press the *PF3 key* and press the *P key*. U: Press the *Alt key* and hold it down while pressing the *P key*. C: *Prints* Description: _.	*DOS Users*
	3. U: Type in Spell, Save, Print and press the *Enter key*. C: *Prints* Macro Def.	
PF2,F8	4. U: Press *Spell*. C: *Prints* Check: 1 Word; 2 Page; 3 Document; 4 New Sup. Dictionary; 5 Look Up; 6 Count: 0.	Ctrl-F2
	5. U: Press *3* for Document. C: *Spell checks Document and then Prints* Word count: x Press any key to continue. *Where x is some number.*	
	6. U: Press *space bar*. C: *Returns to Document.*	
F18 *VMS Users*	7. U: Press *Save* and the *Enter key*. C: *Prints* Saving *file specification and then Returns to Document.* C: *Prints* Replace *pathname?* No (Yes).	F10 *DOS Users*

VMS Users: *Do NOT perform Keystroke Action 8. Continue with Keystroke Action 9.*

DOS Users: *Perform Keystroke Action 8.*

VMS	Keystroke Action	DOS
	8. U: Press *Y* for Yes C: *Prints* Saving *pathname and then Returns to Document.*	

VMS Users:　　*Perform the following Keystroke Actions.*

DOS Users:　　*Perform the following Keystroke Actions.*

VMS	**Keystroke Action**	**DOS**
PF1,F13	9.　U: Press ***Print.*** 　　C: *Displays Print Menu.*	Shift-F7
	10.　U: Press *1* for Full Document. 　　　C: *Prints Document and Returns to Document.*	
PF2,F18	11.　U: Press ***Macro Define.*** 　　　C: *Saves macro.*	Ctrl-F10

The keystrokes that are contained in the "ALTP.WPM" macro are shown on Screen 14-31 or Screen 14-32.

Screen 14-31:　　VMS Users

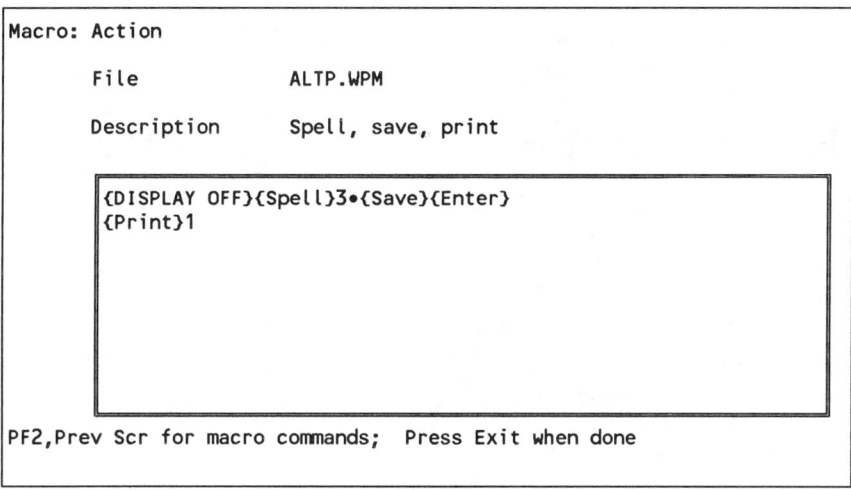

```
Macro: Action

        File           ALTP.WPM

        Description    Spell, save, print

     ┌─────────────────────────────────────────────────┐
     │ {DISPLAY OFF}{Spell}3•{Save}{Enter}              │
     │ {Print}1                                         │
     │                                                  │
     │                                                  │
     │                                                  │
     │                                                  │
     │                                                  │
     │                                                  │
     └─────────────────────────────────────────────────┘

PF2,Prev Scr for macro commands;   Press Exit when done
```

Screen 14-32: **DOS Users**

```
Macro: Action

       File           ALTP.WPM

       Description    Spell, save, print


   {DISPLAY OFF}{Spell}3•{Save}{Enter}
   y{Print}1




Ctrl-V to Insert next key as command;
Ctrl-PgUp for macro commands;  Press Exit when done
```

PF/Alt - Q

This macro quits WordPerfect and saves a named file (where a named file is a document that has been previously saved). Before this macro is defined make sure that the file shown on your screen is a previously saved file.

VMS	Keystroke Action		DOS
PF2,F18	1.	U: Press **Macro Define**. C: *Prints* Define macro: _.	Ctrl-F10
VMS Users	2.	U: Press the **PF3 key** and press the **Q key**. U: Press the **Alt key** and hold it down while pressing the **Q key**. C: *Prints* Description: _.	*DOS Users*
	3.	U: Type in <u>Saves named file - Quits WordPerfect</u> and press the **Enter key**. C: *Prints* Macro Def.	
F13	4.	U: Press **Exit**. C: *Prints* Save Document? <u>Y</u>es (No).	F7
VMS Users	5.	U: Press **Y** for Yes and press the **Enter key**. C: *Prints* Document to be saved: *File Specification*. C: *Prints* Replace *pathname?* <u>N</u>o (Yes).	*DOS Users*
VMS Users	6.	U: Press the **Enter key**. U: Press **Y** for Yes. C: *Prints* Exit WP? <u>N</u>o (Yes).	*DOS Users*

VMS	**Keystroke Action**	**DOS**

7.　U: Press *Y* for Yes.
　　C: *Exits WordPerfect.*

The keystrokes that are contained in the "ALTQ.WPM" macro are shown on Screen 14-33 or 14-34.

Screen 14-33:　VMS Users

```
Macro: Action

     File           ALTQ.WPM

     Description    Saves named file - Quits WordPerfect

    ┌─────────────────────────────────────────────────┐
    │ {Exit}y{Enter}                                  │
    │ y                                               │
    │                                                 │
    │                                                 │
    │                                                 │
    │                                                 │
    └─────────────────────────────────────────────────┘
PF2,Prev Scr for macro commands;   Press Exit when done
```

Screen 14-34:　DOS Users

```
Macro: Action

     File           ALTQ.WPM

     Description    Saves named file - Quits WordPerfect

    ┌─────────────────────────────────────────────────┐
    │ {Exit}y{Enter}                                  │
    │ yy                                              │
    │                                                 │
    │                                                 │
    │                                                 │
    └─────────────────────────────────────────────────┘
Ctrl-V to Insert next key as command;
Ctrl-PgUp for macro commands;   Press Exit when done
```

PF/Alt - R

This macro reports the printer status by displaying the Print: Control Printer Menu.

VMS	Keystroke Action	DOS
PF2,F18	1. U: Press *Macro Define*. C: *Prints* Define macro: _.	Ctrl-F10
VMS Users	2. U: Press the *PF3 key* and press the *R key*. U: Press the *Alt key* and hold it down while pressing the *R key*. C: *Prints* Description: _.	*DOS Users*
	3. U: Type in <u>Reports printer status</u> and press the *Enter key*. C: *Prints* Macro Def.	
PF1,F13	4. U: Press *Print*. C: *Displays Print Menu*.	Shift-F7
	5. U: Press *4* for Control Printer. C: *Displays Print: Control Printer Menu*.	
PF2,F18	6. U: Press *Macro Define*. C: *Saves macro*.	Ctrl-F10
F13	7. U: Press *Exit*. C: *Returns to Document*.	F7

The keystrokes that are contained in the "ALTR.WPM" macro are shown on Screen 14-35 or 14-36.

Screen 14-35: *VMS Users*

```
Macro: Action

      File          ALTR.WPM

      Description   Reports printer status

      ┌─────────────────────────────────────────────┐
      │{Print}4                                       │
      │                                               │
      │                                               │
      │                                               │
      │                                               │
      │                                               │
      │                                               │
      └─────────────────────────────────────────────┘

PF2,Prev Scr for macro commands;  Press Exit when done
```

Screen 14-36: *DOS Users*

```
Macro: Action

      File            ALTR.WPM

      Description     Reports printer status

      ┌──────────────────────────────────────────────┐
      │ {Print}4                                       │
      │                                                │
      │                                                │
      │                                                │
      │                                                │
      │                                                │
      │                                                │
      └──────────────────────────────────────────────┘

Ctrl-V to Insert next key as command;
Ctrl-PgUp for macro commands;  Press Exit when done
```

PF/Alt - S

This macro saves, spell checks, and saves a named file again (where a named file is a document previously saved). Before this macro is defined make sure that the file shown on your screen is a previously saved file.

VMS		**Keystroke Action**	**DOS**
PF2,F18	1.	U: Press *Macro Define*. C: *Prints* Define macro: _.	Ctrl-F10
VMS Users	2.	U: Press the *PF3 key* and press the *S key*. U: Press the *Alt key* and hold it down while pressing the *S key*. C: *Prints* Description: _.	*DOS Users*
	3.	U: Type in <u>Spell checks and saves a named file</u> and press the *Enter key*. C: *Prints* Macro Def.	
F18 *VMS Users*	4.	U: Press *Save* and the *Enter key*. C: *Saves file and Returns to Document.* C: *Prints* Replace *file specification/pathname?* <u>N</u>o (Yes).	F10 *DOS Users*

VMS Users: **Do NOT perform the following Keystroke Action 5. Continue with Keystroke Action 6.**

DOS Users: **Perform Keystroke Action 5.**

VMS	**Keystroke Action**	**DOS**

> 5.   U: Press *Y* for Yes.
>   C: *Saves file and Returns to Document.*

VMS Users: *Perform the following Keystroke Actions.*

DOS Users: *Perform the following Keystroke Actions.*

VMS	**Keystroke Action**	**DOS**

PF2,F8

> 6.   U: Press *Spell.*
>   C: *Prints* Check: 1 Word; 2 Page;
>   3 Document; 4 New Sup. Dictionary;
>   5 Look Up; 6 Count: <u>0</u>.

Ctrl-F2

> 7.   U: Press *3* for Document.
>   C: *Spell checks Document and then prints*
>   Word count: *x* Press any key to continue.
>   *Where x is some number.*

VMS Users: *Spell check your document.*

DOS Users: *Spell check your document.*

VMS	**Keystroke Action**	**DOS**

> 8.   U: Press *space bar.*
>   C: *Returns to Document.*

F18
VMS Users

> 9.   U: Press *Save* and the *Enter key.*
>   C: *Saves file and Returns to Document.*
>   C: *Prints* Replace *file specification/pathname?*
>   <u>N</u>o (Yes).

F10

DOS Users

VMS Users: *Do NOT perform the following Keystroke Action 10. Continue with Keystroke*
            Action 11.

DOS Users: *Perform Keystroke Action 10.*

VMS	**Keystroke Action**	**DOS**

> 10. U: Press *Y* for Yes.
>   C: *Saves file and Returns to Document.*

VMS Users: *Perform the following Keystroke Action.*

DOS Users: *Perform the following Keystroke Action.*

VMS   Keystroke Action   DOS

PF2,F18   11. U: Press *Macro Define*.   Ctrl-F10
                     C: *Saves macro.*

    The keystrokes that are contained in the "ALTS.WPM" macro are shown on
Screen 14-37 or 14-38.

Screen 14-37:   *VMS Users*

```
Macro: Action

        File          ALTS.WPM

        Description   Spell checks and saves a named file

        ┌─────────────────────────────────────────────────┐
        │{DISPLAY OFF}{Save}{Enter}                       │
        │{Spell}3•{Save}{Enter}                           │
        │                                                 │
        │                                                 │
        │                                                 │
        │                                                 │
        │                                                 │
        │                                                 │
        └─────────────────────────────────────────────────┘

PF2,Prev Scr for macro commands;   Press Exit when done
```

Screen 14-38:   *DOS Users*

```
Macro: Action

        File          ALTS.WPM

        Description   Spell checks and saves a named file

        ┌─────────────────────────────────────────────────┐
        │{DISPLAY OFF}{Save}{Enter}                       │
        │y{Spell}3•{Save}{Enter}                          │
        │y                                                │
        │                                                 │
        │                                                 │
        │                                                 │
        │                                                 │
        └─────────────────────────────────────────────────┘

Ctrl-V to Insert next key as command;
Ctrl-PgUp for macro commands;   Press Exit when done
```

PF/Alt - T

This macro moves the cursor to the top of the document after any initial WordPerfect code settings. If you want to move the cursor to the very top before all WordPerfect codes then press the *Home key* three times in Keystroke Action 4.

VMS	Keystroke Action	DOS
PF2,F18	1. U: Press *Macro Define*. C: *Prints* Define macro: _.	Ctrl-F10
VMS Users	2. U: Press the *PF3 key* and press the *T key*. U: Press the *Alt key* and hold it down while pressing the *T key*. C: *Prints* Description: _.	*DOS Users*
	3. U: Type in <u>Moves cursor to top of document</u> and press the *Enter key*. C: *Prints* Macro Def.	
	4. U: Press the *Home key* twice and *Up arrow key* once. C: *Positions cursor at top of document*.	
PF2,F18	5. U: Press *Macro Define*. C: *Saves macro*.	Ctrl-F10

The keystrokes that are contained in the "ALTT.WPM" macro are shown on Screen 14-39 or 14-40.

Screen 14-39:   VMS Users

```
Macro: Action

      File           ALTT.WPM

      Description    Moves cursor to top of document

    ┌────────────────────────────────────────────────────────┐
    │ {DISPLAY OFF}{Home}{Home}{Up}                          │
    │                                                         │
    │                                                         │
    │                                                         │
    │                                                         │
    │                                                         │
    └────────────────────────────────────────────────────────┘

PF2,Prev Scr for macro commands;  Press Exit when done
```

Screen 14-40:   *DOS Users*

```
Macro: Action

       File             ALTT.WPM

       Description      Moves cursor to top of document

   ┌──────────────────────────────────────────────────────┐
   │ {DISPLAY OFF}{Home}{Home}{Up}                          │
   │                                                        │
   │                                                        │
   │                                                        │
   │                                                        │
   │                                                        │
   └──────────────────────────────────────────────────────┘

Ctrl-V to Insert next key as command;
Ctrl-PgUp for macro commands;  Press Exit when done
```

PF/Alt - U

Unlocks or removes a password from a document that was saved with a password. Opposite of macro Alt-L. You must save the document in order to have the password removed from the document.

VMS	Keystroke Action	DOS
PF2,F18	1. U: Press *Macro Define*. C: *Prints* Define macro: _.	Ctrl-F10

VMS Users	2. U: Press the *PF3 key* and press the *U key*.
	    U: Press the *Alt key* and hold it down while pressing the *U key*.
	    C: *Prints* Description: _.
		DOS Users

	3. U: Type in <u>Unlock a document</u> and press the *Enter key*. C: *Prints* Macro Def.	

PF2,F11
VMS Users
	4. U: Press *Text* In/Out.
	    C: *Prints* 1 ASCII Text; 2 Password; 3 Save As; 4 Comment; 5 Spreadsheet; 6 Read Only: <u>0</u>.
	    C: *Prints* 1 DOS Text; 2 Password; 3 Save As; 4 Comment; 5 Spreadsheets: <u>0</u>.
		Ctrl-F5
		
		DOS Users

	5. U: Press *2* for Password. C: *Prints* Password: 1 Add/Change; 2 Remove: <u>0</u>.	

VMS	**Keystroke Action**	**DOS**

| | 6. | U: Press *2* for Remove. | |
| | | C: *Removes password.* | |

| PF2,F18 | 7. | U: Press ***Macro Define***. | Ctrl-F10 |
| | | C: *Saves macro.* | |

The keystrokes that are contained in the "ALTU.WPM" macro are shown on Screen 14-41 or 14-42.

Screen 14-41:   VMS Users

```
Macro: Action

     File           ALTU.WPM

     Description    Unlock a document


     ┌─────────────────────────────────────────────────────────┐
     │ {DISPLAY OFF}{Text In/Out}22                             │
     │                                                          │
     │                                                          │
     │                                                          │
     │                                                          │
     │                                                          │
     │                                                          │
     │                                                          │
     └─────────────────────────────────────────────────────────┘

PF2,Prev Scr for macro commands;  Press Exit when done
```

Screen 14-42:   DOS Users

```
Macro: Action

     File           ALTU.WPM

     Description    Unlock a document


     ┌─────────────────────────────────────────────────────────┐
     │ {DISPLAY OFF}{Text In/Out}22                             │
     │                                                          │
     │                                                          │
     │                                                          │
     │                                                          │
     │                                                          │
     └─────────────────────────────────────────────────────────┘

Ctrl-V to Insert next key as command;
Ctrl-PgUp for macro commands;  Press Exit when done
```

PF/Alt - V

Viewing a document with a macro.

VMS	Keystroke Action	DOS
PF2,F18	1. U: Press *Macro Define*. C: *Prints* Define macro: _.	Ctrl-F10
VMS Users	2. U: Press the *PF3 key* and press the *V key*. U: Press the *Alt key* and hold it down while pressing the *V key*. C: *Prints* Description: _.	*DOS Users*
	3. U: Type in <u>Views document</u> and press the *Enter key*. C: *Prints* Macro Def.	
PF1,F13	4. U: Press *Print*. C: *Displays Print Menu*.	Shift-F7
	5. U: Press *V* for View. C: *Views the Document*.	
PF2,F18	6. U: Press *Macro Define*. C: *Saves macro*.	Ctrl-F10

The keystrokes that are contained in the "ALTV.WPM" macro are shown on Screen 14-43 or 14-44.

Screen 14-43: **VMS Users**

```
Macro: Action

      File          ALTV.WPM

      Description   Views document

    ┌─────────────────────────────────────────────────┐
    │ {Print}v                                          │
    │                                                   │
    │                                                   │
    │                                                   │
    │                                                   │
    │                                                   │
    └─────────────────────────────────────────────────┘

PF2,Prev Scr for macro commands;  Press Exit when done
```

Screen 14-44:   DOS Users

```
Macro: Action

       File            ALTV.WPM

       Description     Views document


     ┌─────────────────────────────────────────────┐
     │ {Print}v                                     │
     │                                              │
     │                                              │
     │                                              │
     │                                              │
     │                                              │
     └─────────────────────────────────────────────┘

Ctrl-V to Insert next key as command;
Ctrl-PgUp for macro commands;   Press Exit when done
```

PF/Alt - W

This macro will split your screen into two windows. The file in Document 1 will be located in the upper window and the file in Document 2 will be shown in the lower window. Corresponds to Alt-O macro. You should be currently editing two documents.

VMS	Keystroke Action	DOS
PF2,F18	1. U: Press **Macro Define**. C: *Prints* Define macro: _.	Ctrl-F10
VMS Users	2. U: Press the **PF3 key** and press the **W key**. U: Press the **Alt key** and hold it down while pressing the **W key**. C: *Prints* Description: _.	*DOS Users*
	3. U: Type in <u>Two Windows</u> and press the **Enter key**. C: *Prints* Macro Def.	
PF2,F9 *VMS Users*	4. U: Press **Screen.** C: *Prints* 1 Window; 2 Line Draw; 3 Rewrite; 4 Screen Size: <u>3</u>. C: *Prints* 1 Window; 2 Line Draw; 3 Rewrite: <u>3</u>.	Ctrl-F3 *DOS Users*
	5. U: Press **1** for Window. C: *Prints* Number of lines in this window: <u>24</u>.	

VMS	**Keystroke Action**	**DOS**

6. U: Press *12* for twelve lines in this window
and press the *Enter key*.
C: *Displays Document 1 and Document 2 in a
split screen setting.*

PF2,F18   7.   U: Press *Macro Define*.   **Ctrl-F10**
C: *Saves macro.*

The keystrokes that are contained in the "ALTW.WPM" macro are shown on Screen 14-45 or 14-46.

Screen 14-45:   *VMS Users*

```
Macro: Action

     File           ALTW.WPM

     Description    Two Windows


     ┌─────────────────────────────────────────────────┐
     │ {DISPLAY OFF}{Screen}112{Enter}                 │
     │                                                 │
     │                                                 │
     │                                                 │
     │                                                 │
     │                                                 │
     │                                                 │
     └─────────────────────────────────────────────────┘

PF2,Prev Scr for macro commands;  Press Exit when done
```

Screen 14-46:   *DOS Users*

```
Macro: Action

        File           ALTW.WPM

        Description    Two Windows


     ┌─────────────────────────────────────────────────┐
     │ {DISPLAY OFF}{Screen}112{Enter}                 │
     │                                                 │
     │                                                 │
     │                                                 │
     │                                                 │
     │                                                 │
     └─────────────────────────────────────────────────┘

Ctrl-V to Insert next key as command;
Ctrl-PgUp for macro commands;  Press Exit when done
```

PF/Alt - X

This macro exits WordPerfect without saving the file.

VMS	Keystroke Action	DOS
PF2,F18	1. U: Press *Macro Define.* C: *Prints* Define macro: _.	Ctrl-F10
VMS Users	2. U: Press the *PF3 key* and press the *X key.* U: Press the *Alt key* and hold it down while pressing the *X key.* C: *Prints* Description: _.	*DOS Users*
	3. U: Type in <u>Exits without saving file</u> and press the *Enter key.* C: *Prints* Macro Def.	
F13	4. U: Press *Exit.* C: *Prints* Save Document? <u>Y</u>es (No).	F7
	5. U: Press *N* for No. C: *Prints* Exit WP? <u>N</u>o (Yes).	
	6. U: Press *Y* for Yes. C: *Exits WordPerfect.*	

The keystrokes that are contained in the "ALTX.WPM" macro are shown on Screen 14-47 or 14-48.

Screen 14-47: *VMS Users*

```
Macro: Action

     File           ALTX.WPM

     Description    Exits without saving file

     ┌─────────────────────────────────────────────────────────────┐
     │{Exit}n                                                       │
     │y                                                            │
     │                                                             │
     │                                                             │
     │                                                             │
     │                                                             │
     │                                                             │
     └─────────────────────────────────────────────────────────────┘

PF2,Prev Scr for macro commands;  Press Exit when done
```

Screen 14-48:   *DOS Users*

```
Macro: Action

       File              ALTX.WPM

       Description       Exits without saving file

      ┌─────────────────────────────────────────────┐
      │ {Exit}n                                       │
      │ y                                             │
      │                                               │
      │                                               │
      │                                               │
      │                                               │
      │                                               │
      └─────────────────────────────────────────────┘

Ctrl-V to Insert next key as command;
Ctrl-PgUp for macro commands;  Press Exit when done
```

PF/Alt - Y

This macro yanks back deletion mistakes into memory. It undoes your last deletion mistake. Delete some characters before you define this macro.

VMS	Keystroke Action	DOS
PF2,F18	1. U: Press *Macro Define*. C: *Prints* Define macro: _.	Ctrl-F10
VMS Users	2. U: Press the *PF3 key* and press the *Y key*. U: Press the *Alt key* and hold it down while pressing the *Y key*. C: *Prints* Description: _.	*DOS Users*
	3. U: Type in <u>Yanks back deletion mistake into memory</u> and press the *Enter key*. C: *Prints* Macro Def.	
F7	4. U: Press *Cancel*. C: *Prints* Undelete: 1 Restore; 2 Previous Deletion: <u>0</u>.	F1
	5. U: Press *1* for Restore. C: *Restores Last Deletion*.	
PF2,F18	6. U: Press *Macro Define*. C: *Saves macro*.	Ctrl-F10

The keystrokes that are contained in the "ALTY.WPM" macro are shown on Screen 14-49 or 14-50.

Screen 14-49: *VMS Users*

```
Macro: Action

      File              ALTY.WPM

      Description       Yanks back deletion mistake into memory

      ┌──────────────────────────────────────────────────────┐
      │ {DISPLAY OFF}{Cancel}1                                │
      │                                                      │
      │                                                      │
      │                                                      │
      │                                                      │
      │                                                      │
      └──────────────────────────────────────────────────────┘

PF2,Prev Scr for macro commands;   Press Exit when done
```

Screen 14-50: *DOS Users*

```
Macro: Action

      File              ALTY.WPM

      Description       Yanks back deletion mistake into memory

      ┌──────────────────────────────────────────────────────┐
      │ {DISPLAY OFF}{Cancel}1                                │
      │                                                      │
      │                                                      │
      │                                                      │
      │                                                      │
      │                                                      │
      └──────────────────────────────────────────────────────┘

Ctrl-V to Insert next key as command;
Ctrl-PgUp for macro commands;   Press Exit when done
```

PF/Alt - Z

This macro zaps a page by deleting the page from the current cursor position to the end of the page. Place the cursor at the beginning of some page when creating and invoking this macro.

VMS	Keystroke Action	DOS
PF2,F18	1. U: Press *Macro Define*. C: *Prints* Define macro: _.	Ctrl-F10

VMS Users	2. U: Press the *PF3 key* and press the *Z key*.
	     U: Press the *Alt key* and hold it down while pressing the *Z key*.
	     C: *Prints* Description: _.
		DOS Users

VMS	**Keystroke Action**	**DOS**

3. U: Type in <u>Zaps a page</u> and press the *Enter key*.
   C: *Prints* Macro Def.

PF2,KP3   4. U: Press the ***Ctrl key*** (DOS users hold it down) and tap the ***PgDn key***.   Ctrl-PgDn
   C: *Prints* Delete Remainder of page? (Y/N) <u>N</u>o.

5. U: Press *Y* for Yes.
   C: *Deletes the remainder of the page after the cursor.*

PF2,F18   6. U: Press ***Macro Define***.   Ctrl-F10
   C: *Saves macro.*

The keystrokes that are contained in the "ALTZ.WPM" macro are shown on Screen 14-51 or 14-52.

Screen 14-51: ***VMS Users***

```
Macro: Action

        File            ALTZ.WPM

        Description     Zaps a page

    ┌──────────────────────────────────────────────┐
    │ {DISPLAY OFF}{Del to EOP}y                     │
    │                                                │
    │                                                │
    │                                                │
    │                                                │
    │                                                │
    └──────────────────────────────────────────────┘

PF2,Prev Scr for macro commands;  Press Exit when done
```

Screen 14-52:   DOS Users

```
Macro: Action

        File          ALTZ.WPM

        Description   Zaps a page

        ┌─────────────────────────────────────────────────────┐
        │ {DISPLAY OFF}{Del to EOP}y                           │
        │                                                     │
        │                                                     │
        │                                                     │
        │                                                     │
        │                                                     │
        └─────────────────────────────────────────────────────┘

Ctrl-V to Insert next key as command;
Ctrl-PgUp for macro commands;   Press Exit when done
```

Advanced Macros

The advanced macros contained in this section are very easy to create and use. You do not have to use the macro programming language for these macros.

Each macro will include the following introduction:

Name:	Name of the macro.
Description:	States the macro's purpose.
Instructions:	How to use the macro.

For all of the advanced macros you want to use you can type in the given code and then do the following to invoke the macro:

VMS	**Keystroke Action**	**DOS**
PF3,F18	1. U: Press *Macro.* C: *Prints* Macro: _.	Alt-F10
	2. U: Type in macro's file specification (VMS) or pathname (DOS) and the name of the macro and press the *Enter key.* C: *Invokes macro.*	

There are seven advanced macros in this chapter. They are:

1.   The Bold a Sentence Macro
2.   The Capitalize the First Letter of a Word Macro
3.   The Font Change Macro
4.   The Margin (L/R) Macro
5.   The Table Calculation Macro
6.   The Table Creation Macro
7.   The Underline a Sentence Macro

1. The Bold a Sentence Macro

Name:	BOLD.WPM
Description:	Bolds the sentence on which your cursor is positioned.
Instructions:	While creating and when using this macro position your cursor on the sentence you want to bold. This sentence cannot be the first sentence in your document.

VMS	**Keystroke Action**	**DOS**
PF2,F18	1. U: Press *Macro Define.* C: Prints Define Macro: .	Ctrl-F10

VMS	Keystroke Action	DOS
	2. U: Type in <u>BOLD</u> and press the *Enter key.* C: *Prints* Description: _.	
	3. U: Type in <u>Bolds a Sentence</u> and press the *Enter key.* C: *Prints* Macro Def.	
PF1,F8	4. U: Press *<-Search.* C: *Prints* <- Srch: _.	Shift-F2
	5. U: Type in . *(period).* C: *Echoes characters.*	
PF1,F8	6. U: Press *<-Search.* C: *Positions cursor after previous search string that was found.*	Shift-F2
PF3,F10 OR F20	7. U: Press *Block.* C: *Prints* Block on.	Alt-F4 OR F12
F8	8. U: Press *->Search.* C: *Prints* -> Srch: _.	F2
	9. U: Type in . *(period).* C: *Echoes characters.*	
F8	10. U: Press *->Search.* C: *Positions cursor after next search string that was found.*	F2
F12	11. U: Press *Bold.* C: *Bolds the sentence.*	F6
PF2,F18	12. U: Press *Macro Define.* C: *Saves macro.*	Ctrl-F10

The keystrokes that are contained in the "BOLD.WPM" macro are shown on Screen 14-53 or Screen 14-54.

Screen 14-53: **VMS Users**

```
Macro: Action

     File            BOLD.WPM

     Description     Bolds a Sentence


     ┌─────────────────────────────────────────────────────────────┐
     │ {DISPLAY OFF}{Search Left}.{Search Left}{Block}{Search}.      │
     │ {Search}{Bold}                                                │
     │                                                               │
     │                                                               │
     │                                                               │
     │                                                               │
     │                                                               │
     └─────────────────────────────────────────────────────────────┘

PF2,Prev Scr for macro commands;  Press Exit when done
```

Screen 14-54: **DOS Users**

```
Macro: Action

     File            BOLD.WPM

     Description     Bolds a Sentence


     ┌─────────────────────────────────────────────────────────────┐
     │ {DISPLAY OFF}{Search Left}.{Search Left}{Block}{Search}.      │
     │ {Search}{Bold}                                                │
     │                                                               │
     │                                                               │
     │                                                               │
     │                                                               │
     │                                                               │
     └─────────────────────────────────────────────────────────────┘

Ctrl-V to Insert next key as command;
Ctrl-PgUp for macro commands;  Press Exit when done
```

2. The Capitalize the First Letter of a Word Macro

Name: CAP.WPM
Description: Capitalizes the first letter of the word on which your cursor is positioned.
Instructions: Position your cursor on the word of which you would like to capitalize the first letter.

VMS	**Keystroke Action**	**DOS**
PF2,F18	1. U: Press *Macro Define.* C: *Prints* Define Macro: _.	Ctrl-F10
	2. U: Type in <u>CAP</u> and press the *Enter key.* C: *Prints* Description: _.	

VMS	**Keystroke Action**	**DOS**
	3. U: Type in <u>Capitalizes First Letter</u> and press the ***Enter key.*** C: *Prints* Macro Def.	
P F 2 , R i g h t arrow key	4. U: Press ***Word Right.*** C: *Positions cursor on the word to the right of the current word.*	C t r l - R i g h t arrow key
P F 2 , L e f t arrow key	5. U: Press ***Word Left.*** C: *Positions cursor on the word to the left of the current word.*	C t r l - L e f t arrow key
PF3,F10 OR F20	6. U: Press ***Block.*** C: *Prints* Block on.	Alt-F4 OR F12
	7. U: Press the ***Right arrow key.*** C: *Blocks first letter of the word.*	
PF1,F9	8. U: Press ***Switch.*** C: *Prints* 1 Uppercase; 2 Lowercase: <u>0</u>.	Shift-F3
	9. U: Press ***1*** for Uppercase. C: *Changes blocked letter to uppercase.*	
PF2,F18	10. U: Press ***Macro Define.*** C: *Saves macro.*	Ctrl-F10

The keystrokes that are contained in the "CAP.WPM" macro are shown on Screen 14-55 or Screen 14-56.

Screen 14-55:   *VMS Users*

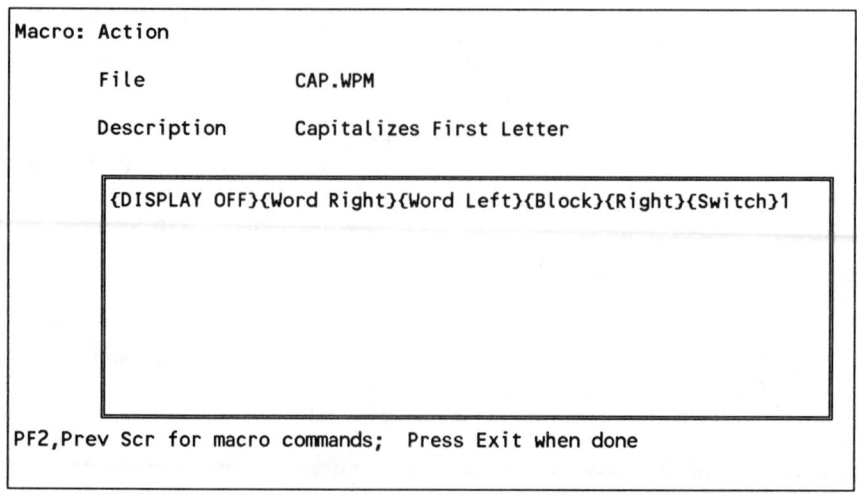

```
Macro: Action

     File          CAP.WPM

     Description   Capitalizes First Letter

     ┌──────────────────────────────────────────────────────────────┐
     │{DISPLAY OFF}{Word Right}{Word Left}{Block}{Right}{Switch}1     │
     │                                                                │
     │                                                                │
     │                                                                │
     │                                                                │
     │                                                                │
     │                                                                │
     │                                                                │
     └──────────────────────────────────────────────────────────────┘

PF2,Prev Scr for macro commands;  Press Exit when done
```

Screen 14-56: **DOS Users**

```
┌─────────────────────────────────────────────────────────────────────┐
│Macro: Action                                                          │
│                                                                       │
│       File            CAP.WPM                                         │
│                                                                       │
│       Description     Capitalizes First Letter                        │
│                                                                       │
│    ┌──────────────────────────────────────────────────────────────┐  │
│    │{DISPLAY OFF}{Word Right}{Word Left}{Block}{Right}{Switch}1     │  │
│    │                                                                │  │
│    │                                                                │  │
│    │                                                                │  │
│    │                                                                │  │
│    │                                                                │  │
│    │                                                                │  │
│    │                                                                │  │
│    └──────────────────────────────────────────────────────────────┘  │
│                                                                       │
│Ctrl-V to Insert next key as command;                                  │
│Ctrl-PgUp for macro commands;  Press Exit when done                    │
└─────────────────────────────────────────────────────────────────────┘
```

3.   The Font Change Macro

Name: FR.WPM
Description: Selects a new base font.
Instructions: Position your cursor in the location where you want to change your base font.
This macro selects a base font on the Digital LN03R (ScriptPrinter) or the HP
LaserJet IIP. For other printers, note the font name you want to use before
you start defining the macro.

VMS	Keystroke Action	DOS
PF2,F18	1. U: Press *Macro Define.* C: *Prints* Define macro: _.	Ctrl-F10
	2. U: Type in <u>FR</u> and press the *Enter key.* C: *Prints* Description: _.	
	3. U: Type in <u>Font - Roman</u> and press the *Enter key.* C: *Prints* Macro Def.	

PF2,F14	4. U: Press *Font.*
	     C: *Prints* 1 Size; 2 Appearance; 3 Normal;
	     4 Base Font; 5 Print Color: <u>0</u>.
		Ctrl-F8

	5. U: Press *4* for Base Font. C: *Displays Base Font Menu.*	
	6. U: Press *n* for Name Search. C: *Highlights current selected font.*	

VMS	Keystroke Action	DOS

7. U: Type in <u>Times Roman</u> *(VMS)*, <u>Dutch Roman 18pt</u> *(DOS)*, or type in as many characters of the new font name that will distinguish it from the other available fonts.
   C: *Highlights chosen font.*

8. U: Press the *Enter key.*
   C: *Prints* 1 Select; N Name search: <u>1</u>.

9. U: Press *1* for Select.
   C: *Selects Font and Returns to Document.*

VMS Users: **On the Digital LN03R (ScriptPrinter) WordPerfect will Print Point size: 12 at which point you should enter in a point size if you want a point size different than the one offered, such as 18, and press the Enter key.**

VMS	Keystroke Action	DOS

PF2,F18   10. U: Press *Macro Define.*   Ctrl-F10
                 C: *Saves macro.*

The keystrokes contained in the "FR.WPM" macro are shown on Screen 14-57 or Screen 14-58.

Screen 14-57: VMS Users - Digital LN03R (ScriptPrinter)

```
Macro: Action

        File            FR.WPM

        Description     Font - Roman


     ┌──────────────────────────────────────────────────────┐
     │ {DISPLAY OFF}{Font}4nTimes•Roman{Enter}              │
     │ 118{Enter}                                            │
     │                                                      │
     │                                                      │
     │                                                      │
     │                                                      │
     └──────────────────────────────────────────────────────┘

PF2,Prev Scr for macro commands;  Press Exit when done
```

Screen 14-58: DOS Users - HP LaserJet IIP

```
Macro: Action

      File            FR.WPM

      Description     Font - Roman


      ┌─────────────────────────────────────────────────────────┐
      │ {DISPLAY OFF}{Font}4nDutch•Roman•18pt{Enter}             │
      │ 1                                                         │
      │                                                           │
      │                                                           │
      │                                                           │
      │                                                           │
      │                                                           │
      └─────────────────────────────────────────────────────────┘

Ctrl-V to Insert next key as command;
Ctrl-PgUp for macro commands; Press Exit when done
```

4.   The Margin (L/R) Macro

Name: MAR.WPM
Description: Sets your left and right margins at 1.5 inches each.
Instructions: Position your cursor at the location where you want to insert the Left/Right
               Margin code of 1.5 inches respectively.

VMS	**Keystroke Action**	**DOS**
PF2,F18	1. U: Press *Macro Define.* C: *Prints* Define macro: _.	Ctrl-F10
	2. U: Type in <u>MAR</u> and press the *Enter key.* C: *Prints* Description: _.	

	3. U: Type in <u>Sets L/R Margins at 1.5 inches</u> and
	       press the *Enter key.*
	    C: *Prints* Macro Def.	

PF1,F14	4. U: Press *Format.* C: *Displays Format Menu.*	Shift-F8
	5. U: Press *1* for Line. C: *Displays Format: Line Menu.*	
	6. U: Press *7* for Margins. C: *Positions cursor to right of Margins - Left.*	

VMS	**Keystroke Action**	**DOS**
	7. U: Type in <u>1.5</u> for 1.5 inches and press the *Enter key.* C: *Displays 1.5" to the right of Margins - Left and positions cursor to right of Margins - Right.*	
	8. U: Type in <u>1.5</u> for 1.5 inches and press the *Enter key.* C: *Displays 1.5" to the right of Margins - Right and Returns to Command Line.*	
F13	9. U: Press *Exit.* C: *Returns to Document.*	F7
PF2,F18	10. U: Press *Macro Define.* C: *Saves macro.*	Ctrl-F10

The keystrokes contained in the "MAR.WPM" macro are shown on Screen 14-59 or Screen 14-60.

Screen 14-59: VMS Users

```
Macro: Action

      File            MAR.WPM

      Description     Sets L/R Margins at 1.5 inches


      ┌─────────────────────────────────────────────────┐
      │ {DISPLAY OFF}{Format}171.5{Enter}               │
      │ 1.5{Enter}                                      │
      │ {Exit}                                          │
      │                                                 │
      │                                                 │
      │                                                 │
      │                                                 │
      │                                                 │
      │                                                 │
      └─────────────────────────────────────────────────┘

PF2,Prev Scr for macro commands;   Press Exit when done
```

Screen 14-60: DOS Users

```
Macro: Action

        File            MAR.WPM

        Description     Sets L/R Margins at 1.5 inches


    ┌──────────────────────────────────────────────────┐
    │ {DISPLAY OFF}{Format}171.5{Enter}                  │
    │ 1.5{Enter}                                         │
    │ {Exit}                                             │
    │                                                    │
    │                                                    │
    │                                                    │
    │                                                    │
    └──────────────────────────────────────────────────┘

Ctrl-V to Insert next key as command;
Ctrl-PgUp for macro commands; Press Exit when done
```

5.   The Table Calculation Macro

Name: TABCALC.WPM
Description: Calculates the formulas located in your table.
Instructions: When creating and using this macro position your cursor in the table where your formulas need to be calculated.

VMS	**Keystroke Action**	**DOS**
PF2,F18	1. U: Press *Macro Define.* C: *Prints* Define macro: _.	Ctrl-F10
	2. U: Type in <u>TABCALC</u> and press the *Enter key.* C: *Prints* Description: _.	
	3. U: Type in <u>Performs table calculations</u> and press the *Enter key.* C: *Prints* Macro Def.	
PF3,F13	4. U: Press *Columns/Table.* C: *Displays the Table Edit Menu.*	Alt-F7
	5. U: Press *5* for Math. C: *Prints* Math: 1 Calculate; 2 Formula; 3 Copy Formula; 4 +; 5 =; 6 *: <u>0</u>.	
	6. U: Press *1* for Calculate. C: *Calculates formulas in table and Displays the Table Edit Menu.*	

VMS	Keystroke Action	DOS
PF3,F13	7. U: Press *Columns/Table.* C: *Returns to Document.*	Alt-F7
PF2,F18	8. U: Press *Macro Define.* C: *Saves macro.*	Ctrl-F10

The keystrokes that are contained in the "TABCALC.WPM" macro are shown on Screen 14-61 or Screen 14-62.

Screen 14-61: VMS Users

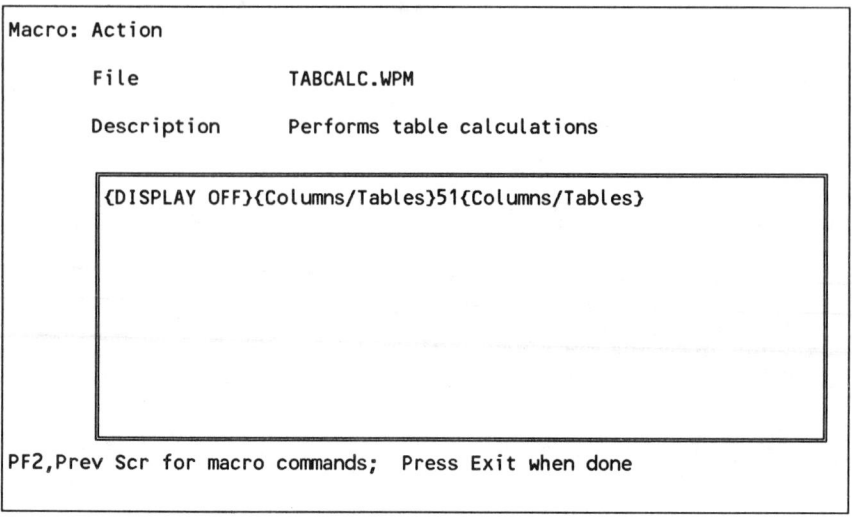

```
Macro: Action

        File            TABCALC.WPM

        Description     Performs table calculations

    ┌──────────────────────────────────────────────────────┐
    │ {DISPLAY OFF}{Columns/Tables}51{Columns/Tables}       │
    │                                                        │
    │                                                        │
    │                                                        │
    │                                                        │
    └──────────────────────────────────────────────────────┘

PF2,Prev Scr for macro commands;  Press Exit when done
```

Screen 14-62: DOS Users

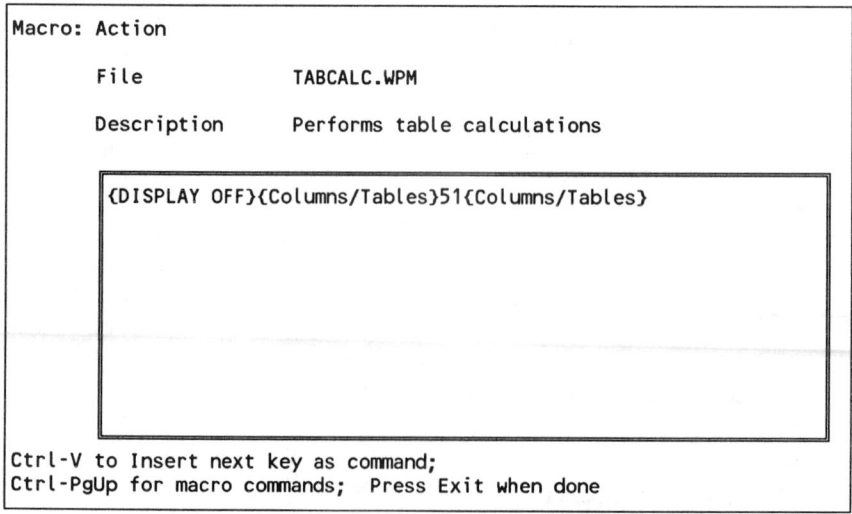

```
Macro: Action

        File            TABCALC.WPM

        Description     Performs table calculations

    ┌──────────────────────────────────────────────────────┐
    │ {DISPLAY OFF}{Columns/Tables}51{Columns/Tables}       │
    │                                                        │
    │                                                        │
    │                                                        │
    │                                                        │
    └──────────────────────────────────────────────────────┘

Ctrl-V to Insert next key as command;
Ctrl-PgUp for macro commands;  Press Exit when done
```

6. The Table Creation Macro

Name: TABLE.WPM
Description: Creates a five row by four column table.
Instructions: Position your cursor where you would like the table to be created.

VMS	Keystroke Action	DOS
PF2,F18	1. U: Press *Macro Define.* C: *Prints* Define macro: _.	Ctrl-F10
	2. U: Type in <u>TABLE</u> and press the *Enter key.* C: *Prints* Description: _.	
	3. U: Type in <u>Creates a 5 Row, 4 Column Table</u> and press the *Enter key.* C: *Prints* Macro Def.	
PF3,F13	4. U: Press *Columns/Table.* C: *Prints* 1 Columns; 2 Tables; 3 Math: <u>0</u>.	Alt-F7
	5. U: Press *2* for Tables. C: *Prints* Table: 1 Create; 2 Edit: <u>0</u>.	
	6. U: Press *1* for Create. C: *Prints* Number of Columns: <u>3</u>.	
	7. U: Press *4* for 4 Columns and press the *Enter key.* C: *Prints* Number of Rows: <u>1</u>.	
	8. U: Press *5* for 5 Rows and press the *Enter key.* C: *Prints Updating Table and Displays the Table Edit Menu.*	
F13	9. U: Press *Exit* to exit from the Table Edit Menu. C: *Returns to Document.*	F7
PF2,F18	10. U: Press *Macro Define.* C: *Saves macro.*	Ctrl-F10

The keystrokes that are contained in the "TABLE.WPM" macro are shown on Screen 14-63 or Screen 14-64.

Screen 14-63: VMS Users

```
Macro: Action

       File            TABLE.WPM

       Description     Creates a 5 Row, 4 Column Table

    ┌────────────────────────────────────────────────────────┐
    │ {DISPLAY OFF}{Columns/Tables}214{Enter}                 │
    │ 5{Enter}                                                │
    │ {Exit}                                                  │
    │                                                         │
    │                                                         │
    │                                                         │
    │                                                         │
    │                                                         │
    │                                                         │
    └────────────────────────────────────────────────────────┘

PF2,Prev Scr for macro commands;   Press Exit when done
```

Screen 14-64: DOS Users

```
Macro: Action

       File            TABLE.WPM

       Description     Creates a 5 Row, 4 Column Table

    ┌────────────────────────────────────────────────────────┐
    │ {DISPLAY OFF}{Columns/Tables}214{Enter}                 │
    │ 5{Enter}                                                │
    │ {Exit}                                                  │
    │                                                         │
    │                                                         │
    │                                                         │
    │                                                         │
    │                                                         │
    │                                                         │
    └────────────────────────────────────────────────────────┘

Ctrl-V to Insert next key as command;
Ctrl-PgUp for macro commands;   Press Exit when done
```

7.   The Underline a Sentence Macro

Name: UND.WPM
Description: Underlines the sentence on which your cursor is positioned.
Instructions: While creating and when using this macro position your cursor on the
                 sentence you want to underline. This sentence cannot be the first sentence in
                 your document.

VMS	Keystroke Action	DOS
PF2,F18	1. U: Press *Macro Define.* C: *Prints* Define Macro: _	Ctrl-F10

VMS	**Keystroke Action**	**DOS**
	2. U: Type in <u>UND</u> and press the *Enter key.* C: *Prints* Description: _.	
	3. U: Type in <u>Underlines a Sentence</u> and press the *Enter key.* C: *Prints* Macro Def.	
PF1,F8	4. U: Press *<-Search.* C: *Prints* <- Srch: _.	Shift-F2
	5. U: Type in . *(period).* C: *Echoes characters.*	
PF1,F8	6. U: Press *<-Search.* C: *Positions cursor after previous search string that was found.*	Shift-F2
PF3,F10 OR F20	7. U: Press **Block.** C: *Prints* Block on.	Alt-F4 OR F12
F8	8. U: Press *->Search.* C: *Prints* -> Srch: _.	F2
	9. U: Type in . *(period).* C: *Echoes characters.*	
F8	10. U: Press *->Search.* C: *Positions cursor after next search string that was found.*	F2
F14	11. U: Press **Underline.** C: *Underlines the sentence.*	F8
PF2,F18	12. U: Press **Macro Define.** C: *Saves macro.*	Ctrl-F10

The keystrokes that are contained in the "UND.WPM" macro are shown on Screen 14-65 or Screen 14-66.

Screen 14-65:   *VMS Users*

```
Macro: Action

      File              UND.WPM

      Description       Underlines a Sentence


  ┌─────────────────────────────────────────────────────────┐
  │ {DISPLAY OFF}{Search Left}.{Search Left}{Block}{Search}.  │
  │ {Search}{Underline}                                       │
  │                                                           │
  │                                                           │
  │                                                           │
  │                                                           │
  │                                                           │
  └─────────────────────────────────────────────────────────┘

PF2,Prev Scr for macro commands;  Press Exit when done
```

Screen 14-66:   *DOS Users*

```
Macro: Action

      File              UND.WPM

      Description       Underlines a Sentence


  ┌─────────────────────────────────────────────────────────┐
  │ {DISPLAY OFF}{Search Left}.{Search Left}{Block}{Search}.  │
  │ {Search}{Underline}                                       │
  │                                                           │
  │                                                           │
  │                                                           │
  │                                                           │
  └─────────────────────────────────────────────────────────┘

Ctrl-V to Insert next key as command;
Ctrl-PgUp for macro commands;  Press Exit when done
```

SECTION IV:

ADDITIONS

NOTES FOR 5.0 USERS

Appendix A is for WordPerfect Version 5.0 Users only. The new WordPerfect 5.1 has included many minor and major changes. These notes document the items that are included in this book that are different in Version 5.0.

Equation Feature

This feature was not available in 5.0.

Font Feature

The Font feature in WordPerfect 5.0 is very similar to the feature in version 5.1. The main improvements are the WordPerfect screens along with their menu options.

Graphics Feature

The graphic images that come with WordPerfect 5.0 for VMS are listed below in Table A-1.

Table A-1

ABAN-SU.WPG;1	ARCHERY.WPG;1
ARROW-10.WPG;1	ARROW-21.WPG;1
BALLOONS.WPG;1	BORDER-6.WPG;1
BULB.WPG;1	CHECKMRK.WPG;1
CLOCK.WPG;1	DINOSAUR.WPG;1
FRAGILE.WPG;1	GLOBE2-M.WPG;1
HANDS-2.WPG;1	HANDS-6.WPG;1
HAPPY.WPG;1	HOUSE.WPG;1
KEY.WPG;1	MOVIECAM.WPG;1
NEWS.WPG;2	NOSIGN.WPG;1
PC3.WPG;1	PEN.WPG;1
PENCIL-1.WPG;1	PHONE.WPG;1
RIBBON.WPG;1	SADFACE.WPG;1
SALE.WPG;1	SANTA.WPG;1
STAR-2.WPG;1	STATES-M.WPG;1

The graphic images that come with WordPerfect 5.0 for DOS are listed below in Table A-2.

Table A-2

AIRPLANE.WPG	AND.WPG
ANNOUNCE.WPG	APPLAUSE.WPG
ARROW1.WPG	ARROW2.WPG
AWARD.WPG	BADNEWS.WPG
BOOK.WPG	BORDER.WPG
CHECK.WPG	CLOCK.WPG
CONFIDEN.WPG	FLAG.WPG
GAVEL.WPG	GOODNEWS.WPG
HAND.WPG	HOURGLAS.WPG
KEY.WPG	MAPSYMBL.WPG
NEWSPAPR.WPG	NO1.WPG
PC.WPG	PENCIL.WPG
PHONE.WPG	PRESENT.WPG
QUILL.WPG	RPTCARD.WPG
THINKER.WPG	USAMAP.WPG

Macro Programming Feature

Depending on what macro programming commands your 5.0 macros contain will depend on whether they will work in 5.1 without modifications.

WordPerfect 5.1 and 6.0 added more keyboard commands to the macro programming language. (See WordPerfect's Reference Manual for 5.1 and the online help facility for 6.0.) Table A-3 is a brief summary of the limited Keyboard Commands in WordPerfect 5.0.

Table A-3

Keyboard Command	Description
{;}	Comment statements. Ignored by WordPerfect during macro execution.
{ASSIGN}	Allows assignment of a value to a variable.
{BELL}	Sounds the computer's bell.
{BREAK}	Terminates macro or escapes from a programming structure.
{CALL}	Executes a subroutine.
{CANCEL OFF}	Turns the Cancel key off.
{CANCEL ON}	Turns the Cancel key on.
{CASE}	Branches to a specified location in the macro depending on the result of an expression.
{CASE CALL}	Branches and returns from a specified location in the macro depending on the result of an expression.
{CHAIN}	Allows another macro to be executed when the current macro is finished.
{CHAR}	Prompts the user via a message for a single keystroke input.
{DISPLAY OFF}	Macro execution is not shown on the screen.
{DISPLAY ON}	Macro execution is shown on the screen.
{ELSE}	Used within an IF or CASE structure. Statements following the ELSE are performed when some conditional expression yields a False answer.

Table A-3 continued.

Keyboard Command	Description
{END IF}	Terminates an IF Structure.
{GO}	Branches to a specified location within the macro.
{IF}	Initiates an IF Structure. Tests some condition expression and then will perform certain statements depending on the conditional expression response.
{IF EXISTS}	Verifies whether or not the specified variable has been assigned a value.
{LABEL}	Marks a location within a macro that the programmer can branch to at any given time.
{LOOK}	Determines whether a key has been pressed or not.
{NEST}	Executes another macro. When the other macro is finished WordPerfect returns to the original macro.
{ON CANCEL}	If the Cancel key has been pressed or a {RETURN CANCEL} command has been issued WordPerfect will perform the indicated action.
{ON ERROR}	When an error has been discovered WordPerfect will perform the indicated action.
{ON NOT FOUND}	When a search fails WordPerfect will perform the indicated action.
{ORIGINAL KEY}	Returns to the original value of the key pressed during macro execution.
{PAUSE}	Macro pauses permanently until the Enter key is pressed.
{PROMPT}	Displays some message on WordPerfect's status line.
{QUIT}	Terminates the execution of a macro.
{RESTART}	Terminates the execution of a macro after the last command in the current nested macro has executed.
{RETURN}	Designates the end of a subroutine. Tells the macro to return to the next item following the command that executed the subroutine.
{RETURN CANCEL}	Designates the end of a subroutine. Tells the macro to return to the next item following the command that executed the subroutine with a cancel indication.
{RETURN ERROR}	Designates the end of a subroutine. Tells macro to return to the item following the command that executed the subroutine with an error indication.
{RETURN NOT FOUND}	Designates the end of a subroutine. Tells macro to return to the item following the command that executed the subroutine with a Not Found indication.
{SPEED}	Indicates the length of time WordPerfect will wait before executing the next macro command.
{STATE}	Indicates the current WordPerfect status.
{STEP OFF}	Turns off the execution of the macro's statements step-by-step.
{STEP ON}	Executes the macro's statements step-by-step. Waits for the user to press a key before continuing on with the next step.

Table A-3 continued.

Keyboard Command	Description
{TEXT}	Prompts the user for input.
{WAIT}	Pauses the execution of the macro for a specified time.

Macro Variables

WordPerfect 5.0 contains only 10 macro variables labeled 0 through 9.

The 10 variables may be assigned to numbers, strings, etc.

In addition to alphabetic and numeric characters, variables may include WordPerfect 5.0's formatting codes such as: Hard Page, Hard Return, ->Indent, Tab, and Hyphen. Any Soft Return codes in a block will be represented as a space in the variable, and any Soft Page codes in a block will be represented as either a Hard Return or a space.

When the user enters WordPerfect 5.0, all the variables are equal to null, that is, they have no value assigned to them.

Macro Editor

Screen A-1 displays the 5.0 Macro Editor Screen. This screen is slightly different in appearance than the new 5.1 screen.

Screen A-1

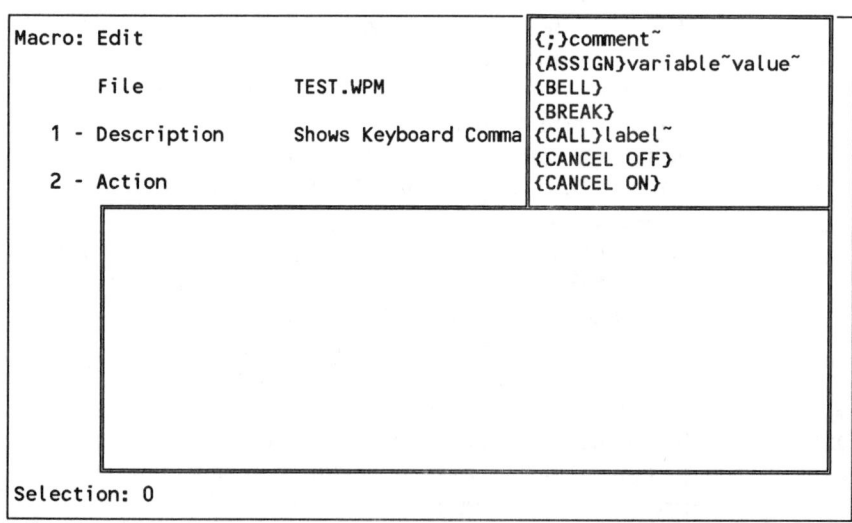

```
Macro: Edit                              {;}comment~
                                         {ASSIGN}variable~value~
       File           TEST.WPM           {BELL}
                                         {BREAK}
   1 - Description     Shows Keyboard Comma{CALL}label~
                                         {CANCEL OFF}
   2 - Action                            {CANCEL ON}




Selection: 0
```

To change the Description of the macro you must select 1.

To actually edit the macro you must select 2.

Merge Feature

In WordPerfect 5.0 there are fourteen possible merge codes which may be inserted into primary or secondary files. These codes are listed in Table A-3.

Table A-4

Syntax:	^C
Purpose:	This merge code allows text to be inserted into the primary or secondary file by the user while the merge process temporarily pauses. To continue the merge process press ^R.
Syntax:	^D
Purpose:	This merge code inserts the current date into the document. The current date must have been entered when the user started the computer or the computer's internal system clock must have been set in order for this code to work.
Syntax:	^E
Purpose:	This merge code usually marks the record's end in a secondary file. However, it may also stop the merge process when entered in a primary file or pressed while the merge process is going on.
Syntax:	^Fn^
Purpose:	This merge code takes the information in the text field n which may be either a number or actual text and merges the information into the final merged file.
Syntax:	^Gmacroname^G
Purpose:	This merge code invokes the macro named macroname at the end of the merge process.
Syntax:	^N
Purpose:	This merge code searches for the secondary file's next record. If this code does not find another record then the merge process will end.
Syntax:	^Omessage^O
Purpose:	This merge code prints the specified message on the command line.
Syntax:	^Pfilename^P
Purpose:	This merge code inserts the specified filename into the final merged document. If this code is not supplied with a filename then the primary file is used as the default file.
Syntax:	^Q
Purpose:	This merge code stops the macro from invoking any further.
Syntax:	^R (PF1,F17,R for VMS or F9 for DOS)
Purpose:	This merge code usually marks the field's end in a secondary file. However, it also finishes input into the final merge file from the ^C merge code.
Syntax:	^Sfilename^S
Purpose:	This merge code inserts the specified filename as the new secondary file to use in the merge process.
Syntax:	^T
Purpose:	This merge code prints the merged document up to this merge code.

Table A-4 continued.

Syntax:	^U
Purpose:	This merge code rewrites the computer screen.
Syntax:	^V
Purpose:	This merge code allows the user to insert merge codes into the final merged document.

WordPerfect Version 5.1 does accept the same merge codes that were used in Version 5.0. However, the new codes for Version 5.1 are easier to use and understand.

Merge Programming

This feature was not available in 5.0.

Pull-Down Menus

Pull-Down Menus were not available in 5.0 unless you created your own.

Styles Feature

WordPerfect 5.0 styles feature does not include the outline style feature.

Tables Feature

This feature was not available in 5.0.

TEMPLATE KEYS

VMS	Template Keys	DOS

VMS   **Template Keys**   **DOS**

PF3,F10
OR
F20

Block
Highlight a selected portion of text so you can
manipulate it as a single unit in a variety of ways.

Alt-F4
OR
F12

F12

Bold
WordPerfect 5.1's method to bold text in your
document.

F6

F7

Cancel
A fail safe procedure to:
1)   Cancel or Quit out of a menu without
selecting an option.
2)   Restore previous deletions that you
have made.

F1

PF1,F12

Center
An arrangement to center a line of text in your
document.

Shift-F6

PF3,F13

Columns/Table
A provision to:
1)   Create columns.
2)   Create tables.
3)   Perform mathematical operations.

Alt-F7

PF1,F11

Date/Outline
Provides a method to:
1)   Use a variety of options to insert the
current date into your document.
2)   Create outlines.
3)   Create numbered paragraphs.

Shift-F5

F17

End Field
Lets you place the Merge code {END FIELD} in
your document.

F9

F13

Exit
You can choose to save or not save your document
and then exit WordPerfect.

F7

PF3,F12

Flush Right
How to push all your text to the right margin.

Alt-F6

VMS	Template Keys	DOS
PF2,F14	**Font** Lets you use different typefaces or print styles in your document.	Ctrl-F8
PF2,F13	**Footnote** With this template key you can create and edit... 1) Footnotes in your document. 2) Endnotes in your document.	Ctrl-F7
PF1,F14	**Format** This arrangement allows you to format... 1) Line options such as Hyphenation, Justification, Line Height, Line Numbering, Line Spacing, Margins Left/Right, Tab Set, and Widow/Orphan Protection. 2) Page options such as Center Page, Force Odd/Even Page, Headers and Footers, Margins Top/Bottom, Page Numbering, Paper Size/Type/Labels, and Suppress. 3) Document options such as Display Pitch, Initial Codes/Font, Redline Method, and Summary. 4) Other options such as Advance, Conditional End of Page, Decimal Characters, Language, Overstrike, Printer Functions, Underline Spaces/Tabs, and Border Options.	Shift-F8
PF3,F17	**Graphics** Inserts WordPerfect 5.1's or other graphics or your mathematical equations into your document.	Alt-F9
F9	**Help** Provides you with extensive on-line help, that is, help is available whenever you need it by pressing the Help key.	F3
PF1,F10	**-> Indent <-** Allows you to indent an equal amount from both the left and right hand margins by indenting to the specified tab set which then becomes your new left and right hand margins until you press the Enter key.	Shift-F4

VMS	Template Keys	DOS

F10

-> Indent
Use this to indent to the specified tab setting and then have the text wrap back around to that tab set which is your new left hand margin until you press the Enter key.

F4

F11

List
Displays the files included in your default directory and allows you to manipulate any of the files shown by highlighting that file (use your arrow keys) and then selecting one of the following options...

F5

1) Retrieve will input your document from your disk into Document One's or Two's memory.

2) Delete will delete your document from your disk.

3) Move/Rename will either erase your file from its current location and move it to another location under the same name OR you can rename the file by typing in a new name.

4) Print will produce a hardcopy of your document on your printer.

5) Short/Long Display shows either a short or long display of files that you see when you invoke the List Files key. Short is the default display that contains two columns of files, that is two files per row. Long is the more descriptive display that contains only one column of files, that is one file per row.

6) Look displays a document on your screen without actually retrieving the document.

7) Other Directory will let you change your default directory.

8) Copy will let you make a duplicate copy of a specified file either in a different location on your disk(s) or associate the file with another filename.

VMS	Template Keys	DOS

List continued.

9)   Find will look through all of the files shown on the screen for certain words or word combinations. It offers you the options of Name, Doc Summary, First Pg, Entire Doc, Conditions, and Undo. If for example, you search the Entire Doc (Document) for some word such as boat then all of the files that are located in that directory listing will be searched through. If WordPerfect finds an occurrence of the word boat it will give you a new directory listing with only the files that contain the word boat.   **F5**

10)   Name Search will help you find the file you are looking for in the list of files. It is used when you have a large number of files listed out on your screen. After you select this option for Name Search your lower menu on the List Files display will vanish and in the lower right hand corner you will see (name Search; Enter or arrows to Exit). All you have to do is start typing the first few characters of the filename and your cursor will start moving to a new position and highlight the file that matches what you type in. When you have typed in enough characters to find your file then you can press the Enter key or the arrow keys to end Name Search. If the file is not found you will see the file selection that is closest to your specified file name.

VMS	Template Keys	DOS
PF2,F18	**Macro Def** Define your macro.	Ctrl-F10
PF3,F18	**Macro** Invoke your macro.	Alt-F10
PF3,F11	**Mark Text** A provision for the insertion of the current date into any location in your document, and helps to create outlines and paragraph numbering.	Alt-F5

VMS	**Template Keys**	**DOS**

PF2,F17	**Merge/Sort**
	Provides the features of...
	    1) Merge: The capability of combining two separate documents into one.
	    2) Sort: Sorting items in your document.
		Ctrl-F9

PF1,F17	**Merge Codes** Displays the options of Field, End Record, Input, Page Off, Next Record which are simple merge commands along with the option of More that offers you more complex merge programming commands that you can use in your merge documents.	Shift-F9
PF2,F10	**Move** The template key used to move, copy, delete, append, or retrieve a block, tabular column, rectangle, sentence, paragraph, or page of data or information.	Ctrl-F4
PF1,F13	**Print** Produces a hardcopy of your document and also allows you to change printer attributes.	Shift-F7
PF3,F8	**Replace** Searches through your document from the position where your cursor is currently located forward to the end of your document for a specified text and replaces that text with revision or an alternate text.	Alt-F2
PF1,F18	**Retrieve** Fetches your document from your disk into WordPerfect.	Shift-F10
PF3,F9 OR F19	**Reveal Codes** Lifts up the WordPerfect curtain so that you can see what's behind your WordPerfect document by seeing the codes that you have placed into your document at various locations. For example, you will see codes in every location where you have pressed the Bold Key.	Alt-F3 OR F11
F18	**Save** Saves or stores your document under the filename that you specify or have specified.	F10

VMS	**Template Keys**	**DOS**

PF2,F9   **Screen**   Ctrl-F3

Provides three different options:

1)   Window: Divides your window into two windows.   One window contains Document 1 and one window contains Document 2.

2)   Line Draw: Allows you to use a line draw feature to draw boxes, tables, or any other item that you can draw with lines.

3)   Rewrite: WordPerfect redraws your editing screen.

PF1,F8   **<- Search**   Shift-F2

Initiates a search of your document from the position where your cursor is currently located backwards to the beginning of your document for some specified text. Once WordPerfect finds your text it will position the cursor one character to the right of the end of the text.

F8   **-> Search**   F2

Initiates a search of your document from the position where your cursor is currently located forward to the end of your document for a specified text.   Once WordPerfect finds your text it will position the cursor one character to the right of the end of the text.

PF1,F7   **Setup**   Shift-F1

Provides the capability of setting WordPerfect defaults that will be defined when you invoke WordPerfect. For instance:

1)   Mouse Settings such as Acceleration, Assisted Pointer Movement, Double Click Interval, Left-Handed Mouse, Port, Submenu Time Delay, and Type.

2)   Display settings include the following items: Attributes/Colors/Fonts; Edit Screen, Menu, and View Document Options; and Graphics and Text Screen Types.

3)   Environment settings like Alternate Keyboard, Backup and Beep Options, Cursor Speed, Document Management and Summary, Fast Unformatted Save,

VMS   Template Keys   DOS

Setup continued.

Hyphenation, Prompt for Hyphenation, and Units of Measure.

4)   Initial Settings of Date Format, Equation, Format Documents Retrieved for the Default Printer, Initial Codes, Merge, Print Options, Repeat Value, and Table of Authorities.

5)   Keyboard Layouts that are available for your use.

6)   File Location default settings for Backup, Documents, Graphics, Keyboard and Macro, Printer, Spreadsheet, Style and Library, and Thesaurus/Spell/Hyphenation Files.

VMS		DOS
PF2,F7	**Shell** The template key used when you need to temporarily exit from WordPerfect to the operating system so you can enter an operating system command.	Ctrl-F1
PF2,F8	**Spell** Allows you to...	Ctrl-F2

     1)   Have WordPerfect check the spelling of a word, page, or document.

     2)   Supply a name for a supplemental dictionary that you wish WordPerfect to use when spell checking your document. The default dictionary that is used is WP{WP}US.SUP. The dictionary you specify will be used until you either specify another dictionary or exit from WordPerfect.

     3)   Look up a word's spelling.

     4)   Have your computer count the number of words you have in your document.

VMS		DOS
PF3,F14	**Style** The means used to create different format templates for your documents. These format templates contain format codes that you can use in your documents once or multiple times.	Alt-F8

VMS	Template Keys	DOS

PF1,F9

Switch

Allows you to edit more than one document simultaneously. You can place a memo in Document One and place a letter in Document Two and then be able to copy or move information back and forth between the two documents by switching from one document to the other.

Shift-F3

PF2,F12

Tab Align

When you use this key you can align characters around the default alignment character of the period. For instance, when you press the key any characters you insert will be inserted to the left then press the alignment character and the characters will be inserted to the right of the alignment character. If you press Tab or the Enter key in place of the alignment character you will automatically be placed at the next Tab stop leaving the text to the left of the missing alignment character in its place.

Ctrl-F6

PF2,F11

Text In/Out

Allows you to...

1) Save or retrieve a DOS Text File. Used for importing and exporting a document from another word processing software package to WordPerfect or from WordPerfect to another word processing software package.

2) Add a password to your document. This is a security feature for your documents. When you add a password to your document it is saved with your document and is used to retrieve it, look at it, print it, etc.

3) Save your document as a generic (all codes removed except for the Tab and Indent codes; Indent codes will be converted into Tab codes), WordPerfect 5.0, or WordPerfect 4.2 document. It is important to remember that WordPerfect is a straight upward compatible software product, meaning that you may retrieve a WordPerfect 4.2 document when using WordPerfect 5.0 or WordPerfect 5.1. However, you

Ctrl-F5

VMS	**Template Keys**	DOS

Text In/Out continued.

                    may not retrieve a WordPerfect 5.1 document when using WordPerfect 5.0 or lower without having major problems, that is why you must save your document as a WordPerfect 5.0 document if you will be using that document in WordPerfect 5.0.

4)   Place comments into your document at key locations to help remind you of certain points. If you would like these comments displayed you may have them displayed on your screen with your document by invoking the SetUp key and selecting 2 for Display, 6 for Edit-Screen Options, and 2 for Comments Display.

5)   Import spreadsheets into your WordPerfect document.

PF3,F7	**Thesaurus** Provides a means for you to find an alternative word, synonym or antonym, for a word in your document.	Alt-F1
F14	**Underline** WordPerfect 5.1's method to underline text in your document.	F8

Other Function Keys

VMS	**Other Function Keys**	DOS
F16	**DO** *(VMS Only)* Same as the Macro key.	
F6	**Escape/Esc** Prompts the user for a Repeat Value that has a default value of 8. After you enter some repeat value number and then press a character that character will be repeated on your document editing screen that specified number of times.	Esc
F15	**Help** *(VMS Only)* Same as the Help key.	

MERGE PROGRAMMING

Merge Programming Feature

Merge power is also available in WordPerfect 5.1 through the merge programming language. This language helps the user create time-saving merge documents by performing the repetitive text manipulation tasks. Multiple letters can be created with specific differences to make each document more individualized for the recipient. Merge programming is different from macro programming through the general concept of macro programming that deals with repetitive keystroke action versus text manipulation action.

The Merge programming language has many similarities to the macro programming language including many of the same keyboard commands.

Variables

Types of Variables

The two types of variables available are system defined and user defined.

System variables contain information about the current state of the WordPerfect software package. These variables are defined by WordPerfect.

The values of user-defined variables are determined by the user's individual needs.

Macro and Merge Variables

All macro variables are global variables, whereas, merge variables can be either global or local variables.

Global variables can be used anytime and anywhere within a macro or merge program. Their value constantly reflects all changes that are made within the macro or merge program.

Local variables can only be used within merge programs not within macro programs. That is, they are local, or used only where they were initially defined for use.

In a merge program local variables always take preference over global variables since they belong to that merge program, or are local to that merge program. Thus, if you have a global variable with the name of NAME assigned to the value of David and a local variable in a merge program with the identical variable name of NAME assigned to the value of Chrysan then the local would take precedence over the global variable so the value of NAME used in the merge program would be Chrysan.

Merge Commands

To insert merge commands into your document you can do one of the following:

VMS	**Reference Keystrokes**	**DOS**
PF1,F17	U: Press **Merge Codes**.	Shift-F9
	C: *Prints* 1 Field; 2 End Record; 3 Input; 4 Page Off; 5 Next Record; 6 More: 0.	
	U: Press **6** for More.	
	C: *Displays Merge Commands Screen.*	

or

VMS	**Reference Keystrokes**	**DOS**
PF1,F17	U: Press **Merge Codes**.	Shift-F9
	C: *Prints* 1 Field; 2 End Record; 3 Input; 4 Page Off; 5 Next Record; 6 More: 0.	
PF1,F17	U: Press **Merge Codes**.	Shift-F9
	C: *Displays Merge Commands Screen.*	

The Merge Commands Screen is shown on Screen C-1 or Screen C-2.

Screen C-1: VMS Users

```
{ASSIGN}var~expr~
{BELL}
{BREAK}
{CALL}label~
{CANCEL OFF}
{CANCEL ON}
{CASE}expr~cs1~lb1~...csN~lbN~~
{CASE CALL}expr~cs1~lb1~...csN~lbN~~
{CHAIN MACRO}macroname~                    (^G)
{CHAIN PRIMARY}filename~




          (Name Search; Arrows; Return to Select)
```

Screen C-2: DOS Users

```
{ASSIGN}var~expr~
{BELL}
{BREAK}
{CALL}label~
{CANCEL OFF}
{CANCEL ON}
{CASE}expr~cs1~lb1~...csN~lbN~~
{CASE CALL}expr~cs1~lb1~...csN~lbN~~
{CHAIN MACRO}macroname~              (^G)
{CHAIN PRIMARY}filename~
```

```
(Name Search; Arrows; Enter to Select)
```

After the Merge Commands Screen appears you can use the Name Search by typing in as many characters of the command you need to find it or use Arrow keys to highlight command then use the Enter key to select the command.

Syntax and Examples of WordPerfect's Keyboard Commands

The Syntax of WordPerfect 5.1's merge keyboard commands are very similar to macro keyboard commands. Some commands are identical. (See Table C-1.)

Table C-1

{ASSIGN}
    Syntax: {ASSIGN}var~expr~
    Description: Allows assignment of a value or formula to a variable.

{BELL}
    Syntax: {BELL}
    Description: Sounds the computer's bell.

{BREAK}
    Syntax: {BREAK}
    Description: Terminates merge or escapes from a programming structure.

{CALL}
    Syntax: {CALL}label~
    Description: Executes a subroutine.

{CANCEL OFF}
    Syntax: {CANCEL OFF}
    Description: Turns the Cancel key off.

Table C-1 continued.

{CANCEL ON}
       Syntax: {CANCEL ON}
       Description: Turns the Cancel key on.

{CASE}
       Syntax: {CASE}expr~cs1~lb1~...csN~lbN~~
       Description: Branches to a specified location in the merge depending on the result of an expression.

{CASE CALL}
       Syntax: {CASE CALL}expr~cs1~lb1~...csN~lbN~~
       Description: Branches and returns from a specified location in the merge depending on the result of an expression.

{CHAIN MACRO}
       Syntax: {CHAIN MACRO}macroname~
       Description: Invokes the macro named macroname at the end of the merge process. Equivalent to WordPerfect 5.0's ^Gmacroname^G command.

{CHAIN PRIMARY}
       Syntax: {CHAIN PRIMARY}filename~
       Description: Executes the primary file that is named after the current primary file is done executing.

{CHAIN SECONDARY}
       Syntax: {CHAIN SECONDARY}filename~
       Description: Takes the records from the secondary file that is named after all the records in the current secondary file are used.

{CHAR}
       Syntax: {CHAR}var~message~
       Description: Prompts the user via a message for a single keystroke input.

{COMMENT}
       Syntax: {COMMENT}comment~
       Description: Comment statements. Ignored by WordPerfect during merge execution.

{CTON}
       Syntax: {CTON}character~
       Description: Converts the character specified from one of WordPerfect's character sets to its individual number. Acronym for Character TO Number.

Table C-1 continued.

{DATE}
>
> Syntax: {DATE}
>
> Description: Inserts the current date into the document. The current date must have been entered when the user started the computer or the computer's internal system clock must have been set in order for this code to work. Equivalent to WordPerfect 5.0's ^D command.

{DOCUMENT}filename~
>
> Syntax: {DOCUMENT}filename~
>
> Description: Places the specified document at the position where the cursor is currently located.

{ELSE}
>
> Syntax: {ELSE}
>
> Description: Used within an IF or CASE structure. Statements following the ELSE are performed when some conditional expression yields a False answer.

{END FIELD}
>
> Syntax: {END FIELD}
>
> Description: Terminates a secondary field. Equivalent to WordPerfect 5.0's ^R command.

{END FOR}
>
> Syntax: {END FOR}
>
> Description: Terminates a FOR Loop.

{END IF}
>
> Syntax: {END IF}
>
> Description: Terminates an IF Structure.

{END RECORD}
>
> Syntax: {END RECORD}
>
> Description: Terminates a secondary record. Equivalent to WordPerfect 5.0's ^E command.

{END WHILE}
>
> Syntax: {END WHILE}
>
> Description: Terminates a WHILE Loop.

{FIELD}
>
> Syntax: {FIELD}field~
>
> Description: The contents of this field is inserted into the merged file. Equivalent to WordPerfect 5.0's ^Fn^ command.

Table C-1 continued.

{FIELD NAMES}
> Syntax: {FIELD NAMES}name1~...nameN~~
> Description: Defines the name and order of these fields in the secondary file.

{FOR}
> Syntax: {FOR}var~start~stop~step~
> Description: Initiates a FOR loop that executes some statements a specified number of times.

{GO}
> Syntax: {GO}label~
> Description: Branches to a specified location within the merge.

{IF}
> Syntax: {IF}expr~
> Description: Initiates an IF Structure. Tests some condition expression and then will perform certain statements depending on the conditional expression response.

{IF BLANK}
> Syntax: {IF BLANK}field~
> Description: If the specified field is blank then the commands that follow this keyboard command are performed.

{IF EXISTS}
> Syntax: {IF EXISTS}var~
> Description: Verifies whether or not the specified variable has been assigned a value.

{IF NOT BLANK}
> Syntax: {IF NOT BLANK}field~
> Description: If the specified field is not blank then the commands that follow this keyboard command are performed.

{INPUT}
> Syntax: {INPUT}message~
> Description: Prompts the user for input that contains variable amounts of keystrokes.

{KEYBOARD}
> Syntax: {KEYBOARD}
> Description: Allows text to be inserted into the primary or secondary file by the user while the merge process temporarily pauses. Equivalent to WordPerfect 5.0's ^C command.

Table C-1 continued.

{LABEL}
    Syntax: {LABEL}label~
    Description: Marks a location within a merge that the programmer can
                                   branch to at any given time.

{LEN}
    Syntax: {LEN}expr~
    Description: Calculates the length or number of characters contained
                                   within a variable or a value.

{LOCAL}
    Syntax: {LOCAL}var~expr~
    Description: Allows assignment of a value to a local variable.

{LOOK}
    Syntax: {LOOK}var~
    Description: Determines whether a key has been pressed or not.

{MID}
    Syntax: {MID}expr~offset~count~
    Description: Extracts a substring from within a string.

{MGR CMND}
    Syntax: {MGR CMND}codes{MGR CMND}
    Description: Allows the user to insert merge codes, commands, and text
                                   into the final merged document. Equivalent to WordPerfect
                                   5.0's ^Vcodes^V command.

{NEST MACRO}
    Syntax: {NEST MACRO}macroname~
    Description: Executes the named macro. When the macro is finished
                                   WordPerfect returns to the merge.

{NEST PRIMARY}
    Syntax: {NEST PRIMARY}filename~
    Description: Executes the named primary file. When the merge is finished
                                   WordPerfect returns to the original primary file. Equivalent
                                   to WordPerfect 5.0's ^Pfilename^P command.

{NEST SECONDARY}
    Syntax: {NEST SECONDARY}filename~
    Description: Uses the named secondary file's records until all records are
                                   used then returns to the original secondary file.

{NEXT}
    Syntax: {NEXT}
    Description: Invokes the next iteration for a FOR or WHILE loop.

Table C-1 continued.

{NEXT RECORD}

    Syntax: {NEXT RECORD}

    Description: Advances to the next record in the secondary file if it exists. Equivalent to WordPerfect 5.0's ^N command.

{NTOC}

    Syntax: {NTOC}number~

    Description: Will return a character that is equivalent to any specified key number on the keyboard.

{ON CANCEL}

    Syntax: {ON CANCEL}action~

    Description: If the Cancel key has been pressed or a {RETURN CANCEL} command has been issued WordPerfect will perform the indicated action.

{ON ERROR}

    Syntax: {ON ERROR}action~

    Description: When an error has been discovered WordPerfect will perform the indicated action.

{OTHERWISE}

    Syntax: {OTHERWISE}

    Description: Use with the {CASE} and {CASE CALL} merge programming statements to be the default for different cases that are not specified in the {CASE} and {CASE CALL} statements.

{PAGE OFF}

    Syntax: {PAGE OFF}

    Description: The hard pages in your final merged document between all primary files will not be automatically inserted.

{PAGE ON}

    Syntax: {PAGE ON}

    Description: The hard pages in your final merged document between all primary files will be automatically inserted. Use this keyboard command after you have used the {PAGE OFF} keyboard command.

{PRINT}

    Syntax: {PRINT}

    Description: Everything located in the merge document at this current time will be printed. Equivalent to WordPerfect 5.0's ^T command.

Table C-1 continued.

{PROCESS}
      Syntax: {PROCESS}codes{PROCESS}
      Description: The codes, commands, or text within this keyboard command are executed when this command is encountered within a secondary merge file.

{PROMPT}
      Syntax: {PROMPT}message~
      Description: Displays some message on WordPerfect's status line. Equivalent to WordPerfect 5.0's ^Omessage^O command.

{QUIT}
      Syntax: {QUIT}
      Description: Terminates the execution of a merge. Equivalent to WordPerfect 5.0's ^Q command.

{RETURN}
      Syntax: {RETURN}
      Description: Designates the end of a subroutine. Tells the merge to return to the next item following the command that executed the subroutine.

{RETURN CANCEL}
      Syntax: {RETURN CANCEL}
      Description: Designates the end of a subroutine. Tells the merge to return to the next item following the command that executed the subroutine with a cancel indication.

{RETURN ERROR}
      Syntax: {RETURN ERROR}
      Description: Designates the end of a subroutine. Tells macro to return to the item following the command that executed the subroutine with an error   indication.

{REWRITE}
      Syntax: {REWRITE}
      Description: Rewrites the computer screen. Equivalent to WordPerfect 5.0's ^U command.

{STATUS PROMPT}
      Syntax: {STATUS PROMPT}message~
      Description: Displays some message on WordPerfect's status line when the status line is there.

{STEP OFF}
      Syntax: {STEP OFF}
      Description: Turns off the execution of the merge statements step-by-step.

Table C-1 continued.

{STEP ON}

      Syntax: {STEP ON}

      Description: Executes the merge statements step-by-step. Waits for the user to press a key before continuing on with the next step.

{STOP}

      Syntax: {STOP}

      Description: Terminates all merge activity.

{SUBST PRIMARY}

      Syntax: {SUBST PRIMARY}filename~

      Description: Executes the named primary file. When the merge is finished WordPerfect does not return to the original primary file.

{SUBST SECONDARY}

      Syntax: {SUBST SECONDARY}filename~

      Description: Inserts the specified filename as the new secondary file to use in the merge process. Equivalent to WordPerfect 5.0's ^Sfilename^S command.

{SYSTEM}

      Syntax: {SYSTEM}sysvar~

      Description: Allows access to system variable's contents.

{TEXT}

      Syntax: {TEXT}var~message~

      Description: Prompts the user for input.

{VARIABLE}

      Syntax: {VARIABLE}var~

      Description: Allows access to your variable's contents.

{WAIT}

      Syntax: {WAIT}10ths second~

      Description: Pauses the execution of the merge for a specified time.

{WHILE}

      Syntax: {WHILE}expr~

      Description: Initiates a WHILE loop that executes while some specified condition is True.

Invoking Merges

To invoke or execute your merge to perform its specified task do the following:

VMS	Reference Keystrokes	DOS
PF2,F17	U: Press *Merge/Sort.* C: *Prints* 1 Merge; 2 Sort; 3 Convert Old Merge Codes: <u>0</u>.	Ctrl-F9
	U: Press *1* for Merge. C: *Prints* Primary file: _.	
	U: Type in primary filename and press the *Enter key.* C: *Prints* Secondary file: _.	
	U: Type in secondary filename and press the *Enter key.* C: *Merges files.*	

KEYBOARD LAYOUT

Keyboard Layout Feature

Initially when WordPerfect 5.1 is invoked, each of the keys have a designated task assigned to them. For example, Function key F9 for VMS and F3 for DOS is the Help key.

The keyboard layout feature allows you to remap, or reassign, any of the keys on the keyboard, in order to assist you in making WordPerfect 5.1 more personalized to meet your specific needs.

Location of Keyboard Layouts

You must tell WordPerfect where WordPerfect's keyboard layout are currently located and where you want your keyboard layouts to be located.

The VMS keyboard layouts are usually located in WPCORP$WP51_KEYBOARDS directory whereas the DOS keyboard layouts are in c:\wp51.

The following keystrokes are used to change the location of the Keyboard/Macro Files:

VMS	Reference Keystrokes	DOS
PF1,F7	U: Press *Setup*. C: *Displays Setup Menu.*	Shift-F1
	U: Press *6* for Location of Files. C: *Displays Setup: Location of Files Menu.*	
VMS Users	U: Press *2* for Keymapping. U: Press *2* For Keyboard/Macro Files.	*DOS Users*
VMS Users	C: *Prints* Location of Keyboard Files: _. C: *Positions cursor to right of Keyboard/Macro Files.*	*DOS Users*
VMS Users WPCORP$ WP51_KEY BOARDS	U: Enter in the location for the Keyboard files and press the *Enter key*.	
	U: Enter in the location for Keyboard and Macro files and press the *Enter key*.	*DOS Users* c:\wp51
VMS Users	C: *Prints* Location of Macro Files: _. C: *Returns to Command Line.*	*DOS Users*

VMS Users: Perform the following Reference Keystrokes.

DOS Users: Do NOT perform the following Reference Keystrokes.

VMS   Reference Keystrokes   DOS

U: Enter in the location for Macro files and press
the *Enter key.*
C: *Returns to Command Line.*

VMS Users: Ask your System Manager for verification for your particular system.

VMS Users: Perform the following Reference Keystrokes.

DOS Users: Perform the following Reference Keystrokes.

VMS   Reference Keystrokes   DOS

F13   U: Press *Exit.*   F7
VMS Users   C: *Returns to Setup Menu.*
                     C: *Returns to Document.*   *DOS Users*

VMS Users: Perform the following Reference Keystrokes.

DOS Users: Do NOT perform the following Reference Keystrokes.

VMS   Reference Keystrokes   DOS

F13   U: Press *Exit.*
                     C: *Returns to Document.*

Once the location of WordPerfect 5.1's and your future keyboard layouts are defined you are all set to reassign the keys.

Keyboard Definitions

To create, select, edit, etc. keyboard layouts do the following:

VMS   Reference Keystrokes   DOS

PF1,F7   U: Press *Setup.*   Shift-F1
                     C: *Displays Setup Menu.*

                     U: Press *5* for Keyboard Layout.
                     C: *Displays Setup: Keyboard Layout Menu.*

The Setup: Keyboard Layout Menu is shown on Screen D-1 or Screen D-2.

Screen D-1: VMS Users

```
Setup: Keyboard Layout

   ALTERNATE
   ENHANCED
   EQUATION
   MACROS
   SHORTCUT
   WPCORP_WP42_DEFAULT













1 Select; 2 Delete; 3 Rename; 4 Create; 5 Copy; 6 Original;
7 Edit; 8 Map; N Name search: 1
```

Screen D-2: DOS Users

```
Setup: Keyboard Layout

   ENHANCED
   EQUATION
   FASTKEYS
   MACROS
   SHORTCUT













1 Select; 2 Delete; 3 Rename; 4 Create; 5 Copy; 6 Original;
7 Edit; 8 Map; N Name search: 1
```

The Setup: Keyboard Layout Menu for both VMS and DOS offers the following nine options:

1. Select: Chooses one of WordPerfect 5.1's predefined keyboard definitions or one of your keyboard layouts, that is highlighted by you, to be used until another one is selected or the original keyboard layout is restored.

2. Delete: Erases the highlighted keyboard layout.

3. Rename: Provides the option to rename the highlighted keyboard layout.

4. **Create:**   Allows you to create a brand new keyboard layout. When you give the keyboard definition a name you may use a maximum of 39 characters for VMS and 8 characters for DOS. By default the extension of the keyboard layout will be .VWPK for VMS and .WPK for DOS unless you specify another extension.

5. **Copy:**   Provides the ability to copy an existing keyboard layout, when highlighted, that you would like to use after you modify several keys to create a new keyboard definition.

6. **Original:**   Selects the original keyboard definition.

7. **Edit:**   Allows you to edit the highlighted keyboard layout.

8. **Map:**   Displays most key definitions and allows you to assign keys for the highlighted keyboard layout.

9. **Name search:**   Allows you to search by keyboard layout name for a particular keyboard definition.

When you edit a keyboard layout you will see what is shown on Screen D-3 or Screen D-4.

Screen D-3: ENHANCED Keyboard Definition - VMS Users

```
Keyboard:  Edit

  Name:   ENHANCED

  Key                Action                Description

  PF4                {KEY MACRO 13}        Home Home Home Left
  KP5                {Home}                Home
  PF1,F19            {KEY MACRO 14}        Italics
  PF1,F20            {KEY MACRO 15}        Retrieve Block
  PF2,KP5            {Goto}                Go To
  PF2,F19            {KEY MACRO 10}        Large
  PF2,F20            {KEY MACRO 11}        Move Block
  PF3,KP2            {KEY MACRO 7}         Move Down by Sentence
  PF3,KP4            {KEY MACRO 4}         Move Left One Column
  PF3,KP6            {KEY MACRO 5}         Move Right One Column
  PF3,KP8            {KEY MACRO 12}        Move Up by Sentence
  PF3,F19            {KEY MACRO 2}         Very Large
  PF3,F20            {KEY MACRO 3}         Copy Block

1 Action; 2 Dscrptn; 3 Original; 4 Create; 5 Move; Macro: 6 Save; 7 Retrieve: 1
```

Screen D-4: ENHANCED Keyboard Definition - DOS Users

```
Keyboard: Edit

  Name:  ENHANCED

  Key              Action                Description

  Home             {KEY MACRO 1}         Home Home Left
  Num 5            {Home}                Home
  Shft-F11         {KEY MACRO 2}         Italics
  Shft-F12         {KEY MACRO 3}         Retrieve Block
  Ctrl-F11         {KEY MACRO 4}         Large
  Ctrl-F12         {KEY MACRO 5}         Move Block
  Alt-F11          {KEY MACRO 6}         Very Large
  Alt-F12          {KEY MACRO 7}         Copy Block
  Ctrl-Num 5       {Goto}                Go To
  Alt-Up           {KEY MACRO 10}        Move Up by Sentence
  Alt-Down         {KEY MACRO 11}        Move Down by Sentence

1 Action; 2 Dscrptn; 3 Original; 4 Create; 5 Move; Macro: 6 Save; 7 Retrieve: 1
```

These key options are described as follows:

Action: Lets the user edit a Key's Action in the Key: Action screen. It operates like the Macro Editor screen used when programming in the macro programming language.

Dscrptn: Provides the option to add or change the description for the specified key.

Original: Selects the original key definition.

Create: With this key you can create a definition for a key and assign its new function.

Move: The user can move the highlighted option to another key when the user presses this new key.

Macro: Save: The key definition will be saved as a macro.

Macro: Retrieve: Allows the user to assign a key to a previously defined macro.

WordPerfect 5.1's Keyboard Definitions

WordPerfect 5.1 offers six layouts for VMS and five layouts for DOS that can be assigned to different functions. These keyboard definitions are contained in files which contain a listing of the specific keys and their associated functions and end with a .VWPK for VMS and .WPK for DOS extension.

The keyboard definitions included with WordPerfect 5.1 for VMS and DOS are shown as follows in the Keyboard: Edit Menus (See Screens D-5 to D-15).

Screen D-5: *ALTERNATE Keyboard Definition - VMS Users ONLY*

```
Keyboard:  Edit

  Name:  ALTERNATE

  Key              Action                 Description

  F6               {Cancel}               Cancel
  F7               {Help}                 Help
  F9               {Esc}                  Esc




1 Action; 2 Dscrptn; 3 Original; 4 Create; 5 Move; Macro: 6 Save; 7 Retrieve: 1
```

Screen D-6: *ENHANCED Keyboard Definition - VMS Users*

```
Keyboard:  Edit

  Name:  ENHANCED

  Key              Action                 Description

  PF4              {KEY MACRO 13}         Home Home Home Left
  KP5              {Home}                 Home
  PF1,F19          {KEY MACRO 14}         Italics
  PF1,F20          {KEY MACRO 15}         Retrieve Block
  PF2,KP5          {Goto}                 Go To
  PF2,F19          {KEY MACRO 10}         Large
  PF2,F20          {KEY MACRO 11}         Move Block
  PF3,KP2          {KEY MACRO 7}          Move Down by Sentence
  PF3,KP4          {KEY MACRO 4}          Move Left One Column
  PF3,KP6          {KEY MACRO 5}          Move Right One Column
  PF3,KP8          {KEY MACRO 12}         Move Up by Sentence
  PF3,F19          {KEY MACRO 2}          Very Large
  PF3,F20          {KEY MACRO 3}          Copy Block

1 Action; 2 Dscrptn; 3 Original; 4 Create; 5 Move; Macro: 6 Save; 7 Retrieve: 1
```

Screen D-7: ENHANCED Keyboard Definition - DOS Users

```
┌─────────────────────────────────────────────────────────────────────────┐
│ Keyboard:  Edit                                                           │
│                                                                           │
│   Name:  ENHANCED                                                         │
│                                                                           │
│   Key              Action                 Description                      │
│                                                                           │
│   Home             {KEY MACRO 1}          Home Home Left                   │
│   Num 5            {Home}                 Home                             │
│   Shft-F11         {KEY MACRO 2}          Italics                         │
│   Shft-F12         {KEY MACRO 3}          Retrieve Block                  │
│   Ctrl-F11         {KEY MACRO 4}          Large                           │
│   Ctrl-F12         {KEY MACRO 5}          Move Block                      │
│   Alt-F11          {KEY MACRO 6}          Very Large                      │
│   Alt-F12          {KEY MACRO 7}          Copy Block                      │
│   Ctrl-Num 5       {Goto}                 Go To                           │
│   Alt-Up           {KEY MACRO 10}         Move Up by Sentence             │
│   Alt-Down         {KEY MACRO 11}         Move Down by Sentence           │
│                                                                           │
│ 1 Action; 2 Dscrptn; 3 Original; 4 Create; 5 Move; Macro: 6 Save; 7 Retrieve: 1 │
└─────────────────────────────────────────────────────────────────────────┘
```

Screen D-8: EQUATION Keyboard Definition - VMS Users

```
Keyboard:  Edit

  Name:  EQUATION

  Key              Action                Description

  PF2,Tab          [←:6,22]              ← (Left Arrow)
  PF2,N            {KEY MACRO 15}        GRAD (Nabla, Gradient)
  PF2,Q            {KEY MACRO 18}        SQRT (Square Root)
  PF2,S            {KEY MACRO 19}        SUM (Sum)
  PF2,a            {KEY MACRO 8}         SUP (Superscript)
  PF2,b            {KEY MACRO 9}         BAR (Bar)
  PF2,d            [Δ:8,8]               DELTA (upper case)
  PF2,e            {KEY MACRO 10}        IN (Member, Element)
  PF2,f            {KEY MACRO 11}        FROM TO (x From a, To b)
  PF2,g            {KEY MACRO 12}        GRAD (nabla, Gradient)
  PF2,i            {KEY MACRO 13}        INT (Integral)
  PF2,l            {KEY MACRO 14}        OVERLINE (Overline)
  PF2,o            {KEY MACRO 16}        OVER (Over)
  PF2,p            {KEY MACRO 17}        PARTIAL (Partial)
  PF2,z            {KEY MACRO 20}        SUB (Subscript)
  PF3,Tab          [→:6,21]              → (Right Arrow)
  PF3,,            {KEY MACRO 4}         <= (Less Than or Equal To)
  PF3,-            {KEY MACRO 6}         CONG (Congruent)
  PF3,.            {KEY MACRO 5}         >= (Greater Than or Equal To)
  PF3,=            {KEY MACRO 7}         != (Not Equal To)
  PF3,\            {KEY MACRO 1}         LINE (Line)
  PF3,`            {KEY MACRO 2}         SIMEQ (Similar or Equal To)
  PF3,a            [α:8,1]               alpha
  PF3,b            [β:8,3]               beta
  PF3,d            [δ:8,9]               delta
  PF3,e            [ε:8,11]              epsilon
  PF3,f            [φ:8,45]              phi
  PF3,g            [γ:8,7]               gamma
  PF3,i            {KEY MACRO 3}         INF (Infinity)
  PF3,l            [λ:8,23]              lambda
  PF3,m            [μ:8,25]              mu
  PF3,n            [ⁿ:8,15]              eta
  PF3,o            [ω:8,51]              omega
  PF3,p            [π:8,33]              pi
  PF3,r            [ρ:8,35]              rho
  PF3,s            [σ:8,37]              sigma
  PF3,t            [θ:8,17]              theta

1 Action; 2 Dscrptn; 3 Original; 4 Create; 5 Move; Macro: 6 Save; 7 Retrieve: 1
```

Screen D-9: EQUATION Keyboard Definition - DOS Users

```
Keyboard:  Edit

  Name:  EQUATION

  Key              Action              Description

  Alt-E            [ε:8,11]            epsilon
  Alt-R            [ρ:8,35]            rho
  Alt-T            [θ:8,17]            theta
  Alt-I            {KEY MACRO 16}      INF (Infinity)
  Alt-O            [ω:8,51]            omega
  Alt-P            [π:8,33]            pi
  Alt-A            [α:8,1]             alpha
  Alt-S            [σ:8,37]            sigma
  Alt-D            [δ:8,9]             delta
  Alt-F            [φ:8,45]            phi
  Alt-G            [γ:8,7]             gamma
  Alt-L            [λ:8,23]            lambda
  Alt-'            {KEY MACRO 27}      SIMEQ (Similar or Equal To)
  Alt-\            {KEY MACRO 33}      LINE (Line)
  Alt-B            [ß:8,3]             beta
  Alt-N            [ʼ:8,15]            eta
  Alt-M            [μ:8,25]            mu
  Alt-,            {KEY MACRO 29}      <= (Less Than or Equal To)
  Alt-.            {KEY MACRO 30}      >= (Greater Than or Equal To)
  Alt--            {KEY MACRO 28}      CONG (Congruent)
  Alt-=            {KEY MACRO 23}      != (Not Equal To)
  Ctrl-Tab         [←:6,22]            (Left Arrow)
  Alt-Tab          [→:6,21]            (Right Arrow)
  Ctrl-A           {KEY MACRO 21}      SUP (Superscript)
  Ctrl-B           {KEY MACRO 22}      BAR (Bar)
  Ctrl-D           [Δ:8,8]             DELTA (upper case)
  Ctrl-E           {KEY MACRO 31}      IN (Member, Element)
  Ctrl-F           {KEY MACRO 36}      FROM TO (x From a, To b)
  Ctrl-G           {KEY MACRO 35}      GRAD (Nabla, Gradient)
  Ctrl-I           {KEY MACRO 15}      INT (Integral)
  Ctrl-L           {KEY MACRO 25}      OVERLINE (Overline)
  Ctrl-N           {KEY MACRO 34}      GRAD (Nabla, Gradient)
  Ctrl-O           {KEY MACRO 19}      OVER (Over)
  Ctrl-P           {KEY MACRO 14}      PARTIAL (Partial)
  Ctrl-Q           {KEY MACRO 17}      SQRT (Square Root)
  Ctrl-S           {KEY MACRO 18}      SUM (Sum)
  Ctrl-Z           {KEY MACRO 20}      SUB (Subscript)

1 Action; 2 Dscrptn; 3 Original; 4 Create; 5 Move; Macro: 6 Save; 7 Retrieve: 1
```

Screen D-10: FASTKEYS Keyboard Definition - DOS Users ONLY

```
Keyboard:  Edit

  Name:  FASTKEYS

  Key              Action            Description

  Ctrl-A           {KEY MACRO 1}     Paste Block
  Ctrl-B           {Bold}            Bold
  Ctrl-C           {Center}          Center
  Ctrl-D           {KEY MACRO 2}     Date Text
  Ctrl-E           {KEY MACRO 3}     Endnote Create
  Ctrl-F           {KEY MACRO 4}     Base Font
  Ctrl-G           {KEY MACRO 5}     Graphics Create
  Ctrl-I           {KEY MACRO 6}     Italics
  Ctrl-K           {KEY MACRO 7}     Copy
  Ctrl-M           {KEY MACRO 8}     Move (Cut)
  Ctrl-N           {KEY MACRO 9}     Normal Text
  Ctrl-P           {KEY MACRO 10}    Preview (View Document)
  Ctrl-R           {Reveal Codes}    Reveal Codes
  Ctrl-S           {Spell}           Spell
  Ctrl-T           {Thesaurus}       Thesaurus
  Ctrl-U           {Underline}       Underline

1 Action; 2 Dscrptn; 3 Original; 4 Create; 5 Move; Macro: 6 Save; 7 Retrieve: 1
```

Screen D-11: MACROS Keyboard Definition - VMS Users

```
Keyboard:  Edit

  Name:  MACROS

  Key              Action            Description

  PF2,c            {KEY MACRO 13}    Pop-Up Calculator
  PF2,d            {KEY MACRO 14}    Create a Memo, Letter, or Itinerary
  PF2,e            {KEY MACRO 15}    Print Name & Address on an Envelope
  PF2,f            {KEY MACRO 12}    Search and Replace Font codes
  PF2,g            {KEY MACRO 16}    Glossary Macro - Expand Abbreviations
  PF2,p            {KEY MACRO 19}    Pointing mode when entering formulas
  PF2,r            {KEY MACRO 6}     Resume Printing when Queue is Paused
  PF2,F14          {KEY MACRO 17}    Font Key
  PF3,b            {KEY MACRO 1}     Restore the previous block
  PF3,c            {KEY MACRO 2}     Capitalize 1st letter of current word
  PF3,d            {KEY MACRO 3}     Delete a line
  PF3,e            {KEY MACRO 4}     Get to Main Editing Screen
  PF3,f            {KEY MACRO 5}     Find the Bookmark
  PF3,g            {KEY MACRO 18}    Resume printing
  PF3,i            {KEY MACRO 7}     Insert a line
  PF3,m            {KEY MACRO 8}     Insert Bookmark
  PF3,n            {KEY MACRO 9}     Edit the Next or Previous Note
  PF3,r            {KEY MACRO 10}    Replace an AFC with a different type
  PF3,t            {KEY MACRO 11}    Transpose 2 visible characters

1 Action; 2 Dscrptn; 3 Original; 4 Create; 5 Move; Macro: 6 Save; 7 Retrieve: 1
```

Screen D-12: MACROS Keyboard Definition - DOS Users

```
Keyboard:  Edit

  Name:  MACROS

  Key            Action            Description

  Alt-E          {KEY MACRO 1}     Return to main editing screen
  Alt-R          {KEY MACRO 2}     Replace Size, Attribute, or Text
  Alt-T          {KEY MACRO 3}     Transpose 2 visible characters
  Alt-I          {KEY MACRO 4}     Insert a line
  Alt-D          {KEY MACRO 5}     Delete a line
  Alt-F          {KEY MACRO 6}     Find the Bookmark (see Alt-m)
  Alt-G          {KEY MACRO 7}     Give printer a GO
  Alt-C          {KEY MACRO 8}     Capitalize 1st letter of current word
  Alt-B          {KEY MACRO 9}     Restore the previous block
  Alt-N          {KEY MACRO 10}    Edit the Next or Previous Note
  Alt-M      .   {KEY MACRO 11}    Insert Bookmark <<MARK>>
  Ctrl-F8        {KEY MACRO 12}    Font key
  Ctrl-C         {KEY MACRO 13}    Calculator
  Ctrl-D         {KEY MACRO 14}    Create a Memo, Letter, or Itinerary
  Ctrl-E         {KEY MACRO 15}    Print Name & Address on an Envelope
  Ctrl-F         {KEY MACRO 19}    Search and Replace Font codes
  Ctrl-G         {KEY MACRO 16}    Glossary Macro - Expand Abbreviations
  Ctrl-P         {KEY MACRO 18}    Pointing mode when entering formulas
  Ctrl-R         {KEY MACRO 17}    Recalculate all formulas in a table


1 Action; 2 Dscrptn; 3 Original; 4 Create; 5 Move; Macro: 6 Save; 7 Retrieve: 1
```

Screen D-13: SHORTCUT Keyboard Definition - VMS Users

```
Keyboard:   Edit

   Name:   SHORTCUT

   Key              Action                Description

   PF2,b            {KEY MACRO 17}        Base Font
   PF2,c            {KEY MACRO 18}        Define Columns
   PF2,d            {KEY MACRO 19}        Double Spacing
   PF2,e            {KEY MACRO 20}        Endnote create
   PF2,f            {KEY MACRO 21}        Footnote create
   PF2,g            {KEY MACRO 22}        Graphic -create a graphic figure
   PF2,h            {KEY MACRO 23}        Header A create
   PF2,i            {KEY MACRO 24}        Document Initial codes
   PF2,j            {KEY MACRO 25}        Justification
   PF2,l            {KEY MACRO 26}        Left/Right Margins
   PF2,m            {KEY MACRO 27}        Margins Top/Bottom
   PF2,o            {KEY MACRO 28}        Footer A create
   PF2,p            {KEY MACRO 29}        Paper Size/Type
   PF2,q            {KEY MACRO 30}        Equation create
   PF2,s            {KEY MACRO 31}        Single Spacing
   PF2,t            {KEY MACRO 32}        Tab Set
   PF3,a            {KEY MACRO 8}         Add an Attribute
   PF3,b            {KEY MACRO 16}        Subscript
   PF3,d            {KEY MACRO 10}        Double Underline
   PF3,e            {KEY MACRO 2}         Edit a Code
   PF3,f            {KEY MACRO 11}        Fine
   PF3,g            {KEY MACRO 12}        Go Printer
   PF3,i     -      {KEY MACRO 5}         Italics
   PF3,l            {KEY MACRO 13}        Large
   PF3,o            {KEY MACRO 6}         Outline
   PF3,p            {KEY MACRO 7}         Superscript
   PF3,r            {KEY MACRO 3}         Redline
   PF3,s            {KEY MACRO 9}         Small
   PF3,t            {KEY MACRO 4}         Strikeout
   PF3,v            {KEY MACRO 1}         Very Large
   PF3,x            {KEY MACRO 15}        Extra Large

 1 Action; 2 Dscrptn; 3 Original; 4 Create; 5 Move; Macro: 6 Save; 7 Retrieve: 1
```

Screen D-14: SHORTCUT Keyboard Definition - DOS Users

```
Keyboard:  Edit

  Name:  SHORTCUT

  Key              Action               Description

  Alt-W            {KEY MACRO 26}       Shadow
  Alt-E            {KEY MACRO 15}       Edit a Code
  Alt-R            {KEY MACRO 8}        Redline
  Alt-T            {KEY MACRO 27}       Strikeout
  Alt-I            {KEY MACRO 1}        Italics
  Alt-O            {KEY MACRO 25}       Outline
  Alt-P            {KEY MACRO 21}       Superscript
  Alt-A            {KEY MACRO 32}       Add an Attribute
  Alt-S            {KEY MACRO 6}        Small
  Alt-D            {KEY MACRO 2}        Double Underline
  Alt-F            {KEY MACRO 7}        Fine
  Alt-G            {KEY MACRO 30}       Go Printer
  Alt-L            {KEY MACRO 5}        Large
  Alt-X            {KEY MACRO 3}        Extra Large
  Alt-V            {KEY MACRO 4}        Very Large
  Alt-B            {KEY MACRO 20}       Subscript
  Ctrl-B           {KEY MACRO 23}       Base Font
  Ctrl-C           {KEY MACRO 19}       Define Columns
  Ctrl-D           {KEY MACRO 24}       Double Spacing
  Ctrl-E           {KEY MACRO 10}       Endnote create
  Ctrl-F           {KEY MACRO 9}        Footnote create
  Ctrl-G           {KEY MACRO 17}       Graphic -create a graphic figure
  Ctrl-H           {KEY MACRO 11}       Header A create
  Ctrl-I           {KEY MACRO 31}       Document Initial codes
  Ctrl-J           {KEY MACRO 18}       Justification
  Ctrl-L           {KEY MACRO 13}       Left/Right Margins
  Ctrl-M           {KEY MACRO 14}       Margins Top/Bottom
  Ctrl-O           {KEY MACRO 22}       Footer A create
  Ctrl-P           {KEY MACRO 28}       Paper Size/Type
  Ctrl-Q           {KEY MACRO 16}       Equation create
  Ctrl-S           {KEY MACRO 29}       Single Spacing
  Ctrl-T           {KEY MACRO 12}       Tab Set


1 Action; 2 Dscrptn; 3 Original; 4 Create; 5 Move; Macro: 6 Save; 7 Retrieve: 1
```

Screen D-15: WPCORP_WP42_DEFAULT Keyboard Definition - VMS Users

```
Keyboard:  Edit

  Name:  WPCORP_WP42_DEFAULT

  Key                 Action                    Description

  Ctrl-J              {KEY MACRO 5}
* Ctrl-P              {Print Screen}
* Back (<X])          {Backspace}
  KP0                 {Cancel}
  KP1                 {End Field}
  KP2                 {Save}
  KP3                 {Page Down}
  KP4                 {List}
  KP5                 {Bold}
* KP6                 {Exit}
* KP7                 {Esc}
  KP8                 {Search}
  KP9                 {Help}
  KPEnter             {SHy}
  KPMinus             {Indent}
  KPComma             {Underline}
  KPPeriod            {Del}
* F6                  {Cancel}
* F7                  {Esc}
* F13                 {Exit}
  Find                {Goto}
* PF1,Ctrl-P          {Capture Screen}
* PF1,PF1             {Change Keypad}
  PF1,KP0             {PF Keyboard Level 0}
  PF1,KP2             {Retrieve}
  PF1,KP3             {Page Up}
  PF1,KP4             {Date/Outline}
  PF1,KP5             {Center}
  PF1,KP6             {Print}
  PF1,KP7             {Setup}
  PF1,KP8             {Search Left}
  PF1,KP9             {Switch}
  PF1,KPEnter         {-}
  PF1,KPMinus         {L/R Indent}
  PF1,KPComma         {Format}
  PF1,KPPeriod        {Del Word}
  PF1,Up              {Screen Up}
  PF1,Down            {Screen Down}
  PF1,Right           {Word Right}
  PF1,Left            {Word Left}
  PF1,Find            {Search}
  PF1,Remove          {Del Word}
  PF2,-               {SHy}
  PF2,KP0             {PF Keyboard Level 0}
  PF2,KP1             {Merge/Sort}
  PF2,KP2             {Macro Define}
  PF2,KP3             {HPg}
  PF2,KP4             {Text In/Out}
  PF2,KP5             {Tab Align}
  PF2,KP6             {Footnote}
  PF2,KP7             {Shell}
  PF2,KP8             {Spell}
  PF2,KP9             {Screen}
  PF2,KPEnter         {Macro Commands}
  PF2,KPMinus         {Move}
  PF2,KPComma         {Font}
* PF2,KPPeriod        {Del to EOL}
1 Action; 2 Dscrptn; 3 Original; 4 Create; 5 Move; Macro: 6 Save; 7 Retrieve: 1
```

Screen D-15: WPCORP_WP42_DEFAULT Keyboard Definition - VMS Users continued.

```
Keyboard:  Edit

  Name:  WPCORP_WP42_DEFAULT

  Key               Action                    Description
  PF2,Up            {Page Up}
  PF2,Down          {Page Down}
  PF2,Right         {End}
  PF2,Left          {KEY MACRO 6}
  PF2,Find          {Search Left}
* PF2,Remove        {Del to EOL}
  PF3,KP0           {PF Keyboard Level 0}
  PF3,KP1           {Graphics}
  PF3,KP2           {Macro}
  PF3,KP3           {Goto}
  PF3,KP4           {Mark Text}
  PF3,KP5           {Flush Right}
  PF3,KP6           {Columns/Tables}
  PF3,KP7           {Thesaurus}
  PF3,KP8           {Replace}
  PF3,KP9           {Reveal Codes}
  PF3,KPEnter       {Typeover}
  PF3,KPMinus       {Block}
  PF3,KPComma       {Style}
* PF3,KPPeriod      {Del to EOP}
  PF3,Up            {KEY MACRO 1}
  PF3,Down          {KEY MACRO 2}
  PF3,Right         {KEY MACRO 4}
  PF3,Left          {KEY MACRO 3}
  PF3,Find          {Replace}
* PF3,Remove        {Del to EOP}

1 Action; 2 Dscrptn; 3 Original; 4 Create; 5 Move; Macro: 6 Save; 7 Retrieve: 1
```

A Useful Keyboard Definition

A useful keyboard definition will be established in this section to assign the Pop-Up Menu macro, in Chapter 17, and the Desk-Top Publishing Menu macro, in Chapter 18, to two keys on the keyboard. This will provide easy access to the two menus. This keyboard definition will assign the regular pop-up menu to the "/" key, and the graphics menu to the F9 key. However, you may opt to assign these menus to two different keys. This may be done by following the same instructions, below, except enter your chosen key in place of the "/" and/or F9 key(s).

To create this definition do the following:

VMS	**Keystroke Action**		**DOS**
PF1,F7	1.	U: Press *Setup*. C: *Displays Setup Menu.*	Shift-F1
	2.	U: Press *5* for Keyboard Layout. C: *Displays Setup: Keyboard Layout Menu.*	
	3.	U: Press *4* for Create. C: *Prints* Keyboard Filename: _.	

VMS   **Keystroke Action**   **DOS**

4. U: Type in <u>menu</u> and press the *Enter key.*
    C: *Displays Setup: Keyboard Layout Menu.*

5. U: Press *7* for Edit.
    C: *Displays Keyboard: Edit Menu.*

6. U: Press *7* for Retrieve.
    C: *Prints* Key: _.

F17   7. U: Press *Merge R.*   F9
    C: *Prints* Macro: _.

8. U: Type in <u>DOC51</u>. Note: All the macros
        used for keyboard layouts should be
        located in the keyboard layout directory.
    C: *Inserts key and function.*

9. U: Highlight *Key F9.*
    C: *Highlights Key, Action, and Description.*

10. U: Press *2* for Description.
    C: *Prints* Description: _.

11. U: Enter <u>Desk-Top Publishing menu</u> and
        press the *Enter key.*
    C: *Echoes characters.*

The Keyboard: Edit Menu should look like Screen D-16, if you used the same keys, otherwise, it will be slightly different depending on what keys you used.

Screen D-16

```
┌─────────────────────────────────────────────────────────────────┐
│ Keyboard:  Edit                                                   │
│                                                                   │
│   Name:  Menu                                                     │
│                                                                   │
│   Key              Action                  Description            │
│                                                                   │
│   F9               {KEY MACRO 2}           Desk-Top Publishing menu. │
│                                                                   │
│                                                                   │
│                                                                   │
│                                                                   │
│                                                                   │
│                                                                   │
│                                                                   │
│                                                                   │
│                                                                   │
│                                                                   │
│ 1 Action; 2 Dscrptn; 3 Original; 4 Create; 5 Move; Macro: 6 Save; 7 Retrieve: 1 │
└─────────────────────────────────────────────────────────────────┘
```

VMS	Keystroke Action	DOS
F13	12. U: Press *Exit*. C: *Returns to Setup: Keyboard Layout Menu.*	F7
	13. U: Highlight *menu*. C: *Highlight menu keyboard layout.*	
	14. U: Press *1* to Select. C: *Displays Setup Menu.*	

The final Setup Menu should show "MENU.WPK" to the right of Keyboard Layout as shown on Screen D-17 or Screen D-18.

Screen D-17: VMS Users

```
Setup

     1 - Mouse

     2 - Display

     3 - Environment

     4 - Initial Settings

     5 - Keyboard Layout              MENU.WPK

     6 - Location of Files




Selection: 0
```

Screen D-18: DOS Users

```
Setup

     1 - Mouse

     2 - Display

     3 - Environment

     4 - Initial Settings

     5 - Keyboard Layout              MENU.WPK

     6 - Location of Files




Selection: 0
```

VMS   Keystroke Action   DOS

F13   15. U: Press *Exit.*   F7
                     C: *Returns to Document.*

PRINTING MACROS

It is essential for programmers to be able to print out the code that is contained in their program. To print out your WordPerfect 5.1 macro you must use the WordPerfect 5.1 Macros to Text Conversion Program in this appendix.

Description of Program

This program converts the characters and codes contained in WordPerfect 5.1's macros into ASCII Text. This text may then be retrieved into WordPerfect 5.1 like you retrieve a normal file. The retrieved document may then be printed like a normal document. The file name will have a .TXT extension. This program, thus, allows the user to obtain a hardcopy of the macro's contents. The user may then edit the actual macro in the Macro Editor to make any changes in the program's code.

Technical Information

WordPerfect 5.1's macros contain two byte codes. The first byte is a unique code for that character or code and the second byte specifies the type of the character or code. For example, the letter A's first byte is the unique number 65. All standard ASCII character's second bytes are the code 00. Thus, the two byte code for the letter A is 65,00. This same reasoning was applied to the macro's keyboard commands, variables, and Alternate macros, along with WordPerfect 5.1's function keys.

Program 1 - DOS

This BASIC program is for DOS Users. Type in what is shown below and then to execute the program type in RUN. The program prompts you for the macro name and the name you want to give the created text file.

```
100 ' PROGRAM:  MACPRT.BAS
110 '
140 ' DESCRIPTION:  This program prompts you for a filename.  Enter a
150 ' macro filename.  The program will convert the macro file to a
160 ' text file that you can retrieve into WordPerfect 5.1.  This
170 ' allows you to print your macro in order to help you debug
180 ' very complex macros.
190 '
300 ' Four arrays serve as lookup tables for the second byte's similar
310 ' characters and codes.  The index to the array is the first byte's
320 ' code.
330 '
340 DIM MAC$(256),COMD$(256),VAR$(20),ALT$(256),LINEDRW$(256)
350 '
360 ' Call initialize string vectors subroutine.
370 '
```

```
380 GOSUB 990
390 '
400 ' Enter the names of the input and output files.
402 CLS
410 '
420 INPUT "What is the Pathname and Name of the Macro (No extension)? ",FILE$
430 INPUT "What is the Pathname and Name of the Target File (No extension)?",TGFILE$
450 '
460 ' Open the two files and initialize the beginning of file.
470 '
480 OPEN FILE$ + ".WPM" AS #1 LEN=1
490 FIELD #1, 1 AS C$
500 OPEN TGFILE$ + ".TXT" AS #2 LEN=1
510 '
520 ' Sets the beginning location of the valid codes.
530 '
540 FIELD #2, 1 AS CH$
550 GET #1,56 : PRINT C$
560 GET #1
570 '
590 ' The description of the macro is stripped from the rest of the code.
600 '
610 WHILE (C$ < > CHR$(0))
620     GET #1
630 WEND
640 COUNT = 1
650 L$ = ""
660 '
670 ' Convert characters and codes until the end of the file is reached.
680 '
690 WHILE NOT EOF(1)
700     GET #1
710     C1$ = C$
720     GET #1 : C2$ = C$
730     IF ((C1$ = CHR$(0)) AND (C1$ = C2$)) THEN GOTO 960
740 '
750 '   ASCII Characters.
760 '
770     IF C2$ = CHR$(0) THEN GOTO 1250
780 '
790 '   Macro Programming Commands.
800 '
810     IF C2$ = CHR$(252) THEN GOTO 1400
820 '
830 '   WordPerfect 5.1's Function Keys.
840 '
850 '   IF C2$ = CHR$(128) THEN GOTO 1530
860 '
870 '   Variables 0 through 9.
880 '
890     IF C2$ = CHR$(255) THEN GOTO 1660
```

```
900 '
910 '   WordPerfect 5.1's Function Keys.
920 '
930     IF C2$ = CHR$(254) THEN GOTO 1790
935     IF C2$ = CHR$(3) THEN GOTO 1850
940     PRINT "Odd Code:  ";ASC(C1$),ASC(C2$)
950 WEND
960 CLOSE #1,#2
970 END
980 '
990 ' Initialize strings.
1000 '
1010 FOR I = 1 TO 256
1012      MAC$(I) = "{**MAC$(" + STR$(I) + ") }"
1014 NEXT I
1015 READ NDX
1020 WHILE (NDX < > 300)
1030      READ MAC$(NDX+1) : READ NDX
1040 WEND
1050 '
1060 FOR I = 1 TO 256
1063      COMD$(I) = "{**COMD$(" + STR$(I) + ") }"
1064 NEXT I
1068 READ NDX
1070 WHILE (NDX < > 300)
1080     READ COMD$(NDX+1) : READ NDX
1090 WEND
1100 '
1110 FOR I = 1 TO 20
1113      VAR$(I) = "{**VAR$(" + STR$(I) + ") }"
1115 NEXT I
1118 READ NDX
1120 WHILE (NDX < > 300)
1130      READ VAR$(NDX+1) : READ NDX
1140 WEND
1150 '
1160 FOR I = 1 TO 256
1163      ALT$(I) = "{**ALT$(" + STR$(I) + ") }"
1165 NEXT I
1168 READ NDX
1170 WHILE (NDX < > 300)
1180      READ ALT$(NDX+1) : READ NDX
1190 WEND
1194 '
1195 FOR I = 1 TO 256
1197      LINEDRW$(I) = "{**LINEDRW$(" + STR$(I) + ") }"
1199 NEXT I
1201 READ NDX
1203 WHILE (NDX < > 300)
1204      READ LINEDRW$(NDX+1) : READ NDX
1207 WEND
```

```
1210 RETURN
1220 '
1230 ' ASCII Codes.
1240 '
1250 IF C1$ < > CHR$(10) THEN GOTO 1310
1260 '
1270 ' Carriage Return is added if code equals a line feed.
1280 '
1290 LSET CH$ = CHR$(13)
1293 '
1294 '
1300 PUT #2, COUNT : COUNT = COUNT + 1
1310 LSET CH$ = C1$
1320 PUT #2, COUNT : COUNT = COUNT + 1
1325 IF C1$ < > CHR$(13) THEN GOTO 1360
1327 LSET CH$ = CHR$(10)
1329 PUT #2, COUNT : COUNT = COUNT + 1
1330 '
1340 ' Go to Main Loop.
1350 '
1360 GOTO 950
1370 '
1380 ' Macro Programming Codes.  TBPTR is the Table Pointer.
1390 '
1400 TBPTR1 = ASC(C1$) + 1
1410 TEMP$ = MAC$(TBPTR1)
1420 FOR I = 1 TO LEN(TEMP$)
1430     LSET CH$ = MID$(TEMP$,I,1)
1440     PUT #2, COUNT : COUNT = COUNT + 1
1450 NEXT I
1460 '
1470 ' Go to Main Loop.
1480 '
1490 GOTO 950
1500 '
1510 ' WordPerfect 5.1's Function Codes.
1520 '
1530 TBPTR2 = ASC(C1$) + 1
1540 TEMP$ = COMD$(TBPTR2)
1550 FOR I = 1 TO LEN(TEMP$)
1560     LSET CH$ = MID$(TEMP$,I,1)
1570     PUT #2, COUNT : COUNT = COUNT + 1
1580 NEXT I
1590 '
1600 ' Go to Main Loop.
1610 '
1620 GOTO 950
1630 '
1640 ' Variables 0 through 9.
1650 '
1660 TBPTR3 = ASC(C1$) + 1
```

```
1670 TEMP$ = VAR$(TBPTR3)
1680 FOR I = 1 TO LEN(TEMP$)
1690    LSET CH$ = MID$(TEMP$,I,1)
1700    PUT #2, COUNT : COUNT = COUNT + 1
1710 NEXT I
1720 '
1730 ' Go to Main Loop.
1740 '
1750 GOTO 950
1760 '
1770 ' Alternate Macros A through Z.
1780 '
1790 TBPTR4 = ASC(C1$) + 1
1800 TEMP$ = ALT$(TBPTR4)
1810 FOR I = 1 TO LEN(TEMP$)
1820    LSET CH$ = MID$(TEMP$,I,1)
1830    PUT #2, COUNT : COUNT = COUNT + 1
1840 NEXT I
1846 '
1850 TBPTR4 = ASC(C1$) + 1
1851 TEMP$ = LINEDRW$(TBPTR4)
1852 FOR I = 1 TO LEN(TEMP$)
1853    LSET CH$ = MID$(TEMP$,I,1)
1854    PUT #2, COUNT : COUNT = COUNT + 1
1855 NEXT I
1857 '
1860 ' Go to Main Loop.
1880 GOTO 950
1890 '
1900 DATA 11,{;},1,{ASSIGN},2,{BELL},3,{BREAK},4,{CALL},5,{CANCEL OFF}
1910 DATA 6,{CANCEL ON},7,{CASE},8,{CASE CALL},9,{CHAIN},10,{CHAR}
1920 DATA 12,{DISPLAY OFF},13,{DISPLAY ON},14,{ELSE},16,{END IF}
1930 DATA 20,{GO},21,{IF},47,{IF EXISTS},22,{LABEL},23,{LOOK}
1940 DATA 24,{NEST},27,{ON CANCEL},28,{ON ERROR},29,{ON NOT FOUND}
1950 DATA 46,{ORIGINAL KEY},30,{PAUSE},31,{PROMPT},32,{QUIT}
1960    DATA    33,{RESTART},34,{RETURN},35,{RETURN    CANCEL},36,{RETURN
ERROR}
1970 DATA 37,{RETURN NOT FOUND},38,{SPEED},41,{STATE},45,{STEP OFF}
1975 DATA 39,{STEP ON},40,{TEXT},42,{WAIT}
1976 DATA 15, {END FOR},17,{END WHILE},18,{FOR},19,{FOR EACH}
1980 DATA 43,{WHILE}
1981    DATA    44,{Macro    Commands},48,{MENU    OFF},49,{MENU    ON},50,{STATUS
PROMPT}
1982 DATA 51,{INPUT},52,{VARIABLE},53,{SYSTEM},54,{MID},55,{NTOK}
1983    DATA    56,{KTON},57,{LEN},59,{PAUSE    KEY},61,{OTHERWISE},62,{SHELL
ASSIGN}
1984 DATA 63,{SHELL VARIABLE}
1985 DATA 25,{NEXT},26,{SHELL MACRO},31,{PROMPT},32,{QUIT}
1990 DATA 300
1999 DATA 9,{Tab},11,{Del to EOL},12,{Del to EOP}
2000 DATA 25,{Left},23,{Up},24,{Right},26,{Down},8,{Home},89,{Page Up}
```

```
2010 DATA 85,{End},90,{Page Down},10,{Enter},32,{Cancel},33,{Search}
2020 DATA 34,{Help},35,{Indent},36,{List},37,{Bold},38,{Exit}
2030 DATA 39,{Underline},40,{End Field},41,{Save},44,{Setup},45,{Search Left}
2040 DATA 46,{Switch},47,{L/R Indent},48,{Date/Outline},49,{Center}
2050 DATA 50,{Print},51,{Format},52,{Merge Codes},53,{Retrieve}
2060 DATA 68,{Shell},69,{Spell},70,{Screen},71,{Move},72,{Text In/Out}
2070 DATA 73,{Tab Align},74,{Footnote},75,{Font},76,{Merge/Sort}
2080 DATA 77,{Macro Define},56,{Thesaurus},57,{Replace},58,{Reveal Codes}
2090 DATA 59,{Block},60,{Mark Text},61,{Flush Right}62,{Columns/Tables}
2100 DATA 63,{Style},64,{Graphics},65,{Macro}
2103 DATA 83,{Word Right},84,{Word Left},99,{Para Up},100,{Para Down}
2104 DATA 101,{Item Left},102,{Item Right},103,{Item Up},104,{Item Down}
2105 DATA 81,{Del},95,{HPg},110,{Block Copy},109,{Block Move},108,{Block Append}
2106 DATA 27,{Esc},80,{Backspace},88,{Goto},93,{Typeover}
2107 DATA 1,{^A},2,{^B},3,{^C},4,{^D},5,{^E},6,{^F},7,{^G}
2108 DATA 13,{^M},14,{^N},15,{^O},16,{^P},17,{^Q},18,{^R},19,{^S},20{^T}
2109 DATA 21,{^U},22,{^V},29,{^]},28,{^\},30,{Keyboard},31,{^_}
2110 DATA 42,{F11},43,{F12},54,{Shft F11},55,{Shft F12},66,{Alt F11},67,{Alt F12}
2111 DATA 78,{Ctrl F11},79,{Ctrl,F12},82,{Del Word},86,{Home-Home-Left}
2112 DATA 87,{Invalid},91,{Screen Down},92,{Screen Up},94,{Left Mar Rel}
2113 DATA 96,{Shy},97,{-},98,{ },105,{Alt Home},106,{Del Word (Row)}
2114 DATA 107,{Menu Bar},0,{Compose}
2115 DATA 300
2120 DATA 0,{VAR 0},1,{VAR 1},2,{VAR 2},3,{VAR 3},4,{VAR 4},5,{VAR 5}
2130 DATA 6,{VAR 6},7,{VAR 7},DATA 8,{VAR 8},9,{VAR 9}
2140 DATA 300
2150 DATA 65,{ALT A},66,{ALT B},67,{ALT C},68,{ALT D},69,{ALT E}
2160 DATA 70,{ALT F},71,{ALT G},72,{ALT H},73,{ALT I},74,{ALT J}
2170 DATA 75,{ALT K},76,{ALT L},77,{ALT M},78,{ALT N},79,{ALT O}
2180 DATA 80,{ALT P},81,{ALT Q},82,{ALT R},83,{ALT S},84,{ALT T}
2190 DATA 85,{ALT U},86,{ALT V},87,{ALT W},88,{ALT X},89,{ALT Y}
2200 DATA 90,{ALT Z}
2210 DATA 300
2215 DATA 0,▓,1,▒,2,▐,3,█,4,▌,5,■,6,▄,7,▖,8,–,9,│
2220 DATA 10,┌,11,┐,12,┘,13,└,14,├,15,┬,16,┤,17,┴,18,┼,19,═
2222 DATA 20,║,21,╔,22,╗,23,╝,24,╚,25,╠,26,╦,27,╣,28,╩,29,╬
2224 DATA 30,┌,31,┐,32,┘,33,└,34,┌,35,┐,36,┘,37,└,38,├,39,┬
2226 DATA 40,┤,41,┴,42,║,43,╦,44,╣,45,╩,46,╬,47,╬,48,>,49,↓,50,<,51,↑
2230 DATA 300
2240 END
```

Program 2 - VMS

This BASIC program is for VMS Users. Type in what is shown below and then compile and link your program to produce the .EXE file. To execute the program use the DCL command RUN and type in the filename. The program prompts you for the macro name and the name you want to give the created text file.

```
100 DIM mac$(256), comd$(256), var$(20), alt$(256), linedrw$(256)
```

```
! PROGRAM:  MACPRT.BAS
!
! DESCRIPTION:  This program prompts you for a filename.  Enter a
! macro filename.  The program will convert the macro file to a
! text file that you can retrieve into WordPerfect 5.1.  This
! allows you to print your macro in order to help you debug
! very complex macros.
!
! Four arrays serve as lookup tables for the second byte's similar
! characters and codes.  The index to the array is the first byte's
! code.
!


110 MAP(infile) STRING in_buffer=128
     MAP (outfile) STRING out_buffer=256
     MAP DYNAMIC (infile) STRING fill1, BYTE currchar, STRING fill2
     MAP DYNAMIC (outfile) STRING fill3, BYTE coutchar, STRING fill4
     DECLARE INTEGER dummy
     DECLARE INTEGER c1, c2, temp_char, temp_getchar
     DECLARE INTEGER tempint
     linepos = 0
     charactercount = 0
     recnum = 0


150 ON ERROR GOTO 955

! Get a character from the file

200 DEF INTEGER GET_CHAR(INTEGER dummychar)
205    IF ipos = 0
     THEN
            GET #1
     END IF
            REMAP (infile) fill1 = ipos, currchar = 1, fill2=(127-ipos)
220    temp_getchar = currchar
225    IF temp_getchar < 0 THEN temp_getchar = temp_getchar + 256
230    IF ipos = 127 THEN ipos = 0
     ELSE ipos = ipos + 1
     END IF
            GET_CHAR = temp_getchar
245 END DEF

! Put a char in the output file.

250 DEF INTEGER PUT_CHAR( INTEGER outchar )
251    IF outchar = 10 OR outchar = 13
     THEN
            PUT #2, COUNT opos
            opos = 0
            GOTO 300
     ENDIF
```

```
255     REMAP (outfile) fill3 = opos, coutchar = 1, fill4=(254-opos)
270     IF outchar > 127 THEN outchar = outchar - 256
275     coutchar = outchar
            opos = opos + 1
285     IF opos = 255
        THEN
                PUT #2
                opos = 0
        END IF
300 PUT CHAR = 1
310 END DEF
```

! Call initialize string vectors subroutine.

```
380 GOSUB 1010
```

! Enter the names of the input and output files.

```
420 INPUT "What is the File Specification and Name of the Macro (With type)", file$
430 INPUT "What is the File Specification and Name of the Target File", tgfile$
```

! Open the two files and initialize the beginning of the file.

```
480 OPEN file$ FOR INPUT as FILE #1,            &
    MAP infile, ORGANIZATION SEQUENTIAL, RECORDTYPE NONE,  &
        RECORDSIZE 128, ACCESS READ, ALLOW NONE

481 OPEN tgfile$ FOR OUTPUT AS #2,              &
        MAP outfile, RECORDTYPE LIST
```

! Sets the beginning location of the valid codes.

```
500 ipos = 0
    opos = 0
510 FOR I = 1 TO 56
        dummy = GET_CHAR(0)
520 NEXT I
```

! The description of the macro is stripped from the rest of the code.

```
600 dummy = 1
610 WHILE ( dummy <> 0 )
        dummy = GET_CHAR(0)
630 NEXT
```

! Convert characters and codes until the end of the file is reached.
! While not end of file 1.

```
700     c1=GET_CHAR(0)
725     c2=GET_CHAR(0)
730     IF ((c2=0) AND (c1=c2)) THEN GOTO 960
```

! ASCII characters.

770   IF c2=0 THEN GOTO 1250

! Macro Programming Commands.

810   IF c2=252 THEN GOTO 1400

! WordPerfect 5.1 Function Keys.

850   IF c2=128 THEN GOTO 1530

! Variables 0 through 9.

890   IF c2=255 THEN GOTO 1660

! WordPerfect 5.1's Function Keys.

930   IF c2 = 254 THEN GOTO 1790

! Line Drawing Codes.

935   IF c2 = 3 THEN GOTO 1850
940   PRINT "ODD CODE: "; c1, c2
950 GOTO 700

955 IF (ERR = 11%) AND (ERL = 700%)   &
        THEN RESUME 960 ELSE ON ERROR GOTO 0

960 dummy = PUT_CHAR(10)
985 CLOSE #1,#2
980 GOTO 2220

! Initialize strings.

1010 READ ndx
1020 WHILE (ndx < > 300)
        READ mac$(ndx+1)
        READ ndx
    NEXT

1060 READ ndx
1070 WHILE (ndx < > 300)
        READ comd$(ndx+1)
        READ ndx
    NEXT

1110 READ ndx
1120 WHILE (ndx < > 300)
        READ var$(ndx+1)
        READ ndx

```
        NEXT

1160 READ ndx
1170 WHILE (ndx < > 300)
        READ alt$(ndx+1)
        READ ndx
     NEXT

1210 READ ndx
1215 WHILE (ndx < > 300)
        READ linedrw$(ndx+1)
        READ ndx
     NEXT

1240 RETURN

! ASCII Codes.

1250 dummy = PUT_CHAR(c1)
1255 GOTO 950

! Macro Programming Codes.  tbptr is the Table Pointer.

1400 tbptr1 = c1 + 1
1410 temp$ = mac$(tbptr1)
1420 FOR i = 1 TO LEN(temp$)
        temp_char = ASC(MID$(temp$, i, 1))
        dummy = PUT_CHAR(temp_char)
     NEXT i
!      Go to main loop.
       GOTO 950

! WordPerfect 5.1 Function Codes.

1530 tbptr2 = c1 + 1
     temp$ = comd$(tbptr2)
1550 FOR i = 1 TO LEN (temp$)
        temp_char = ASC(MID$(temp$, i, 1 ))
        dummy = PUT_CHAR(temp_char)
     NEXT I
!      Go to main loop.
       GOTO 950

! Variables 0 through 9.

1660 tbptr3 = c1 + 1
     temp$ = var$(tbptr3)
1680 FOR i = 1 TO LEN(temp$)
        temp_char = ASC(MID$(temp$, I, 1))
        dummy = PUT_CHAR(temp_char)
     NEXT I
```

```
!       Go to main loop.
        GOTO 950


! Alternate macros A through Z.

1790 tbptr4 = c1 + 1
        temp$ = alt$(tbptr4)
1810 FOR i = 1 TO LEN(temp$)
            temp_char = ASC(MID$(temp$, i, 1))
            dummy = PUT_CHAR(temp_char)
        NEXT i
!       Go to main loop.
        GOTO 950


! Line Drawing.

1850 tbptr5 = c1 + 1
        temp$ = linedrw$(tbptr5)
1860 FOR i = 1 to LEN(temp$)
            temp_char = ASC(MID$(temp$, i, 1))
            dummy = PUT_CHAR(temp_char)
        NEXT i
!       Go to main loop.
        GOTO 950



1900 DATA 11,{;},1,{ASSIGN},2,{BELL},3,{BREAK},4,{CALL},5,{CANCEL OFF}
1910 DATA 6,{CANCEL ON},7,{CASE},8,{CASE CALL},9,{CHAIN},10,{CHAR}
1920 DATA 12,{DISPLAY OFF},13,{DISPLAY ON},14,{ELSE},16,{END IF}
1930 DATA 20,{GO},21,{IF},47,{IF EXISTS},22,{LABEL},23,{LOOK}
1940 DATA 24,{NEST},27,{ON CANCEL},28,{ON ERROR},29,{ON NOT FOUND}
1950 DATA 46,{ORIGINAL KEY},30,{PAUSE},31,{PROMPT},32,{QUIT}
1960    DATA    33,{RESTART},34,{RETURN},35,{RETURN    CANCEL},36,{RETURN
ERROR}
1970 DATA 37,{RETURN NOT FOUND},38,{SPEED},41,{STATE},45,{STEP OFF}
1975 DATA 39,{STEP ON},40,{TEXT},42,{WAIT}
1976 DATA 15, {END FOR},17,{END WHILE},18,{FOR},19,{FOR EACH}
1980 DATA 43,{WHILE}
1981    DATA    44,{Macro   Commands},48,{MENU   OFF},49,{MENU   ON},50,{STATUS
PROMPT}
1982 DATA 51,{INPUT},52,{VARIABLE},53,{SYSTEM},54,{MID},55,{NTOK}
1983    DATA    56,{KTON},57,{LEN},59,{PAUSE   KEY},61,{OTHERWISE},62,{SHELL
ASSIGN}
1984 DATA 63,{SHELL VARIABLE}
1985 DATA 25,{NEXT},26,{SHELL MACRO},31,{PROMPT},32,{QUIT}
1990 DATA 300
1999 DATA 9,{Tab},11,{Del to EOL},12,{Del to EOP}
2000 DATA 25,{Left},23,{Up},24,{Right},26,{Down},8,{Home},89,{Page Up}
2010 DATA 85,{End},90,{Page Down},10,{Enter},32,{Cancel},33,{Search}
2020 DATA 34,{Help},35,{Indent},36,{List Files},37,{Bold},38,{Exit}
2030 DATA 39,{Underline},40,{End Field},41,{Save},44,{Setup},45,{Search Left}
```

```
2040 DATA 46,{Switch},47,{L/R Indent},48,{Date/Outline},49,{Center}
2050 DATA 50,{Print},51,{Format},52,{Merge Codes},53,{Retrieve}
2060 DATA 68,{Shell},69,{Spell},70,{Screen},71,{Move},72,{Text In/Out}
2070 DATA 73,{Tab Align},74,{Footnote},75,{Font},76,{Merge/Sort}
2080 DATA 77,{Macro Define},56,{Thesaurus},57,{Replace},58,{Reveal Codes}
2090 DATA 59,{Block},60,{Mark Text},61,{Flush Right}62,{Columns/Tables}
2100 DATA 63,{Style},64,{Graphics},65,{Macro}
2103 DATA 83,{Word Right},84,{Word Left},99,{Para Up},100,{Para Down}
2104 DATA 101,{Item Left},102,{Item Right},103,{Item Up},104,{Item Down}
2105 DATA 81,{Del},95,{HPg},110,{Block Copy},109,{Block Move},108,{Block Append}
2106 DATA 27,{Esc},80,{Backspace},88,{Goto},93,{Typeover}
2107 DATA 1,{^A},2,{^B},3,{^C},4,{^D},5,{^E},6,{^F},7,{^G}
2109 DATA 13,{^M},14,{^N},15,{^O},16,{^P},17,{^Q},18,{^R},19,{^S},20{^T}
2110 DATA 21,{^U},22,{^V},29,{^]},28,{^\},30,{Keyboard},31,{^_}
2112 DATA 42,{F11},43,{F12},54,{Shft F11},55,{Shft F12},66,{Alt F11},67,{Alt F12}
2113 DATA 78,{Ctrl F11},79,{Ctrl,F12},82,{Del Word},86,{Home-Home-Left}
2114 DATA 87,{Invalid},91,{Screen Down},92,{Screen Up},94,{Left Mar Rel}
2115 DATA 96,{Shy},97,{-},98,{ },105,{Alt Home},106,{Del Word (Row)}
2116 DATA 107,{Menu Bar},0,{Compose}
2119 DATA 300
2120 DATA 0,{VAR 0},1,{VAR 1},2,{VAR 2},3,{VAR 3},4,{VAR 4},5,{VAR 5}
2130 DATA 6,{VAR 6},7,{VAR 7},DATA 8,{VAR 8},9,{VAR 9}
2140 DATA 300
2150 DATA 65,{ALT A},66,{ALT B},67,{ALT C},68,{ALT D},69,{ALT E}
2160 DATA 70,{ALT F},71,{ALT G},72,{ALT H},73,{ALT I},74,{ALT J}
2170 DATA 75,{ALT K},76,{ALT L},77,{ALT M},78,{ALT N},79,{ALT O}
2180 DATA 80,{ALT P},81,{ALT Q},82,{ALT R},83,{ALT S},84,{ALT T}
2190 DATA 85,{ALT U},86,{ALT V},87,{ALT W},88,{ALT X},89,{ALT Y}
2200 DATA 90,{ALT Z}
2210 DATA 300


! Line Drawing characters are mapped to printable characters.


2214 DATA 0,%,1,%,2,%,3,%,4,|,5,-,6,|,7,_,8,-,9,|
2220 DATA 10,/,11,\,12,/,13,\,14,|,15,-,16,|,17,-,18,+,19,=
2222 DATA 20,|,21,/,22,\,23,/,24,\,25,|,26,=,27,|,28,=,29,#
2224 DATA 30,/,31,\,32,/,33,\,34,/,35,\,36,/,37,\,38,|,39,-
2226 DATA 40,|,41,-,42,|,43,=,44,|,45,=,46,+,47,+,48,>,49,V,50,<,51,^
2230 DATA 300
2240 END
```

DOS TO VMS
OR
VMS TO DOS

Changing Environments

If you normally use WordPerfect 5.1 in one environment such as the DOS operating system on a microcomputer it is easy to learn how to use WordPerfect 5.1 under the VMS operating system on a VAX.

Conversion Process

It is always helpful to learn about the operating system under which you are using WordPerfect.

Different WordPerfect 5.1's

There are many minor differences between WordPerfect 5.1 for VMS and for DOS. Some differences are covered below.

Filenames

The length of your document's filename will be different depending on which WordPerfect environment you are working in.

Keyboards

When converting from one environment to the other environment it is important to note that some of the keys on the new keyboard are different.

Template

The templates are similar, however, the keys you use to activate the alternative functions are different.

For DOS Users Converting to VMS

WordPerfect 5.1 for DOS uses the Shift, Alternate, and Control keys to activate alternative selections on the Function Keys, whereas, WordPerfect 5.1 for VMS uses PF1, PF2, and PF3.

The following conversion table will be helpful:

Shift	=	PF1
Alternate	=	PF2
Control	=	PF3

For VMS Users Converting to DOS

WordPerfect 5.1 for VMS uses PF1, PF2, and PF3 to activate alternative selections on the Function Keys, whereas, WordPerfect 5.1 for DOS uses the Shift, Alternate, and Control keys.

The following conversion table will be helpful:

PF1	=	Shift
PF2	=	Alternate
PF3	=	Control

Special Notes

Following the notes in this appendix will give you a jump start on converting from one environment to another. For further help note the special sections throughout the book regarding VMS Users versus DOS users. You should pay special attention to these notes to help you adapt to your new environment.

WORDPERFECT 6.0 for DOS

Appendix G is for people using WordPerfect 6.0 for DOS. These notes document items included in this Version 5.1 book that are different in Version 6.0.

Text Windows

One of the main differences in version 6.0 is the appearance of the WordPerfect interface. Text windows are displayed to help guide you through different features. The text windows provide the information that is required to perform the required function.

Macro Similarities Between WordPerfect 5.1 and 6.0

The major similarities in macros in the WordPerfect 5.1 versus 6.0 environment for DOS are:

- The same file extension of .WPM is used.

- The user uses the same keystrokes to initially create (Ctrl-F10) and then run the macros (Alt-F10) in 6.0 as in 5.1. In 6.0, you can also use the pull-down menus. (Click on "Tools" select "Macro" and "Record" to initially create the macro and click on "Tools" select "Macro" and "Play" to invoke the macro.)

Macro Differences Between WordPerfect 5.1 and 6.0

The major differences in macros in the WordPerfect 5.1 versus 6.0 environment for DOS are:

- The macro's contents are stored differently in 6.0. In version 5.1, every keystroke you typed in or pressed was entered into the macro. In version 6.0, WordPerfect organizes the actions you have performed and summarizes them during macro creation.

- The macro itself, is just another WordPerfect document in 6.0. Macros are created, edited, and printed just like any other WordPerfect document.

- Many new macro programming commands have been incorporated into WordPerfect 6.0. The online help utility has an excellent syntax resource you can use to help you or you can print the help library out. Click on "Help" and select "Macros".

- In 6.0, when you create a macro you will not be prompted for a macro description.

Defining a Macro in 6.0

Defining a macro in WordPerfect 6.0 for DOS will work as indicated throughout the book by using the following:

Mouse	Reference Keystrokes	Keys
	U: Press *Macro Define.*	Ctrl-F10
Mouse	U: Click on *"Tools"* select *"Macro"* and select *"Record"*.	
	C: *Displays Record Macro Text Box (See Screen G-1.)*	

Screen G-1: WordPerfect 6.0 for DOS Users

```
 File    Edit   View   Layout   Tools   Font   Graphics   Window   Help
┌─────────────────────────────────────────────────────────────────────┐
│                                                                       │
│                                                                       │
│        ┌──────────────── Record Macro ──────────────────┐            │
│        │                                                  │           │
│        │  Macro:  ┌──────────────────────────────────┐   │           │
│        │          │ _                               ↓ │   │           │
│        │          └──────────────────────────────────┘   │           │
│        │                                                  │           │
│        │     [ ] Edit Macro                               │           │
│        │                                                  │           │
│        │   ┌─────────────┐ ┌──────────────┐  ┌──────┐ ┌────────┐     │
│        │   │ File List...F5│ │QuickList...F6│  │  OK  │ │ Cancel │     │
│        │   └─────────────┘ └──────────────┘  └──────┘ └────────┘     │
│        │                                                  │           │
│        └──────────────────────────────────────────────────┘           │
│                                                                       │
 Courier 12 pt                              Doc 1 Pg 1 Ln 1" Pos 1"
```

Mouse	Reference Keystrokes	Keys
	U: Type in the name <u>CLOSE</u> and press the *Enter key.*	
	C: *Prints Recording Macro (See Screen G-2.)*	

If you are redefining a macro you will be asked if you want to "Replace" or "Edit" the macro. The "Replace" option will allow you to record over the old macro. The "Edit" option will allow you to edit the macro's contents.

Screen G-2: WordPerfect 6.0 for DOS Users

F̲ile	E̲dit	V̲iew	L̲ayout	T̲ools	F̲ont	G̲raphics	W̲indow	H̲elp

Recording Macro   Doc 1 Pg 1 Ln 1" Pos 1"

Mouse   Reference Keystrokes   Keys

U: Type in the keystrokes you want to include in
    the macro.
C: *Echoes characters.*

| | U: Press ***Macro Define*** again to finish defining the | Ctrl-F10 |

U: Press ***Macro Define*** again to finish defining the   Ctrl-F10
    macro.

Mouse   U: Click on *"Tools"* select *"Macro"* and select
            "Stop".
            C: *Saves macro.*

Note that these are basically the same steps used in WordPerfect 5.1, except that WordPerfect 6.0 does not prompt you for a description for the macro and you see a text window guiding you through the function.

Defining Variables

When you are creating a macro using Macro Define (as shown in the Reference Keystrokes below) or just typing the contents of the macro in a document window you can define a variable by doing the following:

Mouse   Reference Keystrokes   Keys

U: Press and hold down the ***Ctrl key*** and tap the   *Keys*
    PgUp key.
Mouse   U: Click on *"Tools"* select *"Macro"* and *"Control"*.
            C: *Displays the Macro Control Text Box (See Screen
            G-3.)*

Screen G-3: WordPerfect 6.0 for DOS Users

```
┌─────────────────────────────────────────────────────────────────────┐
│ File   Edit   View   Layout   Tools   Font   Graphics   Window   Help │
│ ───────────────────────────────────────────────────────────────────  │
│         ┌──────────────── Macro Control ────────────────┐             │
│         │                                               │             │
│         │   1.   Assign Variable...                     │             │
│         │                                               │             │
│         │   2.   [ ] Macro Record Paused                │             │
│         │                                               │             │
│         │   3.   [ ] Macro Record Document              │             │
│         │                                               │             │
│         │   4.   [ ] Record Abbreviations               │             │
│         │                                               │             │
│         │  ┌──────────────┐  ┌────────┐  ┌──────────┐   │             │
│         │  │Macro Commands...│ │   OK   │  │  Cancel  │  │             │
│         │  └──────────────┘  └────────┘  └──────────┘   │             │
│         └───────────────────────────────────────────────┘             │
│ Recording Macro                        Doc 1 Pg 1 Ln 1" Pos 1"        │
└─────────────────────────────────────────────────────────────────────┘
```

Mouse	**Reference Keystrokes**	**Keys**
	U: Press *1* or *A*.	*Keys*
Mouse	U: Click on *"1"*.	
	C: *Displays the Assign Variable Text Box (See Screen G-4.)*	

Screen G-4: WordPerfect 6.0 for DOS Users

```
┌─────────────────────────────────────────────────────────────────────┐
│ File   Edit   View   Layout   Tools   Font   Graphics   Window   Help │
│ ───────────────────────────────────────────────────────────────────  │
│       ┌──────────────── Macro Control ────────────────┐               │
│    ┌──────────────── Assign Variable ────────────────┐ │             │
│    │                                                 │ │             │
│    │   Variable:   ┌─────────────────────────────┐   │ │             │
│    │               │_                            │   │ │             │
│    │               └─────────────────────────────┘   │ │             │
│    │   Content:                                       │ │             │
│    │                      ┌────────┐   ┌────────┐     │ │             │
│    │                      │   OK   │   │ Cancel │     │ │             │
│    │                      └────────┘   └────────┘     │ │             │
│    └──────────────────────────────────────────────────┘ │             │
│       │  ┌──────────────┐  ┌────────┐  ┌──────────┐  │                │
│       │  │Macro Commands...│ │   OK   │  │  Cancel  │ │                │
│       │  └──────────────┘  └────────┘  └──────────┘  │                │
│       └──────────────────────────────────────────────┘                │
│ Recording Macro                        Doc 1 Pg 1 Ln 1" Pos 1"        │
└─────────────────────────────────────────────────────────────────────┘
```

Mouse   **Reference Keystrokes**   **Keys**

               U: Type in *Variable Name* and press the **Tab Key.**   *Keys*

Mouse   U: Type in *Variable Name* and click on *"Content"*.

               C: *Displays the Assign Variable Text Box (See Screen G-5.)*

Screen G-5: WordPerfect 6.0 for DOS Users

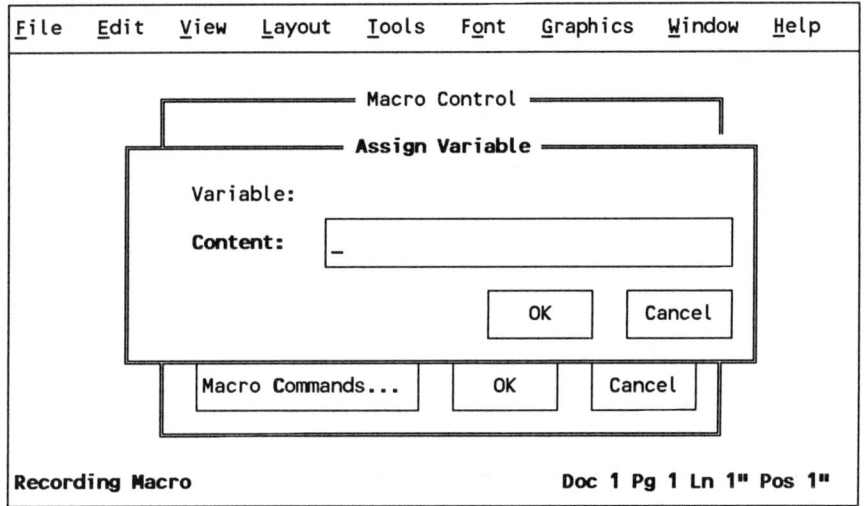

Mouse   **Reference Keystrokes**   **Keys**

               U: Type in the *Contents of the variable* and press the **Enter Key** twice.   *Keys*

Mouse   U: Type in the *Contents of the variable* and click on *"OK"*.

               C: *Displays the Macro Control Text Box.*

               U: Press the **Enter Key.**   *Keys*

Mouse   U: Click on *"OK"*.

               C: *Inserts the variable assignment into the macro.*

Continue with your macro definition.

Inserting Macro Commands and System Variables

When you are creating a macro using Macro Define (as shown in the Reference Keystrokes below) or just typing the contents of the macro in a document window you can insert macro commands by doing the following:

Mouse	**Reference Keystrokes**	**Keys**
	U: Press and hold down the *Ctrl key* and tap the *PgUp key.*	*Keys*
Mouse	U: Click on *"Tools"* select *"Macro"* and *"Control"*.	
	C: *Displays the Macro Control Text Box (See Screen G-6.)*	

Screen G-6: WordPerfect 6.0 for DOS Users

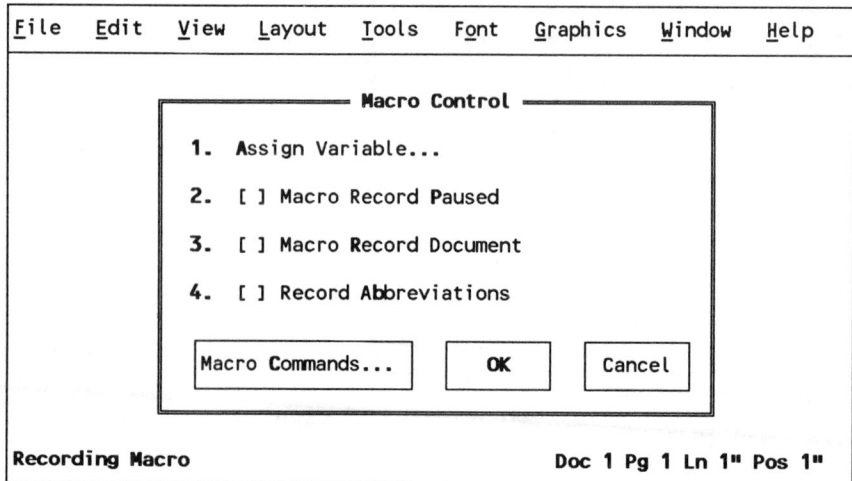

Mouse	**Reference Keystrokes**	**Keys**
	U: Press *C.*	*Keys*
Mouse	U: Click on *"Macro Commands..."*.	
	C: *Displays the Macro Commands Text Box (See Screen G-7.)*	

Screen G-7: WordPerfect 6.0 for DOS Users

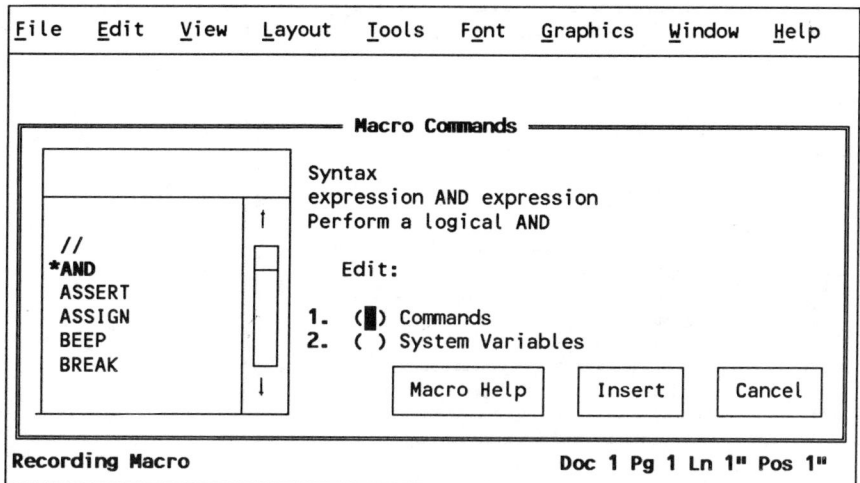

Mouse   **Reference Keystrokes**   **Keys**

Keys

U: Press *1* for Commands or *2* for System Variables. Use the arrow keys to highlight the **Command** or *System Variable* you want to insert and press the ***Enter key***. If you see the Edit Box become active you must modify the syntax for the command and then press the Enter key to insert the command into the macro (See Screen G-8.)

Mouse

U: Click on *"1"* for Commands or *"2"* for System Variables. Click on the **Command** or *System Variable* you want to insert. If you see the Edit Box become active you must modify the syntax for the command and then click on *"Insert"* to insert the command into the macro (See Screen G-8.)

C: *Inserts the Command or System Variable into the macro.*

Screen G-8: WordPerfect 6.0 for DOS Users

```
 File   Edit   View   Layout   Tools   Font   Graphics   Window   Help
┌─────────────────────────────────────────────────────────────────────┐
│                        ── Macro Commands ──                           │
│ ┌──────────────────┐   Syntax                                         │
│ │                  │ ↑ expression and expression                      │
│ ├──────────────────┤   Perform a logical AND                          │
│ │ //               │                                                  │
│ │ AND              │     Edit:  │ASSIGN()                      │       │
│ │ ASSERT           │                                                  │
│ │ *ASSIGN          │    (█) Commands                                  │
│ │ BEEP             │    ( ) System Variables                          │
│ │ BREAK            │     ┌────────────┐  ┌────────┐  ┌────────┐        │
│ └──────────────────┘ ↓   │ Macro Help │  │ Insert │  │ Cancel │       │
│                          └────────────┘  └────────┘  └────────┘       │
│ Recording Macro                        Doc 1 Pg 1 Ln 1" Pos 1"        │
└─────────────────────────────────────────────────────────────────────┘
```

Continue with your macro definition.

Invoking a Macro in 6.0

Invoking a macro in WordPerfect 6.0 for DOS will work as indicated throughout the book by using the following:

Mouse	Reference Keystrokes	Keys
	U: Press *Macro*.	Alt-F10
Mouse	U: Click on *"Tools"* select *"Macro"* and select *"Play"*.	
	C: *Displays Play Macro Text Box (See Screen G-9.)*	

Screen G-9: WordPerfect 6.0 for DOS Users

```
 File    Edit    View    Layout    Tools    Font    Graphics    Window    Help
┌───────────────────────────────────────────────────────────────────────────┐
│                                                                             │
│                                                                             │
│                                                                             │
│                        ═══════ Play Macro ═══════                           │
│                                                                             │
│       Macro:    ┌─────────────────────────────────────────────┐↓           │
│                 │_                                             │            │
│                 └─────────────────────────────────────────────┘            │
│                                                                             │
│     ┌──────────────┐  ┌───────────────┐       ┌──────┐   ┌────────┐         │
│     │File List...F5│  │QuickList...F6 │       │  OK  │   │ Cancel │         │
│     └──────────────┘  └───────────────┘       └──────┘   └────────┘         │
│                                                                             │
│                                                                             │
│                                                                             │
│ Courier 12 pt                            Doc 1 Pg 1 Ln 1" Pos 1"            │
└───────────────────────────────────────────────────────────────────────────┘
```

Mouse   Reference Keystrokes   Keys

U: Type in *macro's pathname* and *name of the macro* and press the *Enter key.*

C: *Invokes macro.*

Note that these are basically the same steps as used in WordPerfect 5.1, except that you see a text window guiding you through the macro's execution.

Macro Editor in 6.0

In WordPerfect 6.0 for DOS the macro editor was removed. Macros are now edited in the same way as a document. To edit a macro you can do the following:

Mouse   Reference Keystrokes   Keys

U: Press *Macro Define* .   Ctrl-F10

Mouse   U: Click on *"Tools"* select *"Macro"* and select *"Record"*.

C: *Displays Record Macro Text Box (See Screen G-10.)*

Mouse	**Reference Keystrokes**	**Keys**

U: Type in *macro's pathname* and *name of the macro.* Press the ***Tab key*** to move to "Edit Macro" and press the ***Space Bar*** to place an "X" in the brackets. Press the ***Tab key*** to move to the "OK" button and press the ***Enter key.***

Mouse U: Type in *macro's pathname* and *name of the macro.* Click on "***Edit Macro***" to place an "X" in the brackets. Click on "***OK***".

C: *Displays the macro's contents (See Screen G-11.)*

Screen G-10: WordPerfect 6.0 for DOS Users

```
┌─────────────────────────────────────────────────────────────┐
│ File   Edit   View   Layout   Tools   Font   Graphics   Window   Help │
│ ┌─────────────────────────────────────────────────────────┐ │
│ │                                                          │ │
│ │                                                          │ │
│ │                ═══════ Record Macro ═══════              │ │
│ │      Macro:  ┌────────────────────────────────────┐ ↓  │ │
│ │              │ _                                   │     │ │
│ │              └────────────────────────────────────┘     │ │
│ │      [ ] Edit Macro                                      │ │
│ │                                                          │ │
│ │   ┌─────────────┐ ┌──────────────┐   ┌──────┐ ┌──────┐  │ │
│ │   │File List...F5│ │QuickList...F6│   │  OK  │ │Cancel│  │ │
│ │   └─────────────┘ └──────────────┘   └──────┘ └──────┘  │ │
│ │                                                          │ │
│ └─────────────────────────────────────────────────────────┘ │
│ Courier 12 pt                      Doc 1 Pg 1 Ln 1" Pos 1"   │
└─────────────────────────────────────────────────────────────┘
```

Screen G-11 displays the contents of Chapter 1's CLOSE.WPM macro.

Screen G-11: WordPerfect 6.0 for DOS Users

```
 File    Edit    View    Layout    Tools    Font    Graphics    Window    Help

DISPLAY(Off!)
Tab
Type("Thank you for purchasing all of your office merchandise
     from Office Supplies, Inc.  Please contact us if you need
     further assistance.  Again, thank you")
Type(" for your patronage.")
HardReturn
HardReturn
Tab
Tab
Tab
Tab
Tab
Tab
Tab
Tab
Tab
Type("Sincerely,")
HardReturn
HardReturn
HardReturn
HardReturn
Tab
Tab
Tab
Tab
Tab
Tab
Tab
Tab
Type("Amanda A. Anderson")
HardReturn
Tab
Tab
Tab
Tab
Tab
Tab
Tab
Tab
Type("Manager")
Edit Macro:  Press Shft+F3 to Record          Doc 1 Pg 1 Ln 1" Pos 1"
```

To change the macro you would use your normal editing keys.
Saving a macro is identical to saving a file.

Converting Macros from 5.1 to 6.0

Conversion Utility

WordPerfect 6.0 for DOS includes a conversion utility for macros. It is very simple to convert 5.1 macros to 6.0 macros. The macro's contents determine whether the macro will immediately work after being converted from 5.1 to 6.0. The simple macros usually can be used immediately, unless they incorporate some function that has changed slightly under 6.0. The more complex macros usually have to be edited to adopt them to the new environment.

The conversion utility is called MCV.EXE and is located in the C:\WP60 directory.

To access the online help guide for this utility type in the following at the DOS prompt:

MCV/h

To convert all the 5.1 macros in the C:\WP51\MACROS subdirectory to 6.0 macros in the C:\WP60\MACROS subdirectory type in the following at the DOS prompt:

C:\WP60\MCV C:\WP51\MACROS*.WPM C:\WP60\MACROS

After you convert the macros you should verify that they work. If they do not work then make the adjustments as required. Use this appendix as a guide to make the adjustments.

Power Macros In WordPerfect 6.0 for DOS

The powerful macros in this book that will work in 6.0 immediately after you convert them are shown in Table G-1.

Table G-1

ALTB.WPM
ALTC.WPM
ALTD.WPM
ALTE.WPM
ALTG.WPM
ALTI.WPM
ALTJ.WPM
ALTK.WPM
ALTN.WPM
ALTO.WPM
ALTR.WPM
ALTT.WPM
ALTV.WPM
ALTW.WPM
ALTY.WPM
ALTZ.WPM
BOLD.WPM
BTOU.WPM
CAP.WPM
CLOSE.WPM
COL51.WPM
COLUMNS.WPM
CRTECAL.WPM
DELMGR51.WPM
HEADFOOT.WPM
IT.WPM
MAR.WPM

Table G-1 continued.

PBLOCK.WPM
PFORMAT.WPM
PMENU.WPM
PUB51.WPM
SEARCH.WPM
TABCALC.WPM
TABLE.WPM
UND.WPM
UTOB.WPM

In the Advanced Features of WordPerfect 6.0 Using Macros section, later in this Appendix, the 6.0 changes have been documented for the following macros shown in Table G-2.

Table G-2

EQUAT.WPM
LINESORT.WPM
MERGER.WPM
MERGSORT.WPM
PARASORT.WPM
PURCHASE.WPM
STYON.WPM
TRAVEL.WPM
WAGES.WPM

Modifying Power Macros Used In This Book

The other powerful macros in this book may be modified to work in WordPerfect 6.0. The changes required usually are very simplistic. For example, shown in Screen G-12 is the newly converted ALTA.WPM macro. This macro will not work immediately after the conversion since the code {Font}2 is unrecognizable to WordPerfect 6.0 for DOS.

The new code for the font menu in WordPerfect 6.0 is FontDlg. The conversion utility will automatically substitute most codes. In WordPerfect 6.0's online help utility Appendix B all the expected WordPerfect 6.0 keystrokes are documented. For instance, Ctrl-F8 is documented as FontDlg.

Note that the slashes (//) represent comments. Comments do not get executed - they are for your benefit only.

Screen G-12: ALTA.WPM

```
 File    Edit    View    Layout    Tools    Font    Graphics    Window    Help

//Description:  Displays Attribute Menu

SAVESTATE PERSISTALL
AutoCodePlacement(OFF!) WP51CursorMovement(ON!) VARERRCHK(OFF!)


//*** Conversion problem ***
//*** Not at main document at end of macro
//*** Cannot convert to matching dialog
//{Font}2




Edit Macro:  Press Shft+F3 to Record          Doc 1 Pg 1 Ln 1" Pos 1"
```

Screen G-13 shows the very simple change that you can make to the ALTA.WPM macro so that it will work in 6.0. To make these changes refer to the Macro Editor in 6.0 section above.

Screen G-13: ALTA.WPM

```
 File    Edit    View    Layout    Tools    Font    Graphics    Window    Help

//Description:  Displays Attribute Menu

FontDlg








Edit Macro:  Press Shft+F3 to Record          Doc 1 Pg 1 Ln 1" Pos 1"
```

Macro Printing

In WordPerfect 6.0 for DOS you can directly print the macro from the editing screen, just like you print a WordPerfect document. Thus, you do not need the special program, provided in Appendix H, to print macros.

Advanced Features of WordPerfect 6.0 Using Macros

Chapters 2 through 12, in this book, contain information about WordPerfect 5.1's advanced features. The changes in these advanced features from 5.1 to 6.0 are briefly described in this section. Also included, for each chapter, is the 6.0 equivalent macro to the ones shown in the related chapter. When you use the step-by-step instructions in the book you should pay attention to the options you are selecting because in 6.0 some of the menu numbers have been changed.

Chapter 2: Search Feature in 6.0

Changes

- Two new wildcard characters are available for use in your search string. You may either use the * to search for any number of characters or use the ? to search for one character. For instance the search string "Macr*" will find all occurrences of words beginning with "Macr" and then having any other group of characters following it like "Macro", "Macros", etc. Whereas the search string "Macro?" will find occurrences of words beginning with "Macr" and then having one single character following it like "Macro", "Macr1", etc. To insert the "*" into the search string press "Home" then "*". To insert the "?" into the search string press "Home" and then "?".

Chapter 2's SEARCH.WPM macro is shown on Screen G-14.

Screen G-14: SEARCH.WPM

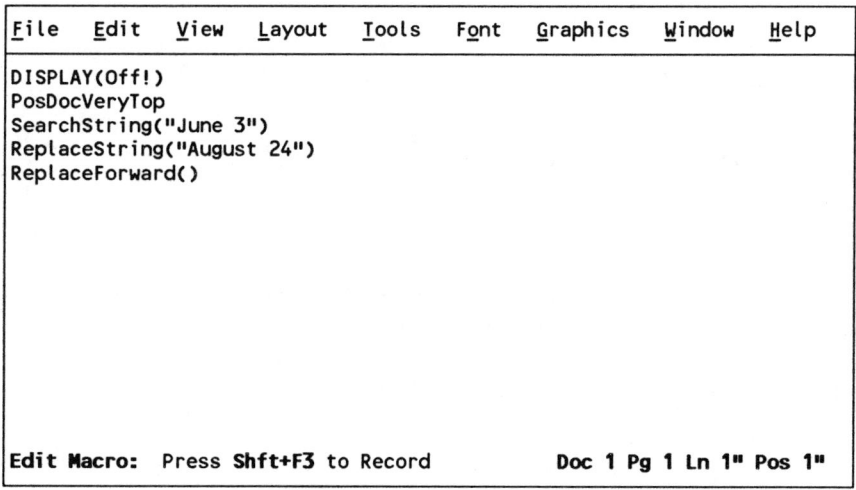

```
File    Edit    View    Layout    Tools    Font    Graphics    Window    Help

DISPLAY(Off!)
PosDocVeryTop
SearchString("June 3")
ReplaceString("August 24")
ReplaceForward()




Edit Macro:   Press Shft+F3 to Record        Doc 1 Pg 1 Ln 1" Pos 1"
```

Chapter 3: Header/Footer Feature in 6.0

Changes

- The menu used to set up Headers and Footers has been modified.
- Press and hold down Ctrl and tap P to insert page numbers into your header or footer.

Chapter 3's HEADFOOT.WPM macro is shown on Screen G-15.

Screen G-15: HEADFOOT.WPM

```
File    Edit    View    Layout    Tools    Font    Graphics    Window    Help

DISPLAY(Off!)
PosDocVeryTop
FooterA(Create!;AllPages!)
Tab
Tab
Tab
Tab
Type("Page ")
PageNumberDisplayFormat
SubstructureExit
PosPageNext
HeaderA(Create!;AllPages!)
Tab
Tab
Tab
Tab
Tab
Tab
Tab
Type("Peters")
SubstructureExit
Edit Macro:  Press Shft+F3 to Record           Doc 1 Pg 1 Ln 1" Pos 1"
```

Chapter 4: Font Feature in 6.0

Changes

- The menu used to set up soft and hard fonts to work with your printer and to insert fonts into your document has been modified.

Chapter 4's IT.WPM macro is shown on Screen G-16.

Screen G-16: IT.WPM

```
File    Edit    View    Layout    Tools    Font    Graphics    Window    Help

DISPLAY(Off!)
PosWordNext
BlockOn(CharMode!)
PosWordPrevious
AttributeAppearanceOn(Italics!)
BlockOff




Edit Macro:   Press Shft+F3 to Record          Doc 1 Pg 1 Ln 1" Pos 1"
```

Chapter 5: Column Feature in 6.0

Changes

- The menu used to set up columns has been modified.
- A new type of column called "Balanced Newspaper" has been added. This column is a slightly modified version of the regular "Newspaper" column. Each column's text is extended to the end of the column.
- In Reveal Codes, the column definition and on code is shown as [Col Def:Parallel;3] and the column off code is shown as [Col Def:Off].

Chapter 5's COLUMNS.WPM macro is shown on Screen G-17.

Screen G-17: COLUMNS.WPM

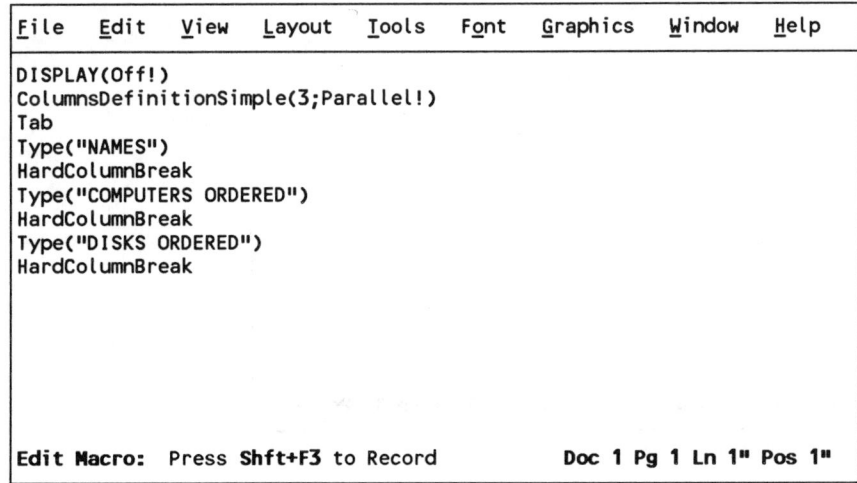

```
File    Edit    View    Layout    Tools    Font    Graphics    Window    Help

DISPLAY(Off!)
ColumnsDefinitionSimple(3;Parallel!)
Tab
Type("NAMES")
HardColumnBreak
Type("COMPUTERS ORDERED")
HardColumnBreak
Type("DISKS ORDERED")
HardColumnBreak




Edit Macro:   Press Shft+F3 to Record          Doc 1 Pg 1 Ln 1" Pos 1"
```

Chapter 6: Tables Feature in 6.0

Changes

- The menu used to set up tables and perform calculations has been modified.
- A wide variety of specialized functions (including spreadsheet functions) have been included to perform different tasks for you automatically.
- Cells can be given a nickname that you can use to reference the cell's contents instead of using the formal cell name of "A1".
- Tables can be used to create spreadsheets. The spreadsheets can have a maximum of 64 columns and over 32,000 rows.

Chapter 6's WAGES.WPM macro is shown on Screen G-18.

Screen G-18: WAGES.WPM

```
 File    Edit    View    Layout    Tools    Font    Graphics    Window    Help

DISPLAY(Off!)
TableCreate(4;8)
TableHeader(Yes!)
TableCellLine(Bottom!;DoubleLine!)
TableBlockOff
PosTableTopCellNext
TableCellLine(Bottom!;DoubleLine!)
TableBlockOff
PosTableTopCellNext
TableCellLine(Bottom!;DoubleLine!)
TableBlockOff
PosTableTopCellNext
TableCellLine(Bottom!;DoubleLine!)
TableBlockOff
PosTableCelllDown
TableFormula("B2*C2")
TableCellCopy(Down!;5)
PosTableCell("D8")
TableFormula("SUM(D2:D7)")
PosTableCell("a1")
Type("Employee")
HardReturn
Type("Name")
PosTableTopCellNext
Type("Hourly")
HardReturn
Type("Rate")
PosTableTopCellNext
Type("Hours")
HardReturn
Type("Worked")
PosTableTopCellNext
Type("Gross")
HardReturn
Type("WagesName")
PosTableTopCellNext
Edit Macro:  Press Shft+F3 to Record          Doc 1 Pg 1 Ln 1" Pos 1"
```

Chapter 7: Graphics Feature in 6.0

Changes

- The menu used to incorporate graphics into your document has been modified.
- The list of graphic boxes that you can use are Button, Equation, Inline Equation, Figure, Table, Text, User, and Watermark.
- Color graphics can be printed on colored printers.
- If you use a mouse you can click and drag a graphic to any new location in your document and the text will wrap automatically around the image.
- The graphic images that come with WordPerfect 6.0 for DOS are listed below in Table G-3.

Table G-3

BORDER4.WPG	BORDER7.WPG
CONDUCT.WPG	DRAGON.WPG
FISHTROP.WPG	GRIZZLY.WPG
HOTAIR.WPG	HOTROD.WPG
HUMBIRD.WPG	INDANCE.WPG
JEEP.WPG	JOCKEY.WPG
LIGHTHS.WPG	MEDICAL1.WPG
MTNCLIMB.WPG	OVERHD1.WPG
PARROT.WPG	PENPUSH.WPG
PHEASANT.WPG	PLAN2.WPG
SKIER1.WPG	SKIPPER.WPG
SUMMRCNR.WPG	TIGERHD.WPG
WATER4.WPG	WATER7.WPG
WINDMILL.WPG	WINRACE.WPG
WIZARD.WPG	WSKIER.WPG

Chapter 7's TRAVEL.WPM macro is shown on Screen G-19.

Screen G-19: TRAVEL.WPM

```
 File    Edit    View    Layout    Tools    Font    Graphics    Window    Help

DISPLAY(Off!)
HardReturn
HardReturn
HardReturn
Tab
Type("Travel the World, Incorporated")
HardReturn
Tab
Type("1 Ocean View Lane")
HardReturn
Tab
Type("Figure Ten Island, NC 19979")
HardReturn
HardReturn
Tab
Type("President:  Arielle Austin")
HardReturn
HardReturn
HardReturn
HardReturn
HardReturn
PosDocTop
PosLineDown
BoxCreate(FigureBox!)
BorderLeftLine(ExtraThickLine!)
BorderRightLine(ExtraThickLine!)
BorderTopLine(ExtraThickLine!)
BorderBottomLine(ExtraThickLine!)
BoxContentType(Image!)
BoxImageRetrieve(MakeInternal!;"LIGHTHS.WPG";
    WordPerfectGraphic_20!)
BoxWidth(AutoWidth!)
BoxHeight(1")
BoxEnd(Save!)
PosDocBottom
Edit Macro:  Press Shft+F3 to Record          Doc 1 Pg 1 Ln 1" Pos 1"
```

Chapter 8: Math Feature in 6.0

Changes

- The menu used to set up math definitions has been modified.
- The math column types are designated by a "C" for Calculation, "N" for Numeric, "X" for Text, and "T" for Total.
- Specialized functions have been added so you can perform many common calculations by using the functions.
- Mathematical order of precedence is now used. For example, all multiplication and division operations are performed first from left to right before addition and subtraction. You can use parentheses to alter the order of calculation.

Chapter 8's PURCHASE.WPM macro is shown on Screen G-20.

Screen G-20: PURCHASE.WPM

```
 File    Edit    View    Layout    Tools    Font    Graphics    Window    Help
DISPLAY(Off!)
Center
Type("PURCHASE ORDER")
HardReturn
HardReturn
Tab
Type("Item Ordered")
Tab
Tab
Type("Quantity")
Tab
Tab
Type("Price")
Tab
Type("Total Price")
HardReturn
HardReturn
MathDefinitionStart
MathColumn(1;MathText!;Parentheses!;2)
MathColumn(4;MathCalculate!;Parentheses!;2;"B*C")
MathDefinitionEnd
TabSet(Relative!;{0";TabLeft!;0.5";TabLeft!;1.5";TabLeft!;4.2";
     TabLeft!;5.5";TabLeft!;6.9";TabLeft!})
Math(On!)
Edit Macro:  Press Shft+F3 to Record          Doc 1 Pg 1 Ln 1" Pos 1"
```

Chapter 9: Equation Feature in 6.0

Changes

- The menu used to set up equations has been modified.
- More commands are available to create complex equations.

Chapter 9's EQUAT.WPM macro is shown on Screen G-21.

Screen G-21: EQUAT.WPM

```
File    Edit    View    Layout    Tools    Font    Graphics    Window    Help

DISPLAY(Off!)
BoxCreate(FigurecBox!)
BoxContentType(Equation!)
BoxContentEdit
Type("INT u~du~=~uv~-~INT v~du")
SubstructureExit
BoxEnd(Save!)




Edit Macro:   Press Shft+F3 to Record          Doc 1 Pg 1 Ln 1" Pos 1"
```

Chapter 10: Merge Feature in 6.0

Changes

- The menu used to set up the primary and secondary files has been modified.
- The codes do not have {} around them.
- The data can be entered into a table structure.
- The list of merge programming commands has been expanded.
- For each record, WordPerfect can generate an envelope.

Chapter 10's MERGER.WPM macro is shown on Screen G-22.

Screen G-22: MERGER.WPM

```
File    Edit    View    Layout    Tools    Font    Graphics    Window    Help

DISPLAY(Off!)
MergeMark(0)
MergeSelect(All!)
MergeBlankField(Leave!)
MergeRepeat(1)
MergePageBreak(On!)
MergeCodesDisplayRun(Hide!)
MergeEnvelope(Off!)
MergeFileAssociate("PRIME.TXT";"SECOND.TXT")
MergeRun(FormFile!;"PRIME.TXT";DataFile!;"SECOND.TXT";
    ToCurrentDoc!)



Edit Macro:   Press Shft+F3 to Record          Doc 1 Pg 1 Ln 1" Pos 1"
```

Chapter 11: Sort Feature in 6.0

Changes

- The menu used to set up sorting has been modified.

Chapter 11's LINESORT.WPM macro is shown on Screen G-23.

Screen G-23: LINESORT.WPM

```
 File    Edit    View    Layout    Tools    Font    Graphics    Window    Help

DISPLAY(Off!)
SortType(LineSort!)
SortSelectString("")
SortAction(Sort!)
SortKeys(1;1;1;Alphanumeric!;Ascending!;1;1;2;Alphanumeric!;
    Ascending!)
Sort()




Edit Macro:   Press Shft+F3 to Record        Doc 1 Pg 1 Ln 1" Pos 1"
```

Chapter 11's PARASORT.WPM macro is shown on Screen G-24.

Screen G-24: PARASORT.WPM

```
 File    Edit    View    Layout    Tools    Font    Graphics    Window    Help

DISPLAY(Off!)
SortType(ParagraphSort!)
SortSelectString("key3=453")
SortKeys(1;1;2;Alphanumeric!;Ascending!;1;1;1;Alphanumeric!;
    Ascending!;2;1;1Numeric!;Ascending!)
Sort()




Edit Macro:   Press Shft+F3 to Record        Doc 1 Pg 1 Ln 1" Pos 1"
```

Chapter 11's MERGSORT.WPM macro is shown on Screen G-25.

Screen G-25: MERGSORT.WPM

```
File    Edit    View    Layout    Tools    Font    Graphics    Window    Help

DISPLAY(Off!)
SortType(MergeSort!)
SortSelectString("")
SortAction(Sort!)
SortKeys(1;1;2;Alphanumeric!;Ascending!;1;1;1;Alphanumeric!;
    Ascending!)
Sort("MERG.TXT")




Edit Macro:  Press Shft+F3 to Record          Doc 1 Pg 1 Ln 1" Pos 1"
```

Chapter 12: Style Feature in 6.0

Changes

- WordPerfect 6.0 for DOS comes with many new system styles and a styles library
  called LIBRARY.STY.

Chapter 12's STYON.WPM macro is shown on Screen G-26.

Screen G-26: STYON.WPM

```
File    Edit    View    Layout    Tools    Font    Graphics    Window    Help

DISPLAY(Off!)
StyleOn(Level1Style!)









Edit Macro:  Press Shft+F3 to Record          Doc 1 Pg 1 Ln 1" Pos 1"
```

INDEX

INDEX

F

G

H

K

L

M

M

M

S

T

T

U

V

V

W

THE MACRO POWER DISK

The Macro Power Disk

The WordPerfect 5.1 for DOS macros in this book are included on a disk to save you time and effort when using macro power. Also included on the disk are some helpful files you can use when you execute the macros referenced in the book.

This disk works on personal computers running DOS. The files can be copied from the disk to a directory on your computer's hard drive or you can use the files directly from the floppy.

Macros on Disk

The macros and documents that are located on the disk are shown in a README.TXT file which contains a reference to the chapter that these macros and documents are used in.

The disk includes additional macros to challenge the reader in his/her particular environment.